A New Star-Rating System & Other Exciting News from Frommer's!

In our continuing effort to publish the savviest, most up-to-date, and most appealing travel guides available, we've added some great new features.

Frommer's guides now include a new **star-rating system.** Every hotel, restaurant, and attraction is rated from 0 to 3 stars to help you set priorities and organize your time.

We've also added **seven brand-new features** that point you to the great deals, in-the-know advice, and unique experiences that separate travelers from tourists. Throughout the guide, look for:

Finds	Special finds—those places only insiders know about
Fun Fact	Fun facts—details that make travelers more informed and their trips more fun
Kids	Best bets for kids—advice for the whole family
Moments	Special moments—those experiences that memories are made of
Overrated	Places or experiences not worth your time or money
Tips	Insider tips—some great ways to save time and money
Value	Great values—where to get the best deals

Here's what critics say about Frommer's:

"Amazingly easy to use. Very portable, very complete."

—*Booklist*

"Detailed, accurate, and easy-to-read information for all price ranges."

—*Glamour Magazine*

"Hotel information is close to encyclopedic."

—*Des Moines Sunday Register*

"Frommer's Guides have a way of giving you a real feel for a place."

—*Knight Ridder Newspapers*

Frommer's®

PORTABLE
New York City from $90 a Day

2nd Edition

by Cheryl Farr Leas

WILEY

Wiley Publishing, Inc.

Published by:

WILEY PUBLISHING, INC.

909 Third Ave.
New York, NY 10022

ISBN 0-7645-6730-6
ISSN 1527-3687

Editor: Kathleen Warnock
Production Editor: Ian Skinnari
Photo Editor: Richard Fox
Cartographer: John Decamillis
Production by Wiley Indianapolis Composition Services

For information on our other products and services or to obtain technical
support, please contact our Customer Care Department within the U.S. at
800-762-2974, outside the U.S. at 317-572-3993 or fax 317-572-4002.

Wiley also publishes its books in a variety of electronic formats. Some con-
tent that appears in print may not be available in electronic formats.

Manufactured in the United States of America

5   4   3   2   1

Contents

List of Maps

ABOUT THE AUTHOR

Cheryl Farr Leas was senior editor at Frommer's before embarking on a free-lance writing career. She also authors the *Frommer's New York City* and *Hawaii For Dummies* travel guides, and has contributed to *Best Places Los Angeles* (Sasquatch Books) and numerous other travel guides. Cheryl also writes about travel, real estate, interior design, and other lifestyle subjects for *Continental, Daily Variety, Travel + Leisure, Bride's,* and other publications. When she's not traveling, she's at home in Park Slope, Brooklyn.

AN INVITATION TO THE READER

In researching this book, we discovered many wonderful places—hotels, restaurants, shops, and more. We're sure you'll find others. Please tell us about them, so we can share the information with your fellow travelers in upcoming editions. If you were disappointed with a recommendation, we'd love to know that, too. Please write to:

> *Frommer's Portable New York City from $90 a Day,* 2nd Edition
> Wiley Publishing, Inc. • 909 Third Ave. • New York, NY 10022

AN ADDITIONAL NOTE

Please be advised that travel information is subject to change at any time—and this is especially true of prices. We therefore suggest that you write or call ahead for confirmation when making your travel plans. The authors, editors, and publisher cannot be held responsible for the experiences of readers while traveling. Your safety is important to us, however, so we encourage you to stay alert and be aware of your surroundings. Keep a close eye on cameras, purses, and wallets, all favorite targets of thieves and pickpockets.

WHAT THE SYMBOLS MEAN

The following abbreviations are used for credit cards:

AE American Express	DISC Discover	V Visa
DC Diners Club	MC MasterCard	

FROMMERS.COM

Now that you have the guidebook to a great trip, visit our website at **www.frommers.com** for travel information on nearly 2,500 destinations. With features updated regularly, we give you instant access to the most current trip-planning information available. At Frommers.com, you'll also find the best prices on airfares, accommodations, and car rentals—and you can even book travel online through our travel booking partners. At Frommers.com, you'll also find the following:

- Online updates to our most popular guidebooks
- Vacation sweepstakes and contest giveaways
- Newsletter highlighting the hottest travel trends
- Online travel message boards with featured travel discussions

Planning an Affordable Trip to New York City

New York, as everyone knows, is perpetually short on space and overflowing with people. The result has been stratospheric prices, generally the highest you'll find in the U.S. If you're used to getting a simple, comfortable motel room for $60 or so, get set for a shock.

That's the bad news—but there's plenty of good news to share, too. You *can* stay in New York City comfortably, eat well, and see and do everything you want without blowing your budget. There are plenty of great deals in New York: more travel and hotel bargains available than there have been in years—if you know where to look.

THE NEW YORK–FROM-$90-A-DAY PREMISE

The idea is this: With good planning and a watchful eye, you can keep your basic daily living costs—accommodations and three meals a day—down to as little as $90. This budget model works best for two adults traveling together who have at least $180 a day to work with and can share a double room. This way, if you aim for accommodations costing around $120 double, you'll be left with about $30 per person per day for food (less drinks and tips).

In defining this premise, we assumed you want to travel comfortably, with your own room rather than a hostel bunk, dining on good food rather than fast food at every meal. This book will also serve you well even if you don't need to keep your budget to a strict $180 a day, but want to get the most for your money at every turn.

Of course, the cost of sightseeing, transportation, and entertainment are all extras. But don't worry—I've got plenty of suggestions on how to keep those bills down, too.

1 35 Money-Saving Tips

1. **Buy a package deal.** In some cases, you'll get airfare, accommodations, and transportation to and from the airport, plus extras—maybe a sightseeing tour or restaurant and shopping

discount coupons—for less than the cost of a hotel room alone had you booked it yourself. For tips on where and how to get the best package, see "Money-Saving Package Deals" on p. 22.

2. **Buy a *New York for Less* guidebook.** The value in this guide ($19.95) is its discount card, which offers discounts from 20% to 50% at restaurants, attractions, shops, theaters, and nightspots. The card is good for up to four people for up to 8 days and comes with a book listing the places that honor the card. It even includes a phone card that gives you $8 in free calls. To order, call € **888/463-6753** or 937/846-1411; or visit **www.for-less.com**, where you can view a list of participating establishments.

3. **Flash your AAA, AARP, military, senior, or student ID card.** American Automobile Association membership is valuable for hotel and car-rental discounts, often in the neighborhood of 10%, but may also score savings on bus tours, harbor cruises, and the like. Seniors and students usually find a valid ID snares reduced-rate admission to most attractions. Military and government folks should always ask about discounts; they can get as much as 40% off. Also check your corporate affiliations; you may get free admission to cultural attractions your company contributes to.

WHEN TO GO

4. **Choose your season carefully.** How much you pay for your hotel room and airfare depends on the season. January to mid-April is the best season for bargains, with summer from June to mid-August being second best. Spring and fall are the busiest, most expensive seasons, as is the Christmas season, but negotiating a decent rate is possible, especially in spring. Budget-minded travelers should skip Christmas and New Year's. Thanksgiving, however, is a bargain hunter's delight.

GETTING TO NEW YORK CITY
AIR TRAVEL

5. **Consider all three airports when you're shopping.** Fares can vary greatly depending on which airport you fly into—LaGuardia, JFK, or Newark—and none of them are that far from Manhattan. Continental, for instance, almost always has cheaper flights into Newark because it's one of their hubs; United is another airline that often has cheaper prices into

Newark. Newark can be more convenient to Manhattan than the other airports, with the Newark AirTrain that links the airport to midtown.

6. **Try the discount carriers.** Don't forget to check with the smaller, no-frills airlines including jetBlue, AirTran, and Southwest (which flies into Long Island's MacArthur Airport, about 50 miles/81km east of Manhattan).

7. **Check for discounted fares with consolidators.** Also known as "bucket shops," consolidators are a good place to find low fares, often below the airlines' discount rates. Consolidators buy airfare in bulk and pass some of the savings on to you. Their tickets are usually nonrefundable or have high cancellation penalties.

   I've found great deals at **Cheap Tickets** ☎ (© 888/922-8849; www.cheaptickets.com); I almost always do better by calling than I do on their website. **Council Travel** (© 800/226-8624; www.counciltravel.com) and **STA Travel** (© 800/781-4040; www.statravel.com) caters to young travelers, but offer discount fares to people of all ages. **The TravelHub** (© 888/AIR-FARE; www.travelhub.com) represents nearly 1,000 travel agencies, many of whom offer consolidator and discount fares. Other reliable consolidators include **1-800-FLY-CHEAP** (www.1800flycheap.com); **TFI Tours International** (© 800/745-8000 or 212/736-1140; www.lowestairprice.com), a clearinghouse for unused seats; and "rebators" like **Travel Avenue** (© 800/333-3335; www.travelavenue.com), which rebate part of their commissions to you.

8. **Search the Internet for cheap fares.** You can tap into the same databases once accessible only to travel agents through sites like **Travelocity.com, Expedia.com,** and **Orbitz.com.** You might also check out **Qixo** (**www.qixo.com**), another search engine that allows you to search for flights and accommodations from some 20 airline and travel-planning sites (such as Travelocity) at once.

   The major carriers frequently offer "Internet only" sales on their websites. A fare can pop up today that wasn't available yesterday, and won't be around tomorrow. Or check sites that have lists of deals, like **Smarter Living** (smarterliving.com) and **WebFlyer** (www.webflyer.com).

If you don't care who your carrier is, consider **Priceline** (www.priceline.com), which lets you "name your price" for airline tickets (as well as hotel rooms and rental cars). For airline tickets, you have to accept any flight between 6am and 10pm on the dates you've selected. Tickets are nonrefundable, and while they say no frequent-flier miles are awarded, we've been given them more than once.

A word of warning: Avoid online auctions. Sites that auction airline tickets and frequent-flier miles are the No. 1 perpetrators of Internet fraud, according to the National Consumers League.

OTHER TRANSPORTATION OPTIONS

9. **Consider taking a train or bus instead of flying.** Traveling by train or bus may be cheaper than flying. You'll come into and out of Midtown without the additional cost of airport transfers. Your cheapest transportation method will always be the bus, but keep in mind that unless it's an express, it can take a lot of time.

10. **Keep an eye out for sales.** Go to **www.amtrak.com** and click on "Rail Sale," where you'll find discounts of up to 90% on select routes. If you register, you'll be notified of sales as they happen. Keep in mind that if you buy a sale ticket, it is not refundable and cannot be exchanged. While you're online, also check the "Savings & Promotions" page for a whole range of discounted and/or value-added deals.

    Greyhound advertises sales at **www.greyhound.com**. They usually have a number of deals, ranging from "Friendly Fares" that let you travel for as little as $49 to free companion fares.

GETTING AROUND NEW YORK CITY

11. **Use the subway and bus to get around the city.** The transit system is safe, relatively clean, quick, efficient, and cheap. Use taxis only late at night, when trains and buses can be few and far between, or when traveling in a group of three or four, when the fare might be less than multiple subway or bus fares.

12. **Buy a MetroCard.** If you're going to be in the city for a few days, or you're traveling in a group (up to four people can use a MetroCard at any given time), buy a $15 pay-per-ride MetroCard, which will get you 11 rides for the price of 10, and allow you to transfer within a 2-hour period of each ride you use. If you're going to do a lot of running around,

consider a $4 daily **Fun Pass** or a $17 **7-Day MetroCard,** each of which allows the cardholder unlimited rides for the life of the card.

13. **In the daytime, walk.** No other American city is more welcoming or as rewarding to explore on foot.

ACCOMMODATIONS

14. **Stay uptown or downtown.** The advantages of a Midtown location are overrated. Manhattan is a petite island, and the subway can whisk you anywhere in minutes. You'll get the best value by staying in the neighborhoods where real New Yorkers live, like Greenwich Village, Chelsea, Murray Hill, or the Upper West Side. These are the neighborhoods where New Yorkers hang out, so you can find good eats and nightlife, too.

15. **Don't be afraid to bargain.** Always ask for a lower price than the first one quoted. Ask whether a less-expensive room is available or if any special rates apply: corporate, student, military, senior. Mention membership in AAA, AARP, frequent-flier programs, corporate or military organizations, or unions, which might entitle you to deals. The chains tend to be good about trying to save you money, but reservations agents often won't volunteer the information; you have to ask them.

16. **Dial direct.** When booking a room in a chain hotel, call the hotel's local line, as well as the toll-free number, and see where you get the best deal. The clerk who runs the place is more likely to know about booking patterns and will often grant deep discounts in order to fill up.

17. **Rely on a qualified professional.** Certain hotels give travel agents discounts in exchange for steering business their way, so if you're shy about bargaining, an agent may be better equipped to negotiate discounts for you.

18. **Shop online.** New York hotels often offer "Internet-only" deals that can save you 10% to 20% over what you'd pay if you booked by telephone. Also, hotels often advertise all of their available weekend and other package deals on their websites.

Also try **Travelocity.com, Expedia.com,** and **Orbitz.com.** I've found that Expedia, in particular, sometimes offers excellent rates that cannot be booked elsewhere. Expedia will require you to pay up front, but you can usually cancel up to 72 hours in advance for a $25 fee. (Check the exact rules for your booking.)

Some of the discount reservations agencies (see tip no. 19) have sites that allow you to book online. **American Automobile Association** members may be able to score the best discounts by booking at **www.aaa.com**.

19. **Investigate reservations services.** These work like consolidators, buying up or reserving rooms in bulk, and then dealing them to customers at a profit. You can get 10% to 50% off; but remember, these discounts apply to rack rates, prices that people rarely end up paying. You may get a decent rate, but call the hotel directly to see if you can do better.

    Start with **Quikbook** (📞 **800/789-9887** or 212/779-7666; www.quikbook.com), the best of the bunch since they book more than 100 hotels, require no prepayment, and allow you to make changes and cancellations (penalties depend on the hotel). Another good bet is **Hotel ConXions** (📞 **800/522-9991** or 212/840-8686; www.hotel conxions. com). Both Quikbook and Hotel ConXions have guaranteed room blocks in select properties, so they can sometimes get you into a hotel that's otherwise sold out. You might also try the **Hotel Reservations Network,** also known as HotelDiscount!com (📞 **800/364-0801;** www.180096HOTEL. com or www.hoteldiscount.com), and **Accommodations Express** (📞 **800/950-4685;** www.accommodationsexpress.com).

    Important tips: Do a little homework; compare the rack rates to the discount rates to see what kind of deal you're getting. That way you'll know whether you're being offered a big savings. Always compare the rate a reservations service offers you with the rate you can get directly from the hotel. If you're being offered a stay in a hotel I haven't recommended, do more research to learn about it. It's not a deal if you end up at a dump.

20. **Take a chance with Priceline.** I'm a little afraid of Priceline (**www.priceline.com**). But I have an aunt who travels constantly, and she won't book a hotel any other way. She's had great luck scoring luxury rooms for as little as $50 through their "name your price" program. Priceline can be a great way to win the budget war. You won't know the name of your hotel until it's paid for, but you can choose your neighborhood and the class of hotel (from economy to deluxe), and Priceline guarantees that you'll stay in a name-brand or independent hotel trusted for their quality, service, and amenities.

21. **Be willing to share a bathroom.** For the best bargains, do as the Europeans do: Share a hall bathroom with your fellow travelers. Usually there are two or three bathrooms to a floor, often with separate rooms for the toilet and the shower and/or tub. If you do this, you can get a lot of bang for your buck. If you're on a tight budget, you'll be able to stay at a nicer hotel than if you insist on a private bathroom. Many rooms have private sinks, so you can brush your teeth or wash your face without leaving your room.

22. **Consider a suite.** If you're traveling with another couple or your family, a suite can be a bargain. They're always cheaper than two hotel rooms. They often feature a sofa bed, and sometimes a kitchenette where you can prepare light meals. Some places charge for extra guests beyond two; some don't.

23. **Save on hotel tax by booking an apartment or home stay.** Booking a hosted or unhosted apartment stay can save you on taxes. These agencies are able to charge 8¼% sales tax, as opposed to 13¼% plus $2 per night for a regular hotel room. Even better: Tax is often included in the rates quoted by agencies; thus, a $130 room is just $130, while a regular hotel will charge you $149.23 per night for a $130 room. A tax loophole eliminated the tax on many 7-night or longer stays (which are classified as short-term leases rather than hotel stays).

     Homestay New York ✆ (℘ and fax **718/434-2071;** www.homestayny.com) can book you into a private room with a family that welcomes travelers. Homes are in residential neighborhoods in Brooklyn, Queens, or Upper Manhattan, all within a half-hour of Midtown or downtown via subway or bus, and most are beautifully restored 19th- and early-20th-century houses. Not only can this save you money, it can be fun, too: Visitors are matched to hosts by age, interests, and occupation, and the hosts are happy to provide advice and assistance. You'll be the only in-house guest. Rates run $100 to $130 single or double, with shared or private bathroom depending on the home. Most rooms have TV, air-conditioning, and a small fridge, and towels are provided. Buffet breakfast is included; also included are free MetroCards and phone cards (values depend on the length of your stay). A 3-night minimum is requested, and no credit cards are accepted.

Manhattan Getaways 🏠 (📞 212/956-2010; www. manhattangetaways.com) maintains a beautifully kept and managed network of bed-and-breakfast rooms (from $105 nightly) and unhosted apartments (from $145) around the city. There's a 3-night minimum, and credit cards are accepted. Other agencies that can book you into a B&B room or a private apartment, with prices starting at $90 nightly, include **A Hospitality Company** (📞 800/987-1235 or 212/965-1102; www.hospitalityco.com), **As You Like It** (📞 800/277-0413 or 212/695-0191; www.furnapts.com), **Abode Apartment Rentals** (📞 800/835-8880 or 212/472-2000; www.abodenyc.com), **Manhattan Lodgings** (📞 212/677-7616; www.manhattanlodgings.com), and **New York Habitat** (📞 212/255-8018; www.nyhabitat.com).

24. **If you're on a shoestring budget, book a hostel bed.** You'll share a room with fellow travelers and all facilities are common—but there's no arguing with the rate. The largest hostel in the **Hostelling International–American Youth Hostels** system houses travelers in bunk-bedded rooms for $29 to $35 per person per night. For more possibilities, surf to **The Hostel Handbook** (www.hostelhandbook.com) and **Hostels.com.**

25. **Try the Y.** The Y isn't as cheap as hostel living, but the facilities are better. The **YMCA of Greater New York** (📞 212/630-9600; www.ymcanyc.org) has eight residences throughout the city's five boroughs. You'll have a private room (some have private bathrooms) and access to the on-site fitness center free. The Y is popular with families, older travelers, and singles. Contact the **West Side YMCA,** adjacent to Central Park at 5 W. 63rd St. (📞 212/875-4100), and the **Vanderbilt Y,** 224 E. 47th St. (📞 212/756-9600), as far in advance as possible. Midtown locations are the most expensive, with prices starting around $80; if you can stay in Harlem, Brooklyn or Queens, rates start as low as $40. For information, visit the Y's website (www.ymcanyc.org), click on "Guest Rooms & Group Rates."

26. **Do as little business as possible through the hotel.** Any service the hotel offers will cost you dearly. Find out before you dial whether your hotel imposes a surcharge on local or long-distance calls; it might be cheaper to use the pay phone in the lobby.

DINING

27. **Book a hotel room with a kitchenette.** Even if you only prepare breakfast, you'll save money this way.

28. **Stay at a hotel, guesthouse, or bed-and-breakfast that includes breakfast.** And be sure to confirm that it's included before you book, because some city guesthouses keep rates down by not offering breakfast. Ask what's included; the offering will most likely be a limited continental breakfast.

29. **Use any coupons you can get your hands on.** The New York Convention & Visitors Bureau offers a free visitor's guide that includes coupons. Even if you order one in advance (see "Visitor Information," below), stop in at the local visitor centers, where the wall racks sometimes have coupons and advertisements for freebies, two-for-ones, and dining discounts. Also consider buying the discount/coupon book recommended in tip no. 2 above. Before you leave home, check the deals offered through the **Playbill Online Theatre Club (www.playbillclub.com)**, which often include a few dining discounts. If you use a dining discount coupon, remember to tip your waiter based on the full value of the meal; he's on a budget, too.

30. **Eat ethnic.** New York probably has the best collection of ethnic restaurants in the country, and the best offer first-class eats for low, low prices. For tips on where to go, see chapter 4.

SIGHTSEEING

31. **Buy a CityPass.** CityPass may be New York's best sightseeing deal. Pay one price ($38, or $31 for kids 12–17) for admission to seven major attractions: The American Museum of Natural History (does not include Space Show); the Solomon R. Guggenheim Museum; the Empire State Building; the *Intrepid* Sea-Air-Space Museum; the Whitney Museum of American Art; MoMA QNS; and a 2-hour Circle Line cruise. If you purchased separate admission to each of these, you'd spend more than twice as much. Even more importantly, CityPass contains actual tickets, so you can bypass long ticket lines. CityPass is good for 9 days from the first time you use it. It's sold at all participating attractions and online at **www. citypass.net**. For more info, call CityPass at ✆ **707/256-0490.** The pricing and attraction list is confirmed through March 2003; call or check the website for updated information if your visit falls later in the year.

32. **Take advantage of freebies.** Many of the best things to do and see in Manhattan are free, from walking the Brooklyn Bridge to riding the Staten Island Ferry to exploring Central Park to attending TV show tapings. Additionally, some organizations offer walking tours at no charge. Many museums and attractions that charge admission have free or pay-as-you-wish programs 1 day or evening a week. See chapter 5 for details.

ENTERTAINMENT

33. **Buy discounted theater tickets through Playbill Online.** Joining Playbill's Online Theater Club (**www.playbillclub. com**) can yield substantial savings on theater tickets, including some of the top draws (even *Oklahoma!,* at press time). It's free to join; all you have to do is register, and you'll have access to discounts that can range from a few dollars to as much as 50% off regular prices. The club also offers deals at some nice hotels as well as a few dining discounts, and you can sign up to receive e-mail updates. Other sites that offer similar services are **TheaterMania** (**www.theatermania.com**) and **Broadway.com** (**www.broadway.com**), although the Broadway.com site wants too much personal information for my taste. At TheaterMania, be sure to click on "Get the Insider Scoop" for instant discounts.

34. **Buy discounted same-day tickets at the TKTS booth.** If your heart is set on seeing a particular show, order your tickets before you come to the city. But if you're flexible, check out TKTS, which sells day-of-show tickets to plays on and Off-Broadway for 25% to 50% off face value, plus a $2.50 per-ticket service charge. In-the-know theatergoers skip the Theater District location for the far-less-crowded downtown booth, where you can also score matinee tickets a day in advance. See chapter 6.

35. **Eschew high-priced, star performances for lesser-known, lower-priced surprises.** Seeing the New York Philharmonic or a Broadway extravaganza is a must if you can afford it. But you'll save money—and maybe enjoy yourself more—by looking beyond the obvious. For instance, the nation's top music education institution, the **Juilliard School,** offers a full slate of free and cheap events, from first-rate student concerts to lectures by celebrities of the performing-arts world.

Off- and Off-Off-Broadway theater is usually significantly less expensive than Broadway, and the quality doesn't have to suffer one bit.

2 Visitor Information

For information before you leave, your best source (besides this book, of course) is NYC & Company, the organization behind the **New York Convention & Visitors Bureau** (NYCVB), 810 Seventh Ave., New York, NY 10019. You can call ℂ **800/NYC-VISIT** or 212/397-8222 to order the **Official NYC Visitor Kit,** which has the *Official NYC Guide* detailing hotels, restaurants, theaters, attractions, events, and more; a fold-out map; a newsletter on the latest goings-on in the city; and brochures on attractions and services. It costs $5.95 to receive the packet (payable by credit card) in 7 to 10 days, $9.95 for rush delivery (3–4 business days) to U.S. addresses and international orders. (*Note:* I have received complaints that packages don't always strictly adhere to these time frames.)

Money-saving tip: You can order the *Official NYC Guide,* the heart of the kit, for free at **www.nycvisit.com** (click on "Visitors"). The site is also a terrific information source. To speak to a travel counselor call ℂ **212/484-1222.**

For visitor-center and information-desk locations once you arrive, see "Visitor Information" in "Orientation," in chapter 2.

FOR U.K. VISITORS   The **NYCVB Visitor Information Center** is at 33–34 Carnaby St., London W1V 1PA (ℂ **0207/437-8300**).

SITE SEEING: THE BIG APPLE ON THE WEB

The New York Convention & Visitors Bureau's official site, **www.nycvisit.com**, is an excellent online resource offering tons of information on the city. But there's much more to be learned about New York in cyberspace than the official line.

Tops these days just may be **New York Metro** ⚜ (**www.nymetro.com**), the online arm of glossy weekly *New York.* New York Metro is currently the most up-to-date site covering happenings in the city. (Although keep in mind that these things can change by the moment in the fickle, poorly funded web world.) The site is particularly strong in restaurant and shopping coverage

Each of the city's high-profile weeklies also maintain sites that are very useful for current happenings, including:

- *The New York Times* www.nytoday.com
- *Time Out New York*: www.timeoutny.com
- *The Village Voice*: www.villagevoice.com
- *The New Yorker*: www.newyorker.com

For the most up-to-date information on Lower Manhattan and Ground Zero, visit the website of the **Alliance for Downtown New York,** the Business Improvement District so productive in Lower Manhattan both before and after 9/11, at **www.downtownny.com**.

3 When to Go

Summer or winter, rain or shine, New York City always has fun things going on, so there's no real "best" time to go.

While hotel prices are more flexible than they've been in years, New York hotels are by no means throwing a fire sale. Therefore, if money is a big concern, you might want to follow these rough seasonal guidelines.

The least expensive time to visit is in winter, between the first of the year and early April. Sure, the weather can be lousy, but hotels are suffering from the post-holiday blues, and rooms often go for a relative song.

Spring and autumn are traditionally the busiest, most expensive, seasons after holiday time. Spring is generally easier than fall; many hotels consider their peak season to be the last 4 months of the year.

The city is drawing more families these days, and they usually visit in the summer. Still, the prospect of heat and humidity keeps some people away, making July and the first half of August a significantly cheaper time to visit than later in the year, and good hotel deals are often available.

Christmas is not a good time for budget-minded travelers. The first two weeks of December—the shopping weeks—are the worst when it comes to scoring an affordable room. But Thanksgiving can be a great time to visit: Business travelers have gone home, and the holiday shoppers haven't yet arrived. It's a little-known secret that most hotels away from the Thanksgiving Day Parade route are usually willing to make great deals to fill them. Hotels practically give away hotel rooms for the week following Thanksgiving.

NEW YORK CITY CALENDAR OF EVENTS

The following is subject to change. Always confirm before you make plans around a specific event. Call the venue, the **NYCVB** at ☎ **212/484-1222,** go to **www.nycvisit.com**.

January

Restaurant Week. This twice-yearly event allows you to lunch for $20.03 at some of New York's finest restaurants. A great way to ring in the New Year! Call ✆ **212/484-1222** or check www.restaurantweek.com for dates and participating restaurants. *Reserve immediately.* Late January or early February.

February

Chinese New Year. Every year Chinatown rings in its own new year with 2 weeks of celebrations, including parades with dragon and lion dancers and costumes. The parade winds through Chinatown along Mott, Canal, and Bayard streets, and along East Broadway. The year 2003 is the Year of the Goat, and Chinese New Year falls on February 1. Call the **NYCVB** hot line at ✆ **212/484-1222** or the **Chinese Information and Culture Center** at ✆ **212/373-1800.**

March

St. Patrick's Day Parade. More than 150,000 marchers join in the world's largest civilian parade, as Fifth Avenue from 44th to 86th streets rings with the sounds of bands and bagpipes, and an inordinate amount of beer is consumed (much of it green). The parade usually starts at 11am, but go extra early if you want a good spot. Call ✆ **212/484-1222.** March 17.

April

Easter Parade. This isn't a traditional parade, per se: There are no bands, baton twirlers, or protesters. Once, New York's gentry came out along Fifth Avenue from 48th to 57th streets to show off their tasteful but discreet toppings. Today, it's more about flamboyant exhibitionism, with hats and costumes that get more outrageous every year—and anybody can join in for free. The parade generally runs Easter Sunday from 10am to 3 or 4pm. Call ✆ **212/484-1222.** April 20.

May

Fleet Week. About 10,000 Navy and Coast Guard personnel are "at liberty" in New York at the end of May. Usually from 1 to 4pm daily, you can visit the ships and aircraft carriers at the piers on the west side of Manhattan, and watch some exhibitions by the U.S. Marines. Even if you don't take in any of the events, you'll know it's Fleet Week because those 10,000 sailors are all over town in their white uniforms. It's like *On the Town* come to life. Call ✆ **212/245-0072,** or visit www.fleetweek.com or www.uss-intrepid.com. Late May.

June

Lesbian and Gay Pride Week and March. A week of cheerful happenings precedes a parade commemorating the Stonewall Riot of June 27, 1969, which for many marks the beginning of the gay liberation movement. Fifth Avenue goes wild as the LGBT community celebrates with bands, marching groups, floats, and plenty of panache. The parade starts on upper Fifth Avenue around 52nd Street and continues into the Village, where a street festival and a dance with fireworks cap the day. Call ✆ **212/807-7433** or check www.nycpride.org. Late June.

Shakespeare in the Park. The Delacorte Theater in **Central Park** is the setting for free performances under the stars—including at least one Shakespeare production each season—often with stars on the stage. For details, call ✆ **212/539-8750** or visit www.publictheater.org. June through August.

Restaurant Week. Lunch for only $20.03 at some of New York's finest restaurants. Participating places vary each year, so call the NYCVB at ✆ **212/484-1222** or check www.restaurantweek.com for the schedule and participants, usually available by mid-May. *Reserve immediately.* One week in late June; some restaurants extend their offers to Labor Day.

July

Independence Day Harbor Festival and Fourth of July Fireworks Spectacular. Start the day amid the crowds at the Great July Fourth Festival in Lower Manhattan, then catch Macy's fireworks over the East River (the best vantage point is from FDR Dr., which closes to traffic several hours before sunset). Call ✆ **212/484-1222** or Macy's Visitor Center at 212/494-2922. July 4th.

August

Lincoln Center Out of Doors. This series of free music and dance performances is held outdoors on the plazas of **Lincoln Center.** Call ✆ **212/875-5108** or 212/546-2656, or visit www.lincolncenter.org for this year's schedule (usually available in mid-July). Throughout August.

New York International Fringe Festival. Held in a variety of Lower East Side venues for a mainly hipster crowd, this arts festival presents alternative and traditional theater, musicals, dance, comedy, and all manner of performance art. Hundreds of events are held over about 10 days in August. The quality can vary, but you'd be surprised at how many shows are *good*. Call

© **888/FRINGE-NYC** or 212/420-8777, or visit www.fringenyc. org. Throughout August.

Harlem Week. The world's largest black and Hispanic cultural festival actually spans almost the whole month to include the Black Film Festival, the Harlem Jazz and Music Festival, and the Taste of Harlem Food Festival. Expect a full slate of music, from gospel to hip-hop, and lots of other festivities. Visit www.discover harlem.com or call *©* **212/484-1222** for this year's schedule of events and locations. Throughout August.

September

West Indian–American Day Parade. This Brooklyn event is New York's largest street celebration. Come for the costumes, pulsating rhythms, bright colors, folklore, food (jerk chicken, oxtail soup, Caribbean soul food), and two million hip-shaking revelers. The route usually runs along Eastern Parkway from Utica Avenue to Grand Army Plaza (at the gateway to Prospect Park). Call *©* **212/484-1222** or 718/625-1515. Labor Day.

Broadway on Broadway. This free afternoon show features the songs and casts from virtually every Broadway show on a stage in the middle of Times Square. This event keeps getting bigger— and is usually broadcast on TV—so you can expect the big stars. Call *©* **212/768-1560** or visit www.timessquarebid.org and click on "Events." One Sunday in mid-September.

October

Greenwich Village Halloween Parade. This is Halloween at its most outrageous. You may have heard Lou Reed singing about it on his classic album *New York*—he wasn't exaggerating. Drag queens and assorted other flamboyant types parade in wildly creative costumes. The parade route starts after sunset at Spring Street and marches up Sixth Avenue to 23rd Street or Union Square. Call the *Village Voice* Parade hot line at *©* **212/475-3333,** ext. 4044, point your browser to www.halloween-nyc.com, or check the papers for the route so you can watch—or participate, if you have the threads and the imagination. October 31.

November

New York City Marathon. Some 30,000 runners from around the world participate in the largest U.S. marathon, and more than a million fans cheer them on as they run through all five New York City boroughs and finish in Central Park. Call *©* **212/423-2249** or 212/860-4455, or surf to www.nyrrc.org for applications. The race is scheduled for November 2 in 2003.

Radio City Music Hall Christmas Spectacular. A gaudy extravaganza starring the Rockettes and a cast that includes live camels. After an extensive 1999 renovation, Radio City itself is a sight to see. For information, call ☎ **212/247-4777,** visit www.radiocity.com; buy tickets at the box office or Ticketmaster's **Radio City Hot Line** (☎ **212/307-1000**), or visit www.ticketmaster.com. Throughout November and December.

Macy's Thanksgiving Day Parade. The procession from Central Park West and 77th Street down Broadway to Herald Square continues to be a national tradition. Huge hot-air balloons of Rocky and Bullwinkle, Snoopy, the Pink Panther, Bart Simpson, and other cartoon favorites are the best part of the fun. The night before, you can see the big blow-up on Central Park West at 79th Street; call in advance to find out whether it will be open to the public. Call ☎ **212/484-1222** or Macy's Visitor Center at 212/494-2922. Thanksgiving Day.

December

Lighting of the Rockefeller Center Christmas Tree. Ice-skating, singing, entertainment, and a crowd accompany the annual ceremony. The tree stays lit around the clock until after the New Year. Call ☎ **212/332-6868** or visit www.rockefeller center.com for this year's date. Early December.

Holiday Trimmings. Stroll down Fifth Avenue and you'll see doormen dressed as wooden soldiers at **FAO Schwarz,** a 27-foot snowflake over the intersection outside **Tiffany's,** the **Cartier** building beribboned in red, wreaths warming the necks of the **New York Public Library**'s lions, and fanciful figures in the windows of **Saks Fifth Avenue** and **Lord & Taylor.** Madison Avenue between 55th and 60th streets is a good bet; **Sony Plaza** usually boasts some fabulous windows, as does **Barneys New York.** Throughout December.

New Year's Eve. The biggest party of them all happens in **Times Square,** where thousands of revelers count down the year's final seconds until the ball drops at midnight at 1 Times Sq. I don't understand it, because it's always a crowded, cold, boozy madhouse, but hey! Call ☎ **212/768-1560** or 212/484-1222, or visit www.timessquarebid.org. December 31.

4 Tips for Travelers with Special Needs
FOR FAMILIES
The first place to look for babysitting is in your hotel (ask about it when you reserve). Many hotels have services or will provide you

with lists of sitters. Or you can call **The Baby Sitters' Guild** (© 212/ 682-0227; www.babysittersguild.com). The sitters are licensed, insured, and bonded, and can even take your child on outings.

FOR TRAVELERS WITH DISABILITIES

Hospital Audiences, Inc. (© 212/575-7676; www.hospitalaudiences.org), arranges attendance and provides details about accessibility at cultural institutions as well as cultural events adapted for people with disabilities. Services include "Describe!," which allows visually impaired theatergoers to enjoy theater events; and the **HAI Hot Line** (© 212/575-7676), which offers accessibility information for hotels, restaurants, attractions, and much more. They also publish *Access for All*, a guidebook on accessibility, available by calling © 212/575-7663 or by sending a $5 check to 548 Broadway, 3rd Floor, New York, NY 10012-3950.

Another good source is **Big Apple Greeter** (© 212/669-8159; www.bigapplegreeter.org). All of its employees are well versed in accessibility issues. They can provide a list of agencies that serve the city's disabled community, and sometimes have discounts to theater and music performances. Big Apple Greeter even offers one-to-one tours that pair volunteers with visitors with disabilities. Reserve at least 1 week ahead.

GETTING AROUND   **Gray Line Air Shuttle** (© 800/451-0455 or 212/315-3006; www.graylinenewyork.com) operates minibuses with lifts from JFK, LaGuardia, and Newark airports to Midtown hotels by reservation; arrange pickup 3 or 4 days in advance. **Olympia Trails** (© 877/894-9155 or 212/964-6233; www.olympia bus.com) provides service from Newark International Airport, with half-price fares for travelers with disabilities. (Prepurchase your tickets to guarantee the discount fare, as drivers can't sell discounted tickets.) Not all buses are appropriately equipped, so call ahead for the daily schedule of accessible buses (press "0" [zero] to reach a real person).

Taxis are required to carry people who have folding wheelchairs and guide or therapy dogs. However, even though you shouldn't have to, you may have to wait for a friendly (or fare-desperate) driver to come along.

All public buses' back doors are supposed to be equipped with wheelchair lifts (though the city has had complaints that not all are in working order). Buses also "kneel," lowering their front steps for people who have difficulty boarding. Passengers with disabilities pay half-price fares (75¢). The **subway** isn't fully wheelchair accessible, but a list of about 30 accessible stations and a guide to wheelchair-accessible subway itineraries is on the MTA website. Call © **718/596-8585** for transit info, or go to **www.mta.nyc.ny.us/nyct** and click on "Accessibility."

FOR SENIOR TRAVELERS

Mention your senior status when you make your reservations, because all major airlines and many hotels offer discounts. Both **Amtrak** (© **800/USA-RAIL;** www.amtrak.com) and **Greyhound** (© **800/229-2424;** www.greyhound.com) offer discounts to persons over 62.

New York subway and bus fares are half price (75¢) for people 65 or older. Many museums and sights (and some theaters and performance halls) offer discounted entrance and tickets to seniors; so do ask for it. Always bring an ID card with proof of age.

Members of **AARP** (© **800/424-3410** or 202/434-2277; www.aarp.org), get discounts on hotels, airfares, and car rentals, as well as other wide-ranging benefits. Anyone over 50 can join.

FOR GAY & LESBIAN TRAVELERS

All over Manhattan, but especially in neighborhoods like the **West Village** (particularly Christopher St., the main drag, so to speak, of New York gay male life) and **Chelsea** (Eighth Ave. from 16th to 23rd sts. and West 17th to 19th sts. from Fifth to Eighth aves.), shops, services, and restaurants have a lesbian and gay flavor. **The Oscar Wilde Bookshop,** 15 Christopher St. (© **212/255-8097;** www.oscarwildebooks.com), is the city's best gay and lesbian bookstore, and a source for information on the city's gay community.

The **Lesbian, Gay, Bisexual & Transgender Community Center** is at 208 W. 13th St., between Seventh and Eighth avenues (© **212/620-7310;** www.gaycenter.org). The center is the meeting place for more than 400 organizations. You can check the online events calendar, which lists hundreds of happenings—lectures, dances, concerts, readings, films—or call. Their site offers links to gay-friendly hotels and guesthouses, plus tons of other information; the staff is also friendly and helpful.

Other good sources are *HX* (www.hx.com), *New York Blade* (www.nyblade.com), *Next* (www.nextnyc.com), *Gay City News* (www.lgny.com); and the *Village Voice* (www.villagevoice.com)—all free weeklies you can pick up in bars, stores, and sidewalk boxes throughout town. The glossy weekly *Time Out New York* (www.timeoutny.com) boasts a terrific gay and lesbian section.

FOR STUDENTS

Many museums, sights, and theaters offer reduced admission to students, so bring your student ID and valid proof of age.

5 Getting There

BY PLANE

Three major airports serve New York City: **John F. Kennedy International Airport** (© 718/244-4444) in Queens, about 15 miles/24km (1 hr.) from Midtown; **LaGuardia Airport** (© 718/533-3400), also in Queens, about 8 miles/13km (30 min.) from Midtown; and **Newark International Airport** (© 973/961-6000) in New Jersey, about 16 miles/26km (45 min.) from Midtown. Information about all three is online at **www.panynj.gov**.

Almost every major domestic carrier serves a New York–area airport; most serve two or all three. Among them are **American** (© 800/433-7300; www.aa.com), **America West** (© 800/235-9292; www.americawest.com), **Continental** (© 800/525-0280; www.continental.com), **Delta** (© 800/221-1212; www.delta.com), **Northwest** (© 800/225-2525; www.nwa.com), **United** (© 800/241-6522; www.united.com), and **US Airways** (© 800/428-4322; www.usairways.com).

In recent years there has been rapid growth in the number of no-frills airlines serving New York. You might check out **AirTran** (© 800/247-8726; www.airtran.com); **ATA** (© 800/435-9282; www.ata.com); **Frontier** (© 800/432-1359; www.flyfrontier.com); **Midway** (© 800/446-4392; www.midwayair.com); **Midwest Express** (© 800/452-2022; www.midwestexpress.com); **National** (© 888/757-5387; www.nationalairlines.com); **Spirit** (© 800/772-7117; www.spiritair.com); and **Vanguard** (© 800/VANGUARD; www.flyvanguard.com). The JFK-based cheap-chic airline **jetBlue** (© 800/JETBLUE; www.jetblue.com) has taken New York by storm with its low fares and high-class service. The nation's leading discount airline, **Southwest** (© 800/435-9792; www.iflyswa.com), flies into MacArthur (Islip) Airport on Long Island, 50 miles east of Manhattan.

Most major international carriers also serve New York.

TRANSPORTATION TO & FROM THE NEW YORK–AREA AIRPORTS

For transportation information for all three airports (JFK, LaGuardia, and Newark), call **Air-Ride** (© 800/247-7433), which

Tips New Air Travel Security Measures

In the wake of the terrorist attacks of September 11, 2001, the airline industry began implementing new security measures. Although regulations vary from airline to airline, you can expedite the process by taking these steps:

- **Arrive early.** Arrive at the airport *at least* 2 hours before your departure time, because you'll have to negotiate lines at the ticket counter and the security gate. E-tickets seldom speed up the check-in process, since interacting with a check-in agent is essential to the new security processes.
- **Try not to drive your car to the airport.** Parking and curbside access to the terminal may be limited. Call ahead and check.
- **Curbside check-in may not be available.** You can't count on handing off your bag to a skycap anymore. For the latest on this, check with the individual airlines.
- **Carry plenty of documentation.** A government-issued photo ID (federal, state, or local) is now required. With an E-ticket, you may be required to have with you printed confirmation of purchase, and the credit card with which you bought your ticket. This varies from airline to airline, so call ahead to make sure you have what you need. Be sure that your ID is **up-to-date:** An expired driver's license or passport may keep you from boarding.
- **Know what you can carry on—and what you can't.** Travelers in the United States are limited to one carry-on bag, plus one personal bag (such as a purse or a briefcase). The Transportation Safety Administration (TSA) has also issued a list of restricted carry-on items that includes knives (yep, including the Swiss Army variety); for the latest restrictions, visit **www.tsa.gov**.
- **Prepare to be searched.** Expect spot-checks, both at the security and boarding gates. Electronic items, such as laptops and cell phones, should be readied for additional screening.
- **Remember: No ticket, no gate access.** Only ticketed passengers will be allowed beyond the screener checkpoints, except for those travelers with specific medical or parental needs.

offers recorded details on bus and shuttle companies and car services 24 hours a day; live operators staff the line Monday through Friday from 8am to 6pm EST. Similar information is online at **www. panynj.gov/airports**.

The Port Authority also runs staffed Ground Transportation Information counters on the baggage claim level in each terminal at each airport. Most transportation companies have courtesy phones near the baggage-claim area.

SUBWAYS & PUBLIC BUSES   Taking the MTA to and from the airport can be a hassle, but it's the cheapest way to go—$1.50 each way. (Note that a fare hike was a possibility at press time.) However, keep in mind that the subways and buses that serve the airports involve transfers and staircases; count on more hauling to your hotel (or a taxi fare) once you arrive in Manhattan. This won't work for travelers with lots of luggage, because you won't have anywhere to store it on the bus or subway. You might not want to take the bus or the subway if you're traveling very early or very late.

For more subway and bus info, see "Getting Around" in chapter 2.

From/to JFK   Upon exiting the terminal, pick up the shuttle bus (marked LONG TERM PARKING LOT); it takes you to the **Howard Beach station,** where you get the A train to Manhattan. Service is every 10 to 15 minutes during rush hour and every 20 minutes at midday, and the subway fare is $1.50. Plan on 2 hours in each direction, maybe more if you're traveling at rush hour: The subway ride from Midtown takes about 75 minutes, and you'll need another 20 to 30 minutes for the shuttle ride to your terminal; also be sure to factor in waiting time at both ends. If you're traveling to JFK from Manhattan, take the A train that says FAR ROCKAWAY or ROCKAWAY PARK—*not* LEFFERTS BOULEVARD. Get off at the Howard Beach/JFK Airport station and connect to the shuttle bus, A or B, which goes to your terminal (they're clearly marked).

From/to LaGuardia   The **M60 bus** serves all LaGuardia terminals. When leaving LaGuardia, follow the GROUND TRANSPORTATION signs and look for the **M60** stop sign at the curb. The bus will take you to Broadway and 116th Street on Manhattan's west side, where you can transfer to a downtown bus or the 1 or 9 subway; you can also pick up the N subway into Manhattan by disembarking at the Astoria Boulevard station in Queens. The bus runs daily between 4am and 1am, leaving at half-hour intervals and taking 40 to 50 minutes. Be sure to allow at least 1¼ hours, however; you

Tips   Money-Saving Package Deals

Before you start your search for the lowest airfare, you may want to consider booking your flight as part of a travel package that includes both airfare and accommodations (and sometimes extras like sightseeing tours and theater tickets) all for one price.

A terrific source for Big Apple packages is **New York City Vacation Packages** (© 888/692-8701 or 570/714-4692; www.nycvp.com), which can sell you a complete package including hotel, theater tickets, and more—usually for much less than you can do on your own. NYCVP can often build a package that includes otherwise sold-out tickets to Broadway shows and sporting events.

One of the biggest packagers in the Northeast, **Liberty Travel** (© 888/271-1584; www.libertytravel.com) offers 2- to 7-night New York packages that usually include freebies like a Circle Line cruise or tickets to the Empire State Building, plus good hotels at every price point.

The major airlines offering good-value packages to New York include **Continental Airlines Vacations** (© 800/634-5555; www.coolvacations.com), **Delta Vacations** (© 800/872-7786; www.deltavacations.com), **US Airways Vacations** (© 800/455-0123; www.usairwaysvacations.com), **United Vacations** (© 800/328-6877; www.unitedvacations.com), **American Airlines Vacations** (© 800/321-2121; www.aavacations.com), and **Northwest WorldVacations** (© 800/800-1504; www.nwa.com/vacpkg).

If you're a late planner, check out the discounted packages offered by **Site59.com.** Their last-minute getaways can save you up to 60% on your entire package, and can be booked anytime between 3 hours and 14 days in advance. Various combinations are available, including flight and hotel, land only (if you've already booked your flight or will be arriving by car), and others that include dining and entertainment.

If you'd prefer to take the train, check with **Amtrak Vacations** (© 800/321-8684; www.amtrak.com/services/amtrak-vacations.html) for all-inclusive ride-and-stay packages.

never know about traffic. *Money-saving tip:* Use a MetroCard to pay your fare and you'll save the extra $1.50 it usually costs for the transfer. For the complete schedule and other pickup and drop-off points, visit **www.mta.nyc.ny.us/nyct**.

PRIVATE BUSES & SHUTTLES   Buses and shuttle services are more expensive than using the MTA for airport transfers, but they're less expensive than taxis if there's only one or two of you (though they're usually more time-consuming).

Gray Line Express Shuttle USA (© 800/451-0455 or 212/315-3006; www.graylinenewyork.com) vans depart JFK, LaGuardia, and Newark every 20 to 30 minutes between 7am and 11:30pm. They will drop you off at most hotels between 21st and 103rd streets in Manhattan. No reservation is required; go to the ground-transportation desk or dial **24** on the Gray Line courtesy phone in the baggage-claim area. Service from mid-Manhattan to all three airports operates daily from 5am to 9pm; call a day in advance to arrange a hotel pickup. The regular one-way fare to and from JFK is $19, to and from LaGuardia is $16, and to and from Newark is $19, but you can save a few bucks by prepaying your round-trip at the airport ($28 for JFK and Newark, $26 for LaGuardia).

The blue vans of **Super Shuttle** (© 800/BLUE-VAN or 212/258-3826; www.supershuttle.com) serve all three area airports, providing door-to-door service to Manhattan and points on Long Island every 15 to 30 minutes around the clock. You don't need to reserve your airport-to-Manhattan ride; go to the ground-transportation desk or use the courtesy phone in the baggage-claim area and ask for Super Shuttle. Hotel pickups for your return trip require 24 to 48 hours' advance booking; you can make reservations online. Fares run $13 to $22 per person, depending on the airport, with discounts available for additional persons in the same party.

New York Airport Service (© 718/875-8200; www.nyairport service.com) buses travel from JFK and LaGuardia to the Port Authority Bus Terminal (42nd St. and Eighth Ave.), Grand Central Terminal (Park Ave. between 41st and 42nd sts.), and to select Midtown hotels between 27th and 59th streets. Follow the GROUND TRANSPORTATION signs to the curbside pickup or look for the uniformed agent. Buses depart the airport every 20 to 70 minutes (depending on your departure point and destination) between 6am and midnight. Buses to JFK and LaGuardia depart the Port

Newark's AirTrain: From Jersey to Manhattan in Minutes

In 2001, there was a new way to get to the airport: the **AirTrain Newark,** which now connects Newark International Airport with Manhattan via a speedy monorail/rail link.

The system is fast, pleasant, and easy to use. Each arrivals terminal at Newark International Airport has a boarding station, so follow the signs once you collect your bags. All AirTrains head to **Newark International Airport Station,** where you transfer to a **NJ Transit** train. NJ Transit will deliver you to New York Penn Station, where you can pick up a cab to your hotel.

The whole process can have you in Manhattan in 20 minutes if you catch a quick connection. NJ Transit trains run 2 to 3 times an hour during peak travel times (once an hour early and late); you can check the schedules on monitors before you leave the terminal, and again at the train station. Tickets can be purchased from vending machines at both the air terminal and the train station (no ticket is required to board the AirTrain). The one-way fare is $11.15 (children under 5 ride free).

Authority and Grand Central Terminal on the Park Avenue side every 15 to 30 minutes. To request direct shuttle service from your hotel, call at least 24 hours in advance. One-way fare for JFK is $13, $23 round-trip; to and from LaGuardia, it's $10 one way, $17 round-trip.

Olympia Airport Express (✆ **877/894-9155** or 212/964-6233; www.olympiabus.com) provides service every 5 to 30 minutes from Newark International Airport to Penn Station (the pickup point is the northwest corner of 34th St. and Eighth Ave. and the drop-off point is the southwest corner), the Port Authority Bus Terminal (on 42nd St. between Eighth and Ninth aves.), and Grand Central Terminal (on 41st St. between Park and Lexington aves.). Passengers to and from Grand Central can connect to shuttle vans servicing select Midtown hotels. Call for the exact schedule for your return trip. The fare is $11 one way, $21 round-trip; it's $5 more to

Even if you have to wait 15 minutes or so to make a connection, you're likely to find the AirTrain transfer from the airport to Manhattan is quicker than taking a cab, especially during rush hours, when car traffic is bumper-to-bumper.

On your return trip, the AirTrain is far more predictable than subjecting yourself to the whims of traffic. What's more, you can check your flight's status at the Newark International Airport Station.

A word of warning: If you have mobility issues, lots of luggage, or small children to keep track of, it's easier to rely on a taxi, car service, or shuttle for a door-to-door transfer.

For more information on AirTrain Newark, call ℂ **888/ EWR-INFO** or go online to **www.airtrainnewark.com**. For connection details, click on the links on the AirTrain website or contact **NJ Transit** (ℂ **800/626-RIDE;** www.njtransit.com) or **Amtrak** (ℂ **800/USA-RAIL;** www.amtrak.com).

connect to the hotel shuttle. Seniors and travelers with disabilities ride for $5.

TAXIS   Taxis are a quick and convenient way to travel to and from the airports, but you'll pay for the convenience. They're available at taxi stands outside the terminals, with dispatchers on hand during peak hours at JFK and LaGuardia, around the clock at Newark. Follow the GROUND TRANSPORTATION or TAXI signs. There may be a line, but it generally moves quickly. Fares, whether fixed or metered, do not include bridge and tunnel tolls ($3.50–$6) or a tip (15%–20% is customary). They include all passengers and luggage—never pay more than the metered or flat rate, except for tolls and a tip (from 8pm–6am a 50¢ surcharge also applies on New York yellow cabs). Taxis have a limit of four passengers. For more on taxis, see "Getting Around" in chapter 2. Fares from the airports to the city are as follows:

- **From JFK:** A flat rate of $35 to Manhattan (plus tolls and tip) is charged. The meter will not be turned on and the surcharge will not be added. The flat rate does not apply on trips from Manhattan to the airport.
- **From LaGuardia:** $16 to $26, metered, plus tolls and tip.
- **From Newark:** The dispatcher gives you a slip of paper with a flat rate ranging from $30 to $38 (toll and tip extra), depending on where you're going, so be precise about your destination. New York yellow cabs aren't permitted to pick up passengers at Newark. The yellow-cab fare from Manhattan to Newark is the meter amount plus $10 and tolls (about $40–$50, perhaps a few dollars more with tip). New Jersey taxis aren't permitted to take passengers from Manhattan to Newark.

Note that a taxi fare increase was being discussed at press time, so fares may be higher by the time you arrive.

PRIVATE CAR SERVICES   Private car companies provide 24-hour door-to-door airport transfers. The advantage they offer over a taxi is that you can arrange your pickup in advance and avoid the hassles of the taxi line. A taxi is virtually always cheaper from JFK thanks to the flat fare; otherwise, as a general rule of thumb, expect to pay a tad less with a car service during rush hour (because there's no ticking meter), slightly more at other times.

Call at least 24 hours in advance (even earlier on holidays), and a driver will meet you near baggage claim (or at your hotel for a return trip). You'll probably be asked to leave a credit-card number to guarantee your ride. You'll likely be offered the choice of indoor or curbside pickup; indoor pickup is more expensive, but makes it easier to hook up with your driver (who usually waits in baggage claim holding a sign with your name on it). You can save a few dollars if you arrange for an outside pickup; call the dispatcher as soon as you land, then take your luggage to the waiting area, where you'll wait for the driver. Besides the wait, the other disadvantage is that curbside can be chaos during prime deplaning hours.

Ask when booking what the fare will be and if you can use your credit card to pay for the ride so there are no surprises at drop-off time. There may be charges tacked on if the driver has to wait an excessive amount of time for your plane to land, but the car companies usually check on your flight beforehand to get an accurate landing time.

I've had the best luck with **Carmel** (© **800/922-7635** or 212/666-6666) and **Legends** (© **888/LEGENDS** or 718/788-1234); **Allstate** (© **800/453-4099** or 212/333-3333) and **Tel-Aviv** (© **800/222-9888** or 212/777-7777) also have reasonable reputations. (Keep in mind, though, that these services are only as good as the individual drivers—and sometimes there's a lemon in the bunch. If you have a problem, report it to the office.)

BY TRAIN

Amtrak (© **800/USA-RAIL;** www.amtrak.com) runs frequent service to New York City's **Penn Station,** on Seventh Avenue between 31st and 33rd streets, where you can pick up a taxi, subway, or bus. Trains can be less hassle than flying, because they take you into Manhattan (thereby avoiding time-consuming and expensive airport transfers).

BY BUS

Buses arrive at the **Port Authority Terminal,** on Eighth Avenue between 40th and 42nd streets, where you can transfer to your hotel by taxi, subway, or bus. **Greyhound Bus Lines** (© **800/229-9424;** www.greyhound.com) is the nation's biggest bus carrier. You'll find a list of their special fares and discounts on their Web page; ask about special deals if you call. **Peter Pan Lines** (© **800/343-9999,** 212/564-8484, or 212/967-2900; www.peterpanbus.com) services the Northeast Corridor; rates are low, and buses are more comfortable than Greyhound's. For a list of carriers that serve the Port Authority Terminal, visit **www.panynj.gov/tbt/busline.htm**.

Although the bus is likely to be the cheapest option, especially for East Coast short hauls, don't just assume. Always compare fares; sometimes, a full-fare bus ticket is no cheaper than the train. If you get lucky, you might even catch an airline fare sale that will make flying the most prudent option.

BY CAR

From the **New Jersey Turnpike** (I-95) and points west, there are three Hudson River crossings: the **Holland Tunnel** (lower Manhattan), the **Lincoln Tunnel** (Midtown), and the **George Washington Bridge** (Upper Manhattan). At press time, cars with only one passenger were prohibited from traveling from New Jersey through the Holland Tunnel during morning rush hour.

From **upstate New York,** take the **New York State Thruway** (I-87), which crosses the Hudson River on the Tappan Zee Bridge and becomes the **Major Deegan Expressway** (I-87) through the Bronx. For the east side, continue to the Triborough Bridge and down the FDR Drive. For the west side, take the Cross Bronx Expressway (I-95) to the Henry Hudson Parkway or the Taconic State Parkway to the Saw Mill River Parkway to the Henry Hudson Parkway south.

From **New England,** the **New England Thruway** (I-95) connects with the **Bruckner Expressway** (I-278), which leads to the Triborough Bridge and the FDR Drive on the east side. For the west side, take the Bruckner to the Cross Bronx Expressway (I-95) to the Henry Hudson Parkway south.

Note that you'll have to pay tolls along some of these roads and at most crossings.

6 For International Visitors

ENTRY REQUIREMENTS

Be sure to check with any U.S. embassy or consulate for the latest requirements, and travel advisories, as there may be changes and more restrictions in the wake of the September 11, 2001, terrorist attacks. You can obtain a visa application online at the **U.S. State Department**'s website, **http://travel.state.gov.** Click on "Visas for Foreign Citizens" for entry info, while "Foreign Consular Offices" and "Links to Foreign Embassies" provides information for U.S. embassies and consulates worldwide.

VISAS   The U.S. State Department has a **Visa Waiver Program** that allows citizens of certain countries to enter the country without a visa for stays of up to 90 days. At press time, this visa waiver program applied to citizens of Andorra, Australia, Austria, Belgium, Brunei, Denmark, Finland, France, Germany, Iceland, Ireland, Italy, Japan, Liechtenstein, Luxembourg, Monaco, the Netherlands, New Zealand, Norway, Portugal, San Marino, Singapore, Slovenia, Spain, Sweden, Switzerland, the United Kingdom, and Uruguay. Citizens of these countries need only a valid passport and a round-trip ticket in their possession upon arrival. Further information is available from any U.S. embassy or consulate. *Note:* This list can change at any time so always check visa requirements well in advance.

Canadian citizens may enter the United States without visas; they need only proof of residence.

Citizens of other countries must have a valid passport that expires at least 6 months later than the scheduled end of their visit, and a tourist visa, which may be obtained from any U.S. consulate.

To obtain a visa, submit a completed application (in person or by mail) with two 1½-inch-square photos and $45, and demonstrate binding ties to a residence abroad. Usually you can obtain a visa at once or within 24 hours, but it may take longer during the summer. If you cannot go in person, contact the nearest U.S. embassy or consulate for directions on applying by mail. Your travel agent or airline may be able to provide you with visa applications and instructions. The U.S. consulate or embassy will determine if you will be issued a multiple- or single-entry visa and any restrictions regarding the length of your stay.

Inquire about visa cases and the application process at ✆ **202/ 663-1225.**

MEDICAL REQUIREMENTS   Unless you're arriving from an area known to be suffering from an epidemic, inoculations or vaccinations are not required for entry. If you have a disease that requires treatment with narcotics or syringe-administered medications, carry a valid signed prescription from your physician.

Upon entering the United States, foreign nationals are required to declare any dangerous contagious diseases they carry, which includes infection with HIV, the AIDS virus. Anyone who has such a disease is excluded from entry as a tourist. You may be able to apply for a waiver if you are attending a conference or have another compelling nontourism reason for your visit (call the **Immigration and Naturalization Service** (INS) at ✆ **800/375-5283** to inquire). Doubtless many HIV-positive visitors come in without declaring their condition.

MONEY

The most common **bills** are the $1 (a "buck"), $5, $10, and $20 denominations. There are $2 bills (seldom encountered), $50 bills, and $100 bills (the last two usually not welcome for small purchases). Redesigned bills were recently introduced, but the old-style bills are still legal tender. There are six denominations of **coins:** 1¢ (1 cent, or a penny); 5¢ (5 cents, or a nickel); 10¢ (10 cents, or a dime); 25¢ (25 cents, or a quarter); 50¢ (50 cents, or a half dollar);

and a gold-toned $1 piece; you may receive one as change from a subway MetroCard machine.

The foreign-exchange bureaus common in Europe are rare in the United States. You'll find them in tourist areas like Times Square, but expect a lousy exchange rate. **American Express** (© **800/AXP-TRIP;** www.americanexpress.com) has many offices in the city, including 1185 Sixth Ave., at 47th Street (© 212/398-8585); at the New York Marriott Marquis hotel, 1535 Broadway, (© 212/575-6580); and at Macy's Herald Square, 34th Street and Broadway (© 212/695-8075). Visit **http://travel.americanexpress.com/travel/personal/resources/tso** to locate additional offices. **Thomas Cook Currency Services** (© **800/CURRENCY;** www.us.thomas cook.com) are at 1590 Broadway at 48th Street (© 212/265-6063); 1271 Broadway, at 32nd Street (© 212/679-4877); 317 Madison Ave. at 42nd Street (© 212/883-0401); and 29 Broadway, south of Wall Street (© 212/363-6206).

2

Getting to Know New York City

This chapter gives you an insider's take on Manhattan's most distinctive neighborhoods and streets, tells you how to get around, and serves as a reference to everything from personal safety to libraries and liquor laws.

1 Orientation

VISITOR INFORMATION
INFORMATION OFFICES

- The **Times Square Visitors Center,** 1560 Broadway, between 46th and 47th streets (where Broadway meets Seventh Ave.), across from the TKTS booth (© **212/768-1560;** www.times squarebid.org), is the city's top info stop. The center features a helpful info desk offering loads of information. There's also a Metropolitan Transportation Authority (MTA) desk that sells MetroCards, offers transit maps, and answers your transit system questions; a Broadway Ticket Center offering show information and selling full-price tickets; ATMs and currency-exchange machines; and computers with free Internet access. It's open daily from 8am to 8pm.

- The New York Convention and Visitors Bureau runs the **NYCVB Visitor Information Center** at 810 Seventh Ave., between 52nd and 53rd streets. In addition to information on attractions and a multilingual counselor, the center has interactive terminals that provide touch-screen access to visitor information via Citysearch and sell advance tickets to major attractions, which can save you from standing in long lines (you can also buy a CityPass using these; see p. 9). There's also an ATM, a gift shop, and phones that connect you directly with American Express card member services. The center is open Monday through Friday from 8:30am to 6pm, Saturday and Sunday from 9am to 5pm. For phone assistance, call © **212/484-1222.**

PUBLICATIONS

For comprehensive listings of films, concerts, sports, museums and art exhibits, fairs, and events, the following are your best bets:

- The *New York Times* (**www.nytimes.com** or **www.nytoday. com**) features great arts and entertainment coverage, particularly in the Friday "Weekend" section and Sunday's "Arts & Leisure" section.

- *Time Out New York* (**www.timeoutny.com**) is my favorite weekly magazine. *TONY* features excellent coverage in all categories, and it's attractive, well organized, and easy to use. A new issue hits newsstands every Thursday.

- The famous free weekly *Village Voice* (**www.villagevoice. com**), is available late Tuesday downtown and early Wednesday elsewhere. The arts and entertainment coverage couldn't be more extensive, but I find the paper a bit unwieldy to navigate.

- *New York* magazine (**www.newyorkmag.com** or **www.ny metro.com**) offers excellent restaurant reviews and the "Cue" section, a selective guide to city arts and entertainment

- The *New Yorker* (**www.newyorker.com**) features "Goings On About Town" with an artsy bent at the front of the magazine.

CITY LAYOUT

New York City is comprised of five boroughs: **Manhattan;** the **Bronx; Queens; Brooklyn;** and **Staten Island.** It is Manhattan, the finger-shaped island just off the mainland, that most visitors think of when they envision New York City. Despite the fact that it's the city's smallest borough (13½ miles/22km long, 2¼ miles/3.5km wide, 22 sq. miles/35 sq. km), Manhattan contains the city's most famous attractions, buildings, and institutions.

In most of Manhattan, finding your way around is a snap because of the grid system by which the streets are numbered. If you can discern uptown and downtown, and East Side and West Side, you can find your way around pretty easily. In real terms, **uptown** means north of where you happen to be and **downtown** means south, although sometimes these labels have deeper meanings (generally speaking, "uptown" chic vs. "downtown" bohemianism).

Avenues run north and south (uptown and downtown). Most are numbered. **Fifth Avenue** divides the East Side from the West Side, and serves as the eastern border of Central Park north of 59th Street. **First Avenue** is all the way east and **Twelfth Avenue** is all the way

Manhattan's Neighborhoods

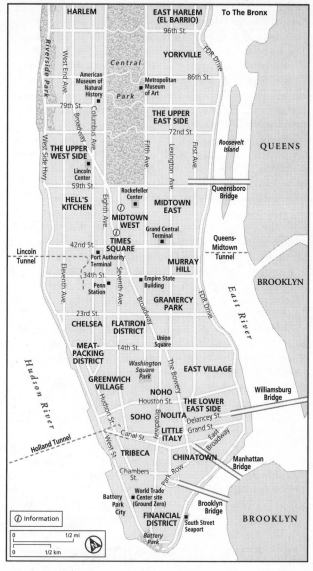

HARLEM

EAST HARLEM
(EL BARRIO)

To The Bronx

96th St.

YORKVILLE

FDR DRIVE

Central

American
Museum of
Natural
History

Metropolitan
Museum
of Art

86th St.

Park

79th St.

THE UPPER
EAST SIDE

72nd St.

Riverside Park

West End Ave.

Columbus Ave.

Broadway

Fifth Ave.

Lexington Ave.

First Ave.

Roosevelt
Island

QUEENS

THE UPPER
WEST SIDE

West Side Hwy.

Lincoln
Center

59th St.

Rockefeller
Center

HELL'S
KITCHEN

Eighth Ave.

MIDTOWN
WEST

Queensboro
Bridge

MIDTOWN
EAST

Grand Central
Terminal

Lincoln
Tunnel

42nd St.

TIMES
SQUARE

Port Authority
Terminal

Eleventh Ave.

34th St.

Penn
Station

Seventh Ave.

MURRAY
HILL

Empire State
Building

Queens-
Midtown
Tunnel

BROOKLYN

East River

Broadway

GRAMERCY
PARK

FDR Drive

23rd St.

CHELSEA

FLATIRON
DISTRICT

Union
Square

14th St.

MEAT-
PACKING
DISTRICT

*Washington
Square
Park*

EAST VILLAGE

GREENWICH
VILLAGE

Hudson St.

NOHO

The Bowery

Williamsburg
Bridge

Houston St.

Hudson River

SOHO

West St.

Broadway

NOLITA

THE LOWER
EAST SIDE

Delancey St.

Canal St.

LITTLE
ITALY

Grand St.

East Broadway

Holland Tunnel

TRIBECA

CHINATOWN

Chambers
St.

Park Row

Manhattan
Bridge

World Trade
Center site
(Ground Zero)

Battery
Park
City

Brooklyn
Bridge

BROOKLYN

FINANCIAL
DISTRICT

South Street
Seaport

(i) Information

*Battery
Park*

0   1/2 mi

0   1/2 km

N

west. The three most important unnumbered avenues on the East Side are between Third and Fifth avenues: **Madison** (east of Fifth), **Park** (east of Madison), and **Lexington** (east of Park, west of Third). Important unnumbered avenues on the West Side are **Avenue of the Americas,** which New Yorkers call Sixth Avenue; **Central Park West,** which Eighth Avenue north of 59th Street as it borders Central Park on the west; **Columbus Avenue,** Ninth Avenue north of 59th Street; and **Amsterdam Avenue,** or Tenth Avenue north of 59th.

Broadway is the exception to the rule—it's the only major avenue that doesn't run uptown to downtown. It cuts a diagonal path across the island, from the northwest tip down to the southeast corner. As it crosses most major avenues, it creates **squares** (Times Sq., Herald Sq., and Union Sq., for example).

Streets run east to west (crosstown) and are numbered as they proceed uptown from Houston (*House*-ton) Street. To go uptown, walk north of, or to a higher-numbered street than, where you are. Downtown is south of (or a lower-numbered street than) your current location. Traffic generally runs east on even-numbered streets and west on odd-numbered streets, with a few exceptions, like the major east-west thoroughfares—**14th, 23rd, 34th, 42nd, 57th, 72nd, 79th, 86th**—which have two-way traffic.

Fifth Avenue is the dividing line between the **East Side** and **West Side** of town (except below Washington Sq., where Broadway serves that function). On the east side of Fifth Avenue, streets are numbered with the distinction "East"; on the west side of Fifth Avenue, they are numbered "West." East 51st Street, for example, begins at Fifth Avenue and runs east to the East River, while West 51st Street begins at Fifth Avenue and runs west to the Hudson River.

Avenue addresses are irregular. For example, 994 Second Ave. is at East 51st Street, but so is 320 Park Ave. Thus, it's important to know a building's cross street to find it.

Unfortunately, the rules don't apply to neighborhoods south of 14th Street—like Wall Street, Chinatown, SoHo, TriBeCa, the Village—since they sprang up before engineers devised this brilliant grid scheme. A good map is essential when exploring these areas.

MANHATTAN'S NEIGHBORHOODS IN BRIEF

Downtown

Lower Manhattan: South Street Seaport & the Financial District   Lower Manhattan is everything south of Chambers

Street. **Battery Park,** the point of departure for the Statue of Liberty, Ellis Island, and Staten Island, is on the south tip of the island. The **South Street Seaport** lies a bit north on the east coast, just south of the Brooklyn Bridge.

The rest of the area is the **Financial District,** but may even be more famous now as **Ground Zero.** Until September 11, 2001, the Financial District was anchored by the **World Trade Center,** with the World Financial Center complex and Battery Park City to the west, and **Wall Street** running crosstown south and to the east.

Despite the devastation, the Financial District deserves to be celebrated as an incredible story of recovery. Within 6 months after that horrific day, the neighborhood was running pretty much normally just about everywhere but the World Trade Center site itself. Since no redevelopment plan is in place, there's no way to know what's to come. However, one thing's for sure: Ground Zero will still be a massive construction zone throughout 2003. Whether viewing platforms will remain in place is anybody's guess; see chapter 5 for information on how to find the latest on the site.

Most major subway lines congregate here before they end or head to Brooklyn. At this writing, all lines were running again; the 1 and 9 resumed service in September 2002.

TriBeCa   Bordered by the Hudson River to the west, the area north of Chambers Street, west of Broadway, and south of Canal Street is the *Tri*angle *Be*low *Ca*nal Street, or TriBeCa. Since the 1980s, as SoHo became saturated with chic, the spillover transformed TriBeCa into one of the city's hippest neighborhoods, where celebrities and families coexist in cast-iron warehouses converted into spacious, expensive loft apartments. Artists' lofts and galleries as well as hip antique and design shops pepper the area, as do as some of the city's best restaurants. Standing in the north shadow of the World Trade Center, TriBeCa suffered greatly in the wake of the disaster; however, it has recovered beautifully.

The main uptown-downtown drag is **West Broadway** (2 blocks to the west of Broadway). Consider the Franklin Street subway station on the 1/9 line to be your gateway to the heart of the action.

Chinatown   The former marshlands northeast of City Hall and below Canal Street, from Broadway to the Bowery, are where Chinese immigrants were forced to live in the 1870s. This booming neighborhood is a conglomeration of Asian populations. It offers tasty cheap eats in cuisines from Sichuan to Hunan to

Cantonese to Vietnamese to Thai. Exotic shops offer strange foods, herbs, and souvenirs. The area is also home to sweatshops and doesn't have quite the character you'd find in San Francisco, although it does feel authentic. Walking down Canal Street, peering into the myriad stores and exotic fish markets, is some of the city's best free entertainment.

The Canal Street (J, M, Z, N, R, 6, Q, W) station will get you to the heart of the action. The streets are crowded during the day and empty out after around 9pm; they remain quite safe, but the neighborhood is more enjoyable during the bustle.

Little Italy Near Chinatown is Little Italy, just as ethnic if not quite so vibrant, and compelling for its own culinary treats. Traditionally the area east of Broadway between Houston and Canal streets, the community is shrinking, due to the encroachment of Chinatown. It's now limited mainly to **Mulberry Street,** where you'll find most restaurants, and a few offshoots. The best way to reach Little Italy is to walk east from the Spring Street station, on the no. 6 line, to Mulberry Street; turn south for Little Italy (you can't miss the year-round red, green, and white street decorations).

The Lower East Side Of all the waves of immigrants and refugees who passed through this tenement neighborhood from the mid–19th century to the 1920s, eastern European Jews left the most lasting impression. Drugs and crime supplanted the Jewish communities, which first popped up between Houston and Canal streets, east of the Bowery, dragging the Lower East Side into the gutter—until recently. The neighborhood has experienced a hipster renaissance over the last few years, and makes a fascinating stop for both nostalgia and nightlife hounds.

There are some remnants of what was once the largest Jewish population in America along **Orchard Street,** where you'll find great bargain hunting in old-world fabric, clothing, and accessories stores still thriving between the boutiques and hipster lounges. The trendy set can be found in the blocks between Allen and Clinton streets south of Houston and north of Delancey, with more shops, bars, and restaurants popping up every day.

Your best bet is to take the F train to Second Avenue and walk east on Houston; when you see Katz's Deli, you've arrived. You can also reach the neighborhood from the Delancey Street station on the F line, and the Essex Street station on the J, M, and Z lines.

SoHo & Nolita **SoHo** got its name as an abbreviation of "*So*uth of *Ho*uston Street." This fashionable neighborhood extends down to Canal Street, between Sixth Avenue to the west and Lafayette Street (1 block east of Broadway) to the east. Take the N or R to Prince Street; the C, E, or 6 to Spring Street; or the F or V train to the Broadway-Lafayette stop.

An industrial zone during the 19th century, SoHo retains the cast-iron architecture of the era. It's now a prime example of urban gentrification and a major attraction thanks to its impeccably restored buildings, fashionable restaurants, and stylish boutiques. On weekends, the cobbled streets and narrow sidewalks are crowded with shoppers, with the prime action between Broadway and Sullivan Street north of Grand Street.

SoHo is one of the best shopping neighborhoods in the city, and few are more fun to browse. High-end street peddlers set up along the boutique-lined sidewalks, hawking jewelry, coffee-table books, and their own art. At night, the neighborhood is a terrific, albeit pricey, dining and barhopping neighborhood (I recommend some affordable options in chapter 6).

In recent years SoHo has been crawling east, taking over Mott and Mulberry streets—and Elizabeth Street in particular—north of Kenmare Street, an area now known as **Nolita** (*No*rth of *Li*ttle I*ta*ly). Some of the city's most promising clothing designers have set up shop, but don't expect bargains. Good, affordable restaurants abound. Taking the 6 to Spring Street will get you closest by subway, but it's a short walk east from SoHo proper.

The East Village & NoHo The **East Village,** which extends between 14th Street and Houston Street, from Broadway east to First Avenue and beyond to Alphabet City—avenues A, B, C, and D—is where the city's bohemia has gone. The East Village is a mix of ethnic and trendy restaurants, upstart clothing designers and kitschy boutiques, punk-rock clubs (yep, still), and folk cafes—plus a half-dozen or so Off-Broadway theaters—all of which give the neighborhood a youthful vibe and a low-budget appeal for visitors and locals alike. In fact, you'll find the city's highest concentration of high-quality budget dining in these precincts.

Gentrification has made a huge impact on the East Village, but there's still a seedy element that some won't find appealing—and some will. The neighborhood still embraces ethnic diversity, with elements of its Ukrainian and Irish heritage, while more recent immigrants have taken over 6th Street between First and Second avenues, now called "Little India."

Unless you're traveling along 14th Street (the L line will drop you off at Third and First aves.), take the 4, 5, 6, N, R, Q, or W to 14th Street/Union Square; the N, R to 8th Street; or the 6 to Astor Place and walk east.

Greenwich Village Tree-lined streets crisscross and wind, following ancient streams and cow paths. Each block reveals yet another row of Greek Revival town houses, a well-preserved Federal-style house, or a peaceful courtyard or square. This is "the Village," from Broadway west to the Hudson River, bordered by Houston Street to the south and 14th Street to the north. It defies Manhattan's orderly grid system with streets that predate it, and unless you live here, it may be impossible to master the lay of the land—so take a map along.

The Seventh Avenue line (1, 2, 3, 9) is the area's main subway artery, while the West 4th Street stop (where the A, C, and E lines meet the F and V lines) serves as its central hub.

The Village is the roost of choice for the young celebrity set, with the likes of Gwyneth Paltrow, Matthew Broderick and Sarah Jessica Parker drawn by its historic, low-rise charms. Gentrification and escalating real-estate values conspire to push out the artistic element, but culture and counterculture still rub shoulders in cafes, jazz clubs, neighborhood bars, off-Broadway theaters, and an endless variety of tiny shops and restaurants.

The Village is probably the most chameleon-like of Manhattan's neighborhoods. Some of the highest-priced real estate in the city runs along lower Fifth Avenue, which dead-ends at **Washington Square Park.** Serpentine **Bleecker Street** stretches through most of the neighborhood and is emblematic of the area's historical bent. The anything-goes attitude in the Village has fostered a large gay community around **Christopher Street** and Sheridan Square. The streets west of Seventh Avenue, an area known as the **West Village,** boast a more relaxed vibe and some of the city's most charming and historic brownstones. Three colleges—New York University, Parsons School of Design, and the New School for Social Research—keep the area thinking young, which explains the popularity of 8th Street, lined with shops selling cheap, hip clothes.

Midtown

Chelsea Chelsea has come on strong in recent years as a hip address, especially for the gay community. A low-rise composite of town houses, tenements, lofts, and factories, the neighborhood comprises roughly the area west of Sixth Avenue from 14th to 30th streets. Chelsea has also evolved into one of the city's best-value accommodations neighborhoods for travelers looking for something special as well as affordable. Its main arteries are Seventh and Eighth avenues, and it's primarily served by the C, E and 1, 9 subway lines.

The **Chelsea Piers** sports complex to the far west and a host of shops (both unique boutiques and big names), well-priced bistros, and bars have contributed to the area's rebirth. You'll find several popular flea markets in parking lots along Sixth Avenue, between 24th and 27th streets on the weekends.

The Flatiron District, Union Square & Gramercy Park These adjoining and at places overlapping neighborhoods are some of the city's most appealing.

The **Flatiron District** lies south of 23rd Street to 14th Street, between Broadway and Sixth Avenue, and centers around the historic Flatiron Building on 23rd (named for its triangular shape) and Park Avenue South, which has become a sophisticated Restaurant Row. Below 23rd Street along Sixth Avenue, discounters like Filene's Basement, Bed Bath & Beyond, and others have moved in. The shopping gets classier on Fifth Avenue and along Broadway, the city's home-furnishings alley.

Union Square is the hub of the area; the N, R, 4, 5, 6, and L trains stop here, as do Q and W trains (until 2004), making it easy to reach. Union Square is the setting for New York's premier greenmarket every Monday, Wednesday, Friday, and Saturday. In-line skaters take over the space in the after-work hours. A number of hip and affordable restaurants rim the square, as do Toys "R" Us, the city's best Barnes & Noble, and a Virgin Megastore.

From about 16th to 23rd streets, east from Park Avenue South to about Second Avenue, is the leafy, largely residential district known as **Gramercy Park.**

Midtown West & Times Square Midtown West, the area from 34th to 59th streets west of Fifth Avenue to the Hudson River, encompasses several famous names: Madison Square Garden, the Garment District, Rockefeller Center, the Theater District, and Times Square. This is New York's tourism central, where you'll find the bright lights and bustle that draw people from all over the world. This is the city's biggest hotel neighborhood, with a lot of budget and midpriced choices in the mix.

The 1, 2, 3, 9 subway line serves the massive neon station at the heart of Times Square, at 42nd Street between Broadway and Seventh Avenue, while the F, V line runs up Sixth Avenue to Rockefeller Center (B and D lines also serve Rockefeller Center, but travel no farther south than 34th St. until 2004). The N/R line cuts diagonally across the neighborhood, following the path of Broadway before heading up Seventh Avenue at 42nd Street (the Q and W trains also use this line until 2004). The A, C, E line serves the west side, running along Eighth Avenue.

If you know New York but haven't been here in a few years, you'll be quite surprised by the "new" **Times Square.** Longtime New Yorkers kvetch about the glory days of the peep-show-and-porn-shop Times Square that this cleaned-up version supplanted, but the truth is that it's a successful regentrification. Most of the Broadway theaters light up the streets just off Times Square, in the West 40s just east and west of Broadway. Expect dense crowds.

Midtown East & Murray Hill Midtown East, the area including Fifth Avenue and everything east from 34th to 59th streets, is the more upscale side of Midtown. It's a bit short of subways, served mostly by the Lexington Avenue 4, 5, 6 line.

The stretch of **Fifth Avenue** from Saks at 49th Street extending to FAO Schwarz at 59th is home to the city's most high-profile haute shopping, including Tiffany & Co. and Bergdorf Goodman, but midpriced names like Banana Republic and Liz Claiborne have moved in. The stretch of 57th Street between Fifth and Lexington avenues is also known for high-fashion boutiques (Chanel, Hermès) and galleries, as is **Madison Avenue.**

Claiming territory east from Madison Avenue, **Murray Hill** begins somewhere north of 23rd Street (the line between it and Gramercy Park is fuzzy), and is most clearly recognizable north of 30th Street to 42nd Street. This brownstone-lined quarter is largely residential, notable for its handful of budget and midpriced hotels.

Uptown

The Upper West Side North of 59th Street and encompassing everything west of Central Park, the Upper West Side contains **Lincoln Center,** one of the world's premier performing-arts venues; the **American Museum of Natural History,** whose Dinosaur Halls and Rose Center for Earth and Space garner rave reviews; and a growing number of affordable hotels whose larger-than-Midtown rooms and nice residential location make them some of the best values in the entire city. Unlike the more stratified Upper East Side, the Upper West Side is home to an egalitarian mix of middle-class yuppiedom, laid-back wealth (lots of celebs and moneyed media types call Central Park West home), and ethnic families who were here before the gentrification.

Two subway lines serve the area: The 1, 2, 3, 9 line runs up Broadway, while the B and C trains go up Central Park West.

Upper East Side North of 59th Street and east of Central Park is New York at its most gentrified: Walk along Fifth and Park avenues, especially between 60th and 80th streets, and you're sure to encounter some of the wizened WASPs and Chanel-suited socialites that make up the most rarefied of the city's population. Madison Avenue from 60th Street well into the 80s is the mon-eyed crowd's main shopping strip. The main attraction of this neighborhood is **Museum Mile,** the stretch of Fifth Avenue fronting Central Park that's home to no fewer than 10 cultural institutions, anchored by the **Metropolitan Museum of Art.** The Upper East Side is served by the crowded Lexington Avenue line (4, 5, 6 trains) and rather slow buses, so wear your walking shoes (or bring taxi fare) if you head here to explore.

Harlem Harlem is really two areas. Harlem proper stretches from river to river, beginning at 125th Street on the West Side and 96th Street on the East Side. East of Fifth Avenue, **Spanish Harlem** (El Barrio) runs between East 100th and East 125th streets. Harlem proper is benefiting from the revitalization that has swept much of the city, with national retailers moving in, restaurants and nightspots opening, and visitors touring historic sites related to the Golden Age of African-American culture.

Do come to Harlem—it's one of the city's most vital, his-toric neighborhoods, and no other feels quite so energized. Your best bet is to take a guided tour (see chapter 5); if you come on your own, don't wander without a plan.

2 Getting Around

Manhattan's transportation systems are a marvel. It's miraculous that so many people can gather on this little island and move around on it. For the most part, you can get where you're going pretty eas-ily using some combination of subways, buses, cabs, and walking.

BY SUBWAY

Run by the **Metropolitan Transit Authority** (MTA), the much-maligned subway system is actually the best way to travel around New York, especially during rush hours. The subway runs 24 hours a day, 7 days a week.

PAYING YOUR WAY The subway fare is $1.50 (half price for seniors and those with disabilities), and children under 44 inches tall ride free (up to three per adult). *Note:* At press time, a fare

---

Tips On the Sidewalks

New Yorkers stride across wide, crowded pavements without any regard for the traffic lights, weaving through crowds, dodging taxis and buses. **Never take your walking cues from the locals.** Wait for walk signals and always use crosswalks. Do otherwise and you could end up as a flattened statistic.

Always pay attention to the traffic flow. Walk as if you're driving, staying to the right. At intersections, keep an eye out for drivers who don't yield, turn without looking, or think a yellow light means "Hurry up!" Unfortunately, many bicyclists blithely fly through red lights and dash the wrong way on one-way streets, so be on your guard.

---

increase was being discussed, so it's possible that the fare might be higher by the time you visit.

While **tokens** still exist (they'll be phased out eventually), most people pay fares with the **MetroCard,** a magnetically encoded card that debits the fare when swiped through the turnstile (or the fare box on a bus). Once you're in the system, you can transfer to any subway line that you can reach without exiting your station. MetroCards—*not* tokens—also allow you **free transfers** between the bus and subway within a 2-hour period.

MetroCards come in a few different configurations:

Pay-Per-Ride MetroCards, which can be used for up to four people by swiping up to four times (bring the whole family). You can put any amount from $3 (two rides) to $80 on your card. Every time you put $15 on your Pay-Per-Ride MetroCard, it's automatically credited 10%—that's one free ride for every $15.

Unlimited-Ride MetroCards, which can't be used for more than one person at a time or more frequently than 18-minute intervals, are available in four values: the **daily Fun Pass,** which allows you a day's worth of unlimited subway and bus rides for $4; the **7-Day MetroCard,** for $17; and the **30-Day MetroCard,** for $63. Seven- and 30-day Unlimited-Ride MetroCards can be purchased at any subway station or MetroCard merchant. Fun Passes cannot be purchased at token booths—you can only buy them from a MetroCard vending machine; from a MetroCard merchant; or at the MTA information desk at the Times Square Visitor Center.

USING THE SYSTEM   The subway system basically mimics the lay of the land above ground, with most lines in Manhattan running north and south, and a few lines east and west.

Lines have assigned colors on subway maps and trains—red for the 1, 2, 3, 9 line; green for the 4, 5, and 6 trains; and so on—but nobody refers to them by color. Always use the number or letter when asking questions. Within Manhattan, the distinction between numbered trains that share the same line is usually that some are express and others are local. **Express trains** often skip about three stops for each one that they make; express stops are indicated on subway maps with a white (rather than solid) circle. Local stops usually come about 9 blocks apart.

Directions are almost always indicated using "Uptown" (north-bound) and "Downtown" (southbound), so be sure to know what direction you want to head in. The outsides of some subway entrances are marked UPTOWN ONLY or DOWNTOWN ONLY; read carefully, as it's easy to head in the wrong direction. Once you're on

---

Tips **For More Bus & Subway Information**

For transit information, call the Metropolitan Transit Authority's **MTA/New York City Transit's Travel Information Center** at ✆ **718/330-1234.** Automated information is available 24 hours a day, and agents are on hand daily from 6am to 9pm. For online information, visit **www.mta.nyc.ny.us**; kudos to the MTA, because the information on the site is always current.

To request maps, call the Customer Assistance Line at ✆ **718/330-3322** (although recent service changes may not be reflected on printed maps). Riders with disabilities should direct inquiries to ✆ **718/596-8585;** hearing-impaired riders can call ✆ **718/596-8273.** For MetroCard information, call ✆ **212/638-7622** weekdays from 7 to 11am, weekends from 9am to 5pm, or go online to **www.mta.nyc.ny.us/metrocard**.

You can get bus and subway maps and additional information at most information centers (see "Visitor Information," earlier in this chapter). An MTA transit information desk is located at the Times Square Visitor Center, 1560 Broadway, between 46th and 47th streets, where you can also buy MetroCards. Maps are sometimes available in subway stations (ask at the token booth), but rarely on buses.

the platform, check the signs overhead to make sure that the train you're waiting for will be traveling in the right direction. If you do make a mistake, it's a good idea to wait for an express station, like 14th Street or 42nd Street, so you can get off and change for the other direction without paying again.

BY BUS

Less expensive than taxis and more pleasant than subways (they provide a sightseeing window on Manhattan), MTA buses are a good transportation option. Their big drawback: They can get stuck in traffic, sometimes making it quicker to walk. They also stop every couple of blocks, rather than the eight or nine blocks that local subways traverse between stops. So for long distances, the subway is best; but for short distances or traveling crosstown, try the bus.

PAYING YOUR WAY   Like the subway fare, **bus fare** is $1.50, half price for seniors and riders with disabilities, free for children under 44 inches (up to three per adult). As of this writing, a fare increase was being discussed, so it's possible that the fare might be higher by the time you visit. The fare is payable with a **MetroCard,** a **token,** or **exact change.** Bus drivers don't make change, and fare boxes don't accept dollar bills or pennies. You can't purchase MetroCards or tokens on the bus, so get them before you board; for details on where to get them, see "Paying Your Way" under "By Subway," above.

USING THE SYSTEM   You can't hail a city bus—you have to wait at a bus stop. **Bus stops** are located every 2 or 3 blocks on the right-side corner of the street. They're marked by a curb painted yellow and a blue-and-white sign with a bus emblem and the route

---

Value **Money-Saving Transit Tips: Free Transfers**

If you pay your subway or bus fare with a **MetroCard,** you can transfer to another bus or to the subway (or from the subway to a bus) for up to 2 hours. Just swipe your card at the token box or turnstile, and the automated system keeps track.

If you use a token or coins to board a bus and need to transfer to another line, request a free **transfer slip** that allows you to change to an intersecting bus route only (transfer points are listed on the transfer itself) within 1 hour of issue. Transfer slips cannot be used to enter the subway.

number or numbers. Guide-A-Ride boxes at most stops show a route map and a somewhat optimistic schedule.

Almost every major avenue has its own **bus route.** They run either north or south. **Crosstown buses** run along all major east-west streets. Some bus routes, however, are erratic: The M104, for example, starts at the East River, then turns at Eighth Avenue and goes up Broadway. The buses of the Fifth Avenue line go up Madison or Sixth and follow various routes around the city. Most routes operate 24 hours a day, but service is infrequent at night.

To make sure the bus you're boarding goes where you're going, check the maps on the sign at the bus stop, get your hands on a route map (see "For More Bus & Subway Information," above), or **just ask.** The drivers are helpful, as long as you don't hold up the line.

BY TAXI

Official New York City taxis, licensed by the Taxi and Limousine Commission, are yellow, with the rates printed on the door and a light with a medallion number on the roof. You can hail a taxi on any street. *Never* accept a ride from any other car except an official yellow cab (livery cars are not allowed to pick up fares on the street).

If you're planning to take taxis, be prepared to pay. The base fare on entering the cab is $2. The cost is 30¢ for every one-fifth mile or 20¢ per minute in stopped or very slow-moving traffic (or for wait-ing time). There's no extra charge for each passenger or for luggage. However, you must pay bridge or tunnel tolls (sometimes the driver will front the toll and add it to your bill at the end; most times, however, you pay the driver before the toll). You'll also pay a 50¢ night surcharge after 8pm and before 6am. A 15% to 20% tip is customary.

Tips **Taxi-Hailing Tips**

When you're waiting on the street for a taxi, look at the **medallion light** on the top of the coming cabs. If the light is out, the taxi is in use. When the center part (the number) is lit, the taxi is available—then raise your hand to flag the cab. If all the lights are on, the driver is off-duty.

Note: A taxi can't take more than four people.

Note: Taxi drivers were lobbying for a fare increase at press time, and the mayor supports it, so don't be surprised if you find higher fares when you arrive.

Because it's going to cost you at least $2 just to get in the car, taxis are far more expensive than other forms of transportation. Visitors on a limited budget are generally better off relying on subways and buses, using taxis only late at night (after 11pm or midnight, when buses and subway trains start getting fewer and farther between) or to reach an out-of-the-way destination. You'll also get your money's worth out of a taxi at night, when there's little traffic to keep them from speeding you to your destination.

The TLC has posted a **Taxi Rider's Bill of Rights** in every cab. Drivers are required to take you anywhere in the five boroughs, to Nassau or Westchester counties, or to Newark Airport. They are supposed to know how to get you to any address in Manhattan and major points in the outer boroughs. They are required to provide air-conditioning and turn off the radio on demand, and they cannot smoke while you're in the cab. They are required to be polite.

You are allowed to dictate the route that is taken. It's a good idea to look at a map before you get in a taxi. Taxi drivers have been known to jack up the fare on visitors who don't know better by taking very circuitous routes. On the other hand, listen to drivers who propose an alternate route. A knowledgeable driver will know how to get you to your destination quickly and efficiently.

Always make sure the meter is turned on at the start of the ride. You'll see the readout register the initial $2 and start calculating the fare as you go. I've witnessed unscrupulous drivers hauling unsuspecting visitors around with the meter off, and then overcharging them at drop-off time. And **always ask for the receipt**— it comes in handy if you need to make a complaint or leave something behind.

For driver complaints and lost property, call the 24-hour Consumer Hot Line at ✆ **212/NYC-TAXI.** For further taxi information— including a complete rundown of your rights as a taxi rider—visit **www.ci.nyc.ny.us/taxi**.

3 Playing It Safe

New York has experienced a dramatic drop in crime and is safer than many other major U.S. cities these days, especially in the neighborhoods that visitors are prone to frequent. While that's quite encouraging, it's still important to take precautions. Criminals are expert at spotting newcomers who appear disoriented or vulnerable.

Tips The Top Safety Tips

Trust your instincts, because they're usually right. You'll rarely be hassled, but it's always best to walk with a sense of purpose, and don't stop in the middle of the sidewalk to look at your map. If you find yourself on a deserted street that feels unsafe, leave as quickly as possible. If you do find yourself accosted by someone with or without a weapon, remember to keep your anger in check and that the most reasonable response (maddening though it may be) is not to resist.

Men should carry their wallets in their front pockets and women should keep hold of their purse straps. Cross camera and purse straps over one shoulder, across your front, and under the other arm. Never hang a purse on the back of a chair or on a hook in a bathroom stall; keep it in your lap or between your feet with one foot through a strap. Avoid carrying large amounts of cash. You might carry your money in several pockets so that if one is picked, the others might escape. Skip the flashy jewelry and keep valuables out of sight on the street.

Panhandlers are seldom dangerous and can usually be ignored (more aggressive pleas can be answered, "Not today"). If a stranger walks up to you on the street with a sob story ("I live in the suburbs and was attacked and don't have the money to get home. . . ."), it's likely a scam. Be wary of an individual who "accidentally" falls in front of you or causes some other commotion, because he or she may be working with someone else who will take your wallet when you try to help. And remember: You _will_ lose if you place a bet on a sidewalk card game or shell game.

There's a good police presence on the street, so don't be afraid to stop an officer, or even a friendly-looking New Yorker (trust me—you can tell) if you need help getting your bearings.

When using the subway, **do not wait for trains near the edge of the platform** or on extreme ends of a station. During non-rush hours, wait for the train in view of the token-booth clerk or under the yellow DURING OFF HOURS TRAINS STOP HERE signs, and ride in the train operator's or conductor's car (usually in the center of the train; you'll see his or her head stick out of the window when the doors open). Choose crowded cars over empty ones—there's safety in numbers.

Avoid subways late at night, and take a cab after about 10 or 11pm—it's money well spent to avoid a long wait on a deserted platform. Or take the bus.

 ## FAST FACTS: New York City

American Express Travel service offices are at many Manhattan locations, including 1185 Sixth Ave., at 47th Street (✆ 212/398-8585); at the New York Marriott Marquis, 1535 Broadway, in the 8th-floor lobby (✆ 212/575-6580); on the mezzanine level at Macy's Herald Square, 34th Street and Broadway (✆ 212/695-8075); and at 374 Park Ave., at 53rd St. (✆ 212/421-8240). Call ✆ **800/AXP-TRIP** or go online to **www.americanexpress.com** for other locations or information.

Area Codes There are four area codes in the city: two in Manhattan, **212** and **646,** and two in the outer boroughs, **718** and **347.** Also common is the **917** area code, which is assigned to cell phones, pagers, and a few land lines. All calls between these area codes are local calls, but you'll have to dial 1 + the area code + the seven digits if the number you're calling is not within your area code.

Emergencies Dial ✆ **911** for fire, police, and ambulance.

Hospitals The following hospitals have 24-hour emergency rooms. Don't forget your insurance card.

Downtown: New York Downtown Hospital, 170 William St., between Beekman and Spruce streets (✆ 212/312-5063 or 212/312-5000); **St. Vincents Hospital and Medical Center,** 153 W. 11th St., at Seventh Avenue (✆ 212/604-7000); and **Beth Israel Medical Center,** First Avenue and 16th Street (✆ 212/420-2000).

Midtown: Bellevue Hospital Center, 462 First Ave., at 27th Street (✆ 212/562-4141); **New York University Medical Center,** 560 First Ave., at 33rd Street (✆ 212/263-7300); and **Roosevelt Hospital,** 425 W. 59th St., between Ninth and Tenth avenues (✆ 212/523-6800).

Uptown: St. Luke's Hospital Center, Amsterdam Avenue and 113th Street (✆ 212/523-3335); **Columbia Presbyterian Medical Center,** 622 W. 168th St., between Broadway and Fort Washington Avenue (✆ 212/305-2500); **Lenox Hill Hospital,** 100 E. 77th St., between Park and Lexington avenues (✆ 212/

434-2000); and **Mount Sinai Medical Center,** Fifth Avenue at 100th Street (📞 212/241-6500).

Liquor Laws The legal age to purchase and consume alcoholic beverages in New York is 21. Liquor and wine are sold only in licensed stores, which are closed on Sundays, holidays, and election days while polls are open. Beer can be purchased in grocery stores and delis 24 hours a day, except Sundays before noon. Last call in bars is at 4am.

Pharmacies **Duane Reade** (www.duanereade.com) has 24-hour pharmacies in Midtown at 224 W. 57th St., at Broadway (📞 **212/541-9708**); on the Upper West Side at 2465 Broadway, at 91st Street (📞 **212/799-3172**); and on the Upper East Side at 1279 Third Ave., at 74th Street (📞 **212/744-2668**).

Police Dial 📞 **911** in an emergency; otherwise, call 📞 **646/610-5000** or 718/610-5000 for the number of the nearest precinct.

Smoking Smoking is prohibited on public transportation, in the lobbies of hotels and office buildings, in taxis, and most shops. It also may be restricted or not permitted in restaurants. At this writing, a ban on smoking in all bars and restaurants is being considered by city government.

Taxes **Sales tax** is 8.25% on meals, most goods, and some services, but not charged on clothing and footwear under $110. **Hotel tax** is 13.25% plus $2 per room per night (including sales tax). **Parking-garage tax** is 18.25%.

Weather For the current temperature and next day's forecast, look in the upper-right corner of the front page of the *New York Times* or call 📞 **212/976-1212**. If you want to know how to pack before you arrive, point your browser to **www.cnn.com/weather** or **www.weather.com**.

3

Accommodations You Can Afford

There are more hotel bargains these days than there have been in a decade, due both to a recent building boom, and a downslide in tourism in the city in the aftermath of the World Trade Center attacks. Visitors have more bargaining power than they've had in years. Still, don't expect cheap. If you only want to spend 100 or so bucks a night—a very budget-basic rate in this city—you're going to have to live with some inconveniences.

First, be aware that many of New York's budget hotels have **shared bathrooms.** There are a few exceptions—but in general, don't count on a double room with a bathroom for less than $100.

Even if you're willing to spend a bit more, don't expect much in the way of **space.** Don't be surprised if your hotel room isn't much bigger than the bed in it, the closet is a rack screwed to the wall, and the bathroom is the smallest you've ever seen.

It's almost always more expensive to stay in the Theater District than in a residential **neighborhood** like Chelsea, Murray Hill, or the Upper West Side. Staying in a residential area is almost always quieter, and will give you better access to affordable restaurants where locals eat.

The **rates** quoted in the listings are the rack rates (the maximum rates that a hotel charges). But rack rates are only guidelines, and there are ways around them. Before you start calling, review the "35 Money-Saving Tips" in chapter 1.

The hotels below have provided us with their best rate estimates for 2003, and all quoted rates were correct at press time. **Rates can change at any time,** subject to availability, season, and plain old increases. All bets are off at Christmas. Remember: Hotel rooms are subject to **13.25% tax plus $2 per night,** unless otherwise noted.

Where to stay in TriBeCa, the Bowery, the Lower East Side, East Village and Greenwich Village

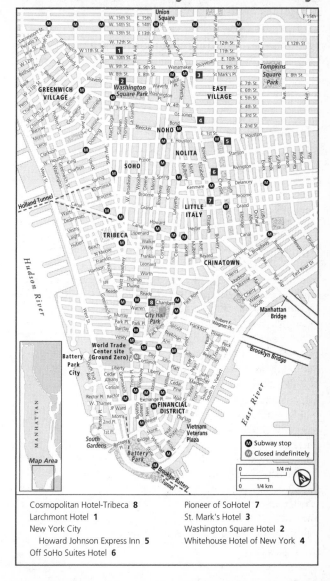

Cosmopolitan Hotel-Tribeca **8**
Larchmont Hotel **1**
New York City
  Howard Johnson Express Inn **5**
Off SoHo Suites Hotel **6**

Pioneer of SoHotel **7**
St. Mark's Hotel **3**
Washington Square Hotel **2**
Whitehouse Hotel of New York **4**

1 TriBeCa

Cosmopolitan Hotel–Tribeca ✵ *Value*   Hiding behind a plain-vanilla TriBeCa awning is one of the best hotel deals in Manhattan for travelers who insist on a private bathroom. The IKEA-ish furniture includes a work desk and an armoire (a few rooms have a dresser and hanging rack instead). Beds are comfy, and sheets and towels are of good quality. Rooms are small but make the most of the limited space, and the place is pristine. The two-level minilofts have lots of character, but expect to duck on the second level: Downstairs is the bathroom, TV, closet, desk, and club chair, while upstairs is a low-ceilinged bedroom. Management keeps everything fresh. The TriBeCa location is safe, hip, and subway-convenient. Services are minimal, to keep costs down, so you must be a low-maintenance guest to be happy here. If you are, this place is a great deal.

95 W. Broadway (at Chambers St.), New York, NY 10007. ✆ **888/895-9400** or 212/566-1900. Fax 212/566-6909. www.cosmohotel.com. 113 units. $119–$159 double. Inquire about discounts. AE, DC, MC, V. Parking $20, 1 block away. Subway: 1, 2, 3, 9 to Chambers St. *In room:* A/C, TV, dataport, ceiling fan.

2 On the Bowery

Off SoHo Suites Hotel *Value*   Once you had to put up with an industrial, edge-of-Chinatown neighborhood to enjoy Off SoHo Suites—a hotel with clean, welcoming rooms with full kitchen facilities at surprisingly low prices. But the neighborhood is getting nicer by the minute, and it's a stone's throw from the city's coolest dining, shopping, and nightlife: Nolita's Elizabeth Street is 2 blocks west, and the Lower East Side's Orchard and Ludlow streets are a half-dozen blocks east, not to mention Chinatown's nearby cheap eats. Each deluxe suite has a living and dining area with a pullout sofa, kitchen, private bathroom with hair dryer, and separate bedroom. In the economy suites, kitchens and bathrooms (with hair dryers) are shared with another room; if four of you are traveling, you can combine two economy suites. Everything is basic and the beds are a bit harder than I like, but the whole place is nicely kept. Telephones have voice mail and dataports. *Note:* If you don't like a youth-oriented, gentrifying scene, stay elsewhere.

11 Rivington St. (btwn Chrystie St. and the Bowery), New York, NY 10002. ✆ **800/ OFF-SOHO** (633-7646) or 212/979-9808. Fax 212/979-9801. www.offsoho.com. 38 units (10 with shared bathroom). $66–$89.50 economy suite (2 people maximum), $99–$199 deluxe suite (4 people maximum). AE, MC, V. Parking $20 nearby. Subway: F to Second Ave., 6 to Spring St. Pets allowed (in deluxe suites only).

Amenities: Cafe for breakfast and lunch; exercise room; access to nearby health club; activities desk; limited room service; dry cleaning/laundry; coin-op laundry. *In room:* A/C, TV w/free movies, dataport, kitchen with fridge and coffeemaker, hair dryer, iron.

Pioneer of SoHotel ⓚ *Finds*   One of my favorite finds is this little Euro-style hotel, which offers clean, quiet, friendly accommodations with private bathrooms for as little as $77 double (plus tax, or $89 nightly) on a year-round basis.

This older hotel has improved and come into its own, and the manager continues to make improvements. The same can be said for the neighborhood: The hotel is in a four-story walkup off a stretch of the Bowery that was crusty and desolate a few years ago. But these days it's clean, safe, and convenient.

It's one level up to the lobby. Decorative painting adds an attractive flair to rooms, and hanging plants add color in the halls. Rooms have black linoleum floors, mix-and-match lamps and chairs, ceiling fans, and fresh and firm platform beds. Most rooms have a tiny but spotless bathroom with a shower stall. Shared-bathroom units (which have small sinks) are petite, but spacious configurations are available, and the standard doubles are a good size. A few rooms have no windows, but they're blissfully silent and will even save you a few dollars. Ask for a renovated room. Service is delightfully old-fashioned; a wake-up call consists of a clerk who'll knock on your door (BYO alarm and hair dryer if you'll want them).

341 Broome St. (btwn Elizabeth St. and the Bowery), New York, NY 10013. Ⓒ **212/ 226-1482.** Fax 212/226-3525. www.pioneerhotel.com. 125 units (about 35 with shared bathroom). $69–$89 single or double with shared bathroom, $99 quad with shared bathroom; $89–$99 double with private bathroom, $116–$158 triple, quad, or family room with private bathroom. Rates include tax. AE, DC, DISC, MC, V. Parking $10–$15 nearby. Subway: F to Second Ave., 6 to Spring St. **Amenities:** Morning coffee in lobby. *In room:* A/C, TV, ceiling fan, no phone.

3 The Lower East Side

New York City Howard Johnson Express Inn ⓚⓚ *Value*   This brand-new hotel is a boon to travelers looking for quality at a great price, a trendy location, or both. It sits on a wide thoroughfare next to the gentrifying neighborhood's new state-of-the-art movie complex. Bars, live-music clubs and restaurants abound on the surrounding blocks. The building was completed in 2001, so everything is new. Rooms are small, but furnishings and textiles are attractive and of good quality: Mattresses are firm, work desks boast desk-level inputs and an ergonomic chair, and the granite

bathrooms are nicer than those in some luxury hotels (some even have Jacuzzis). The staff is more attentive than most working in this price range.

Most rooms have queen beds, while some have two doubles; don't expect much room in either configuration. Those with room numbers ending in 01, 02, or 03 are the largest. Request a back-facing or high-floor room for total quiet.

135 E. Houston St. (at Forsyth St.), New York, NY 10002. ℂ **800/406-1411** or 212/358-8844. Fax 212/473-3500. www.hojo.com. 54 units. $119–$149 double. Rates include continental breakfast. Inquire about AAA, AARP, and corporate discounts. AE, DC, DISC, MC, V. Parking $29, 4 blocks away. Subway: F to Second Ave. **Amenities:** Dry cleaning/laundry. *In room:* A/C, TV, dataport, hair dryer, iron.

4 The East Village

St. Mark's Hotel 𝒜 This renovated hotel from the folks behind the Chelsea Savoy (p. 56) is a welcome addition to the scene. It's in a four-story walkup on St. Marks Place, the hot spot for the East Village's youth, lined with stores, restaurants and bars, and a parade of tattooed hipsters. Anybody interested in being at the heart of the action will love it.

In a city where dingy paint and 20-year-old carpet is the norm in budget hotels, St. Mark's pretty Parisian mural, lighting, finished oak, and marble floors are a welcome sight. Rooms are basic and furnishings are simple, but even the smallest—one double bed—is a decent size and boasts new carpet, a firm bed, a TV, a phone with voice mail, and a tiled bathroom with a tiny sink, shower, and nice towels; butter-yellow walls and framed prints brighten most rooms. Services are minimal, but the staff is professional. Some of New York's best affordable restaurants are within shouting distance.

2 St. Marks Place (at Third Ave.), New York, NY 10003. ℂ **212/674-0100** or 212/674-2192. Fax 212/420-0854. www.stmarkshotel.qpg.com. 70 units. $80–$150 single or double. No credit cards. Subway: 6 to Astor Place. *In room:* A/C, TV.

Whitehouse Hotel of New York 𝒜 *Value* This renovated, youth-oriented hotel offers private rooms at hostel prices, and the location is smashing. Rooms are tiny and plain, each with either a full bed or twins, so expect no perks; but everything is clean, well maintained, and relatively new. Good quality linens and towels are provided. All rooms share simple shower-stall bathrooms off the hall. There's a lounge with a TV, tables and chairs for lounging, a cafe area selling continental-style breakfast items, and friendly service around the clock. A coin-op laundry and an Internet-access machine in the lobby add to the convenience. The city's best budget dining lines the East Village blocks; the heart of Greenwich Village is to the west, and SoHo and the Lower East Side are both just a 5-minute walk away. No smoking allowed, and no travelers under 18.

340 Bowery (btwn 2nd and Great Jones/3rd sts.), New York, NY 10012. ✆ 212/477-5623. Fax 212/473-3150. www.whitehousehotelofny.com. 468 beds (all with shared bathroom). $30–$32 single; $58–$63 double; $75–$91 triple. Rates include tax. AE, DC, MC, V. Subway: 6 to Bleecker St. No children under 18 accepted. **Amenities:** Common kitchen w/microwave; Internet access machine and dataport in lobby; coin-op laundry; continental breakfast for a charge (daily 6–10am). *In room:* A/C.

5 Greenwich Village

Larchmont Hotel 🏛🏛 *Value*   On a tree-lined block in the Village, this European-style hotel is a gem. If you're willing to share a bathroom, it's hard to do better for the money. The entire place has an air of warmth and sophistication. Each bright guest room is done in rattan and outfitted with a writing desk, a minilibrary, an alarm clock, a washbasin, and a few extras you normally have to pay a lot more for, such as bathrobes, slippers, and ceiling fans. Every floor has two shared bathrooms (with hair dryers) and a small kitchen. Everything feels clean and fresh. Those looking for a hip downtown base couldn't be better situated, because some of the city's best shopping, dining, and sightseeing—plus your choice of subway lines—is all close. A free continental breakfast that includes fresh-baked goods every morning is the crowning touch. Book *well* in advance (the management suggests 6–7 weeks' lead time).

27 W. 11th St. (btwn Fifth and Sixth aves.), New York, NY 10011. ✆ 212/989-9333. Fax 212/989-9496. www.larchmonthotel.com. 58 units (all with shared bathroom). $70–$95 single; $90–$125 double. Rates include continental breakfast. Children under 13 stay free in parents' room. AE, DC, DISC, MC, V. Parking $18 nearby. Subway: A, C, E, F, V to W. 4th St. (use 8th St. exit); F to 14th St. **Amenities:** Common kitchenette; tour desk; fax service; room service (10am–6pm). *In room:* A/C, TV, hair dryer, safe, washbasin, ceiling fan.

Washington Square Hotel   Popular with a young international crowd, this hotel faces Washington Square Park (the heart of New York University). A marble-and-brass lobby leads to tiny rooms that benefited from freshening in 2000. Each comes with a firm bed, private bathroom, and a small closet with a pint-size safe. It's worth paying extra for a south-facing room on a high floor, because others can be dark. Both the Union Square Inn and Murray Hill's Thirty Thirty offer a bit more for a similar price; but the heart-of-campus location is ideal for travelers who want to be near Village restaurants, bars, and clubs. On site is a very good restaurant and lounge, **C3.**

103 Waverly Place (btwn Fifth and Sixth aves.), New York, NY 10011. ✆ **800/222-0418** or 212/777-9515. Fax 212/979-8373. www.wshotel.com. 170 units. $101–$131 single; $118–$151 double; $145–$188 quad. Rates include continental breakfast. Inquire about special rates and jazz packages. Rollaway $20 extra. AE, MC, V. Parking $20 nearby. Subway: A, C, E, F, V to W. 4th St. (use 3rd St. exit). **Amenities:** Restaurant; lounge; exercise room; dry cleaning/laundry. *In room:* A/C, TV, dataport, hair dryer, iron, safe.

6 Chelsea

Chelsea Lodge ★★ *Finds* In a brownstone on a landmarked block, this small hotel is charming and a terrific value—arguably the best in the city for budget-minded travelers. The husband-and-wife owners, Paul and GG Weisenfeld, have restored original woodwork and created a country-in-the-city vibe with beautiful wallpapers and wainscoting, vintage furniture, and touches like Hershey's Kisses on the pillows. The beds are the finest and best outfitted I've seen in this price category.

The only place with a similar grown-up sensibility for the same money is Greenwich Village's Larchmont (p. 55), but there, bathroom facilities are shared; at Chelsea Lodge, each room has its own sink and in-room shower stall, so you only have to share a toilet. I won't kid you—rooms are petite, the closets are small, and beds are full-size (queens wouldn't cut it). But considering the stylishness, the amenities—which include TV, a ceiling fan, a desk, and an alarm clock—and the neighborhood, you'd be hard-pressed to do better. *Tip:* Try to book 2A, which is bigger than most, or one of the first-floor rooms, whose high ceilings make them feel more spacious.

318 W. 20th St. (btwn Eighth and Ninth aves.), New York, NY 10011. ✆ **800/373-1116** or 212/243-4499. Fax 212/243-7852. www.chelsealodge.com. 24 units (all with semiprivate bathroom). $90 single; $105 double. AE, DC, DISC, MC, V. Parking about $20 nearby. Subway: 1, 9 to 18th St.; C, E to 23rd St. *In room:* A/C, TV, ceiling fan.

Chelsea Savoy Hotel ★★ *Kids* This hotel has been a welcome addition to Chelsea, a neighborhood abloom with galleries, restaurants, nightclubs, and flea markets. The Savoy was built in 1995, so it isn't subject to the eccentricities of older hotels. The hallways are attractive and wide, the elevators swift and silent, and the cheery rooms of good size with big closets and roomy, immaculate bathrooms. The reasonably priced quad rooms are suitable for a family of four (children stay free). Creature comforts abound: The rooms boast mattresses, furniture, and linens of high quality, plus the kinds of amenities you usually have to pay more for, like minifridges, in-room safes, and toiletries. Free continental breakfast makes a good value even better. Most rooms are street facing and sunny; corner rooms tend to be brightest but noisiest. The staff is young and helpful, and the hip neighborhood makes a good base for exploring Midtown and downtown. A sitting room off the lobby makes an excellent place to enjoy your morning coffee over a selection of newspapers and magazines.

204 W. 23rd St. (at Seventh Ave.), New York, NY 10011. ℂ 866/929-9353 or 212/ 929-9353. Fax 212/741-6309. www.chelseasavoy.qpg.com or www.chelseasavoy nyc.com. 90 units. $99–$115 single; $125–$175 double; $145–$195 quad. Children stay free in parents' room. AE, MC, V. Parking $25 nearby. Subway: 1, 9 to 23rd St. *In room:* A/C, TV, dataport, fridge, hair dryer, iron, safe.

Colonial House Inn ✪   This 1850 brownstone, on a residential block in the heart of Chelsea is a four-story walk-up catering to a largely gay and lesbian clientele, but the staff welcomes everyone. The place is beautifully maintained and run. Rooms are small and basic but clean; all have radios and those that share a hall bathroom (at a ratio of about three rooms per bathroom) have in-room sinks. Deluxe rooms—those with private bathrooms—have minifridges, and a few have working fireplaces. Both private and shared bathrooms are basic but nice. A terrific art collection brightens the public spaces. Book at least a month in advance for weekend stays. At parlor level is a breakfast room where a continental spread is put out from 8am to noon daily; coffee and tea are available all day. Rooms don't have hair dryers and irons, but the front desk will lend them. There's a nice roof deck split by a privacy fence (the area behind the fence is clothing optional). The neighborhood is full of great restaurants, shopping, and close to good public transportation.

318 W. 22nd St. (btwn Eighth and Ninth aves.), New York, NY 10011. ℂ 800/689-3779 or 212/243-9669. Fax 212/633-1612. www.colonialhouseinn.com. 20 units (12 with shared bathroom). $80–$99 single or double with shared bathroom; $125–$140 double with private bathroom. Rates include expanded continental breakfast. 2-night minimum on weekends. Extra person $15. Weekly rates available. MC, V. Parking $20 nearby. Subway: C, E to 23rd St. **Amenities:** Internet-access PC in lounge; fax service. *In room:* A/C, TV, dataport.

SUPERCHEAP SLEEPS

Chelsea International Hostel   The well-managed, well-maintained Chelsea International consists of a warren of low-rise buildings around a central courtyard. It's popular with international travelers. Accommodations and shared bathrooms are older and plain but fine; the shared rooms come with nice extras such as wall hooks, sinks, and in-room lockers big enough for most backpacks

Where to stay in Union Square, Times Square, Chelsea, Midtown West & East

Americana Inn **9**
Big Apple Hostel **6**
Broadway Inn **4**
Chelsea International Hostel **20**
Chelsea Lodge **33**
Chelsea Savoy Hotel **19**
Colonial House Inn **32**
Comfort Inn Midtown **5**
Gershwin Hotel **18**
Hotel Edison **3**
Hotel Grand Union **12**
Hotel Metro **10**
Hudson **1**
Murray Hill Inn **14**
Ramada Inn Eastside **13**
Red Roof Inn **11**
Skyline Hotel **2**
Super 8 Hotel Times Square **7**
The Marcel **17**
Thirty Thirty **15**
Travel Inn **8**
Union Square Inn **16**

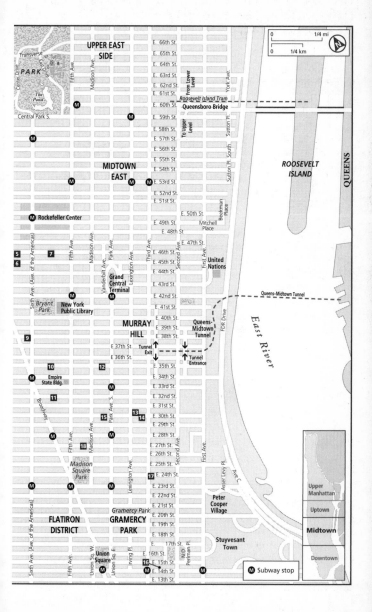

Tips Deal-Making with the Chains

Most hotels—particularly chains like Comfort Inn, Holiday Inn, and Best Western—will negotiate good rates to fill rooms at the last minute and in slow seasons. The chains are also where you can take advantage of discounts, from auto-club membership to senior status. Most chain hotels let the kids stay with parents for free.

Your chances of getting a deal aren't great if you're visiting in a busy season. But if you're willing to make a few extra calls, or spend some time online—which might net you a 10% discount for booking online—you might get a deal at hotels that would otherwise be out of your price range.

Best Western's (© **800/528-1234**; www.bestwestern. com) rack rates for their New York hotels are higher than you'd expect. At the **Best Western President Hotel,** in the Theater District at 234 W. 48th St. (© **800/826-4667** or 212/246-8800), doubles go for $129 to $229 but can drop to $99.

At these and other franchised hotels—like the ones run by **Apple Core Hotels** (© **800/567-7720**; www.applecore hotels.com), which handles the **Comfort Inn Midtown** (p. 64), the **Red Roof Inn** (p. 66), and **Super 8 Hotel Times Square** (p. 67), and the **Best Western Manhattan,** 17 W.

(BYO combination lock and towels). The tiny private rooms have little more than a double bed and shelves, but you can call one your own for just 60 bucks. Some rooms have air-conditioning, so request one if it matters to you.

The two fully equipped common kitchens (with microwaves) are the best I've seen in a hostel, and free coffee, tea, sugar, and cream is on hand. The courtyard has tables and barbecues. There are also dining and lounge areas with TV, Internet access, self-service laundry, and soda machines; free luggage storage is another plus. The neighborhood is great, the desk is attended 24 hours. At press time, free pizza was part of the package for Wednesday-night guests.

251 W. 20th St. (btwn Seventh and Eighth aves.), New York, NY 10011. © **212/647-0010.** Fax 212/727-7289. www.chelseahostel.com. 223 dorm beds; 57 private units (all with shared bathroom). $25 dorm bed; $60–$65 double. Rates include tax. AE, MC, V. Subway: 1, 9 to 18th St. **Amenities:** 2 kitchens; dining areas; Internet access; fax; coin-op laundry. *In room:* No phone.

32nd St. (☎ **212/736-1600**), doubles can go for as little as $89. Check with the franchiser if you're not quoted a good rate or through the management company's online reservations system; their 800 and online reservations systems can garner you a better rate.

A good source for deals is **Choice Hotels** (☎ **800/4-CHOICE**; www.hotelchoice.com), which oversees Comfort Inn, Quality Hotel, and Clarion Hotel chains.

Also try **Holiday Inn** (☎ **800/HOLIDAY**; www.holiday-inn. com), which has a handful of hotels in Manhattan, all of which carry rack rates that are too high for most budget travelers. However, discounted weekend and slow-season rates can drop as low as $109 double—at the **Holiday Inn Wall Street,** 15 Gold St. (☎ **212/232-7800**; www.holidayinn wsd.com). Shoppers might like the **Holiday Inn Downtown/ SoHo,** 138 Lafayette St. (☎ **212/966-8898**; www.holidayinn-nyc.com).

Also try the **Days Hotel Midtown,** 790 Eighth Ave., at 48th Street (☎ **800/544-8313** or 212/581-7000; www.days inn.com). The rooms are worth the $105-to-$130 rate you might be able to snare in slower seasons.

7 Union Square, the Flatiron District & Gramercy Park

Gershwin Hotel 🅐 🅚ids If you see glowing horns protruding from a lipstick-red facade, you're in the right place. This hotel caters to up-and-coming artistic types—and names with an eye for good value—with its art collection and wild style. The lobby is a post-modern cartoon of kitschy furniture and pop art. The standard rooms are clean and bright, with Picasso-style wall murals, Philippe Starck–ish takes on motel furnishings, and more modern art. Superior rooms are best, worth the extra $10; all have either a queen bed, two twins, or two doubles, plus a newish private bathroom with colorful tile. Families and small groups will love the family room, a two-room suite that accommodates four with a queen bed in one room, two twins in the other.

One of the best things about the Gershwin is its vibe: There's always something going on, whether it's jazz in the **Living Room,** nightly happy hour (7–9pm) in the **Red Room** beer bar, or a show at the hotel's own art gallery. The hotel is more service-oriented than you usually see at this price level, and the staff is very professional.

7 E. 27th St. (btwn Fifth and Madison aves.), New York, NY 10016. ✆ 212/545-8000. Fax 212/684-5546. www.gershwinhotel.com. 121 units. $99–$189 double (usually less than $150); $189–$219 family unit. Check website for discounts, 3rd-night-free specials, or other value-added packages. Extra person $10. AE, MC, V. Parking $25, 3 blocks away. Subway: N, R, 6 to 28th St. **Amenities:** Cafe (breakfast only); beer bar; tour desk; Internet-access PC; dry cleaning/laundry. *In room:* A/C, TV, dataport, hair dryer, iron.

The Marcel ★★ *Value*   This Gramercy Park hotel offers style and a superhip scene at low prices. Thanks to designers Goodman Charlton, who love to infuse retro styles with futuristic freshness, the Marcel sits on the cutting edge style-wise. Fab faux *Mod Squad*-era Scandinavian stylings in the lobby lead to guest rooms boasting blond-wood built-ins that make clever use of limited space, and a geometric cushioned headboard adds a luxurious flair. The designer furnishings and textiles look and feel expensive, even if the lumpy-ish beds don't; still, budget travelers will be thrilled. And trust me—you're going to have to look long and hard for another hotel in town that supplies marble bathrooms, dual-line phones, and CD players at this price. Even if the service isn't fabulous or the little details aren't perfect, you should feel like you're getting a great deal here.

One of the strongest appeals of the Marcel is **Spread** (www.spread nyc.com), a restaurant/lounge hybrid offering a small-plates menu, a sushi bar, cocktails, and a blast of an after-dark scene.

201 E. 24th St. (at Third Ave.), New York, NY 10011. ✆ 888/66-HOTEL (664-6835) or 212/696-3800. Fax 212/696-0077. www.nychotels.com. 97 units. $125–$175 double. AE, DISC, MC, V. Parking $24. Subway: 6 to 28th St. **Amenities:** Restaurant; lounge; coffee/cappuccino bar; limited room service; dry cleaning/laundry. *In room:* A/C, TV w/pay movies, CD player, dataport, hair dryer, iron.

Union Square Inn ★★ *Value*   East of Union Square on the fringe of the East Village, this unassuming hotel is a welcome addition. Comforts are of excellent quality, every unit has a private bathroom, and everything feels fresh and new. Four standard rooms are tiny twins with trundle beds while a handful in the deluxe category are spacious double/doubles. Most fall in the moderate category, with one double bed and little room to spare. All rooms boast brand-new pillow-top mattresses and good-quality sheets (probably the best you'll find in this price category), autumn-hued textiles and art, contemporary redwood furnishings, bedside lamps, and all-new Italian-tile bathrooms. On the downside, all rooms lack views, open wall racks substitute for closets, most bathrooms have shower only, halls are narrow, and there's no elevator.

Services are virtually nonexistent to keep costs down, but everything you'll need, from restaurants to dry cleaners to subway lines is at hand in the hip, central-to-everything location.

209 E. 14th St. (btwn Second and Third aves.), New York, NY 10003. ℂ 212/614-0500. Fax 212/614-0512. www.unionsquareinn.com. 40 units. $99–$169 double. Rates include continental breakfast. Extra person $20. AE, MC, V. Parking $25 nearby. Subway: L to Third Ave.; or 4, 5, 6, N, R to 14th St./Union Sq. **Amenities:** Coffee bar w/light meals. In room: A/C, TV, dataport.

8 Times Square & Midtown West

Americana Inn ⋆ (Value The cheapest hotel from the Empire Hotel Group is a star in the budget category. Linoleum floors give the rooms a somewhat institutional quality, but the hotel is well run and immaculate. Rooms are spacious, with good-size closets and private sinks, and an alarm built into the TV; the beds are the most comfortable I've found at this price. Most come with a double bed or two twins; a few can accommodate three guests in two twin beds and a pullout sofa or three twins. One hall bathroom accommodates every three rooms or so; all are spacious and spotless, and the front desk lends hair dryers. Every floor has a kitchenette with microwave, stove, and fridge (BYO cooking utensils). The five-story building has an elevator, and four rooms are accessible for travelers with disabilities. Ask for a back-facing room away from the street noise.

69 W. 38th St. (at Sixth Ave.), New York, NY 10018. ℂ 888/HOTEL-58 (468-3558) or 212/840-6700. Fax 212/840-1830. www.newyorkhotel.com. 50 units (all with shared bathroom). $65–$75 single; $75–$115 double. Check website for specials (winter rates as low as $60 double). Extra person $10. AE, MC, V. Parking $25–$35 nearby. Subway: B, D, F, V to 34th St. **Amenities:** Common kitchen. In room: A/C, TV.

Broadway Inn ⋆⋆ (Finds This lovely, welcoming inn is a charmer. The second-floor lobby sets the homey tone with bookcases, cushy seating, and cafe tables where free continental breakfast is served. The rooms are basic but comfy, outfitted in a neo-Deco style with firm beds, good-quality linens and textiles, and nice bathrooms (about half have showers only). The place is impeccably kept. The standard doubles are fine for couples; the suites—with pullout sofa, microwave, minifridge, and lots of closet space—are a great deal. Double-paned windows keep the rooms surprisingly peaceful.

The inn's biggest asset is its staff, who go above and beyond the call to make guests happy; they'll even give you a hot-line number so you can call while you're out for directions, advice, and other assistance. Service just doesn't get any better in this price range. This nicely gentrified corner of the Theater District makes a great base. The inn has a loyal following, so reserve early. Note that there's no elevator in the four-story building.

264 W. 46th St. (at Eighth Ave.), New York, NY 10036. $\textcircled{C}$ 800/826-6300 or 212/997-9200. Fax 212/768-2807. www.broadwayinn.com. 41 units (about half with shower only). $99–$139 single; $135–$225 double; $199–$299 suite. Rates include continental breakfast. Check the website for special deals (as low as $79 single, $99 double at press time). Extra person $10. Children under 12 stay free in parents' room. AE, DC, DISC, MC, V. Parking $20, 3 blocks away. Subway: A, C, E to 42nd St. **Amenities:** 2 nearby restaurants offer guest discounts; concierge; fax and copy service. *In room:* A/C, TV, dataport, fridge, hair dryer, iron.

Comfort Inn Midtown
As of August 1, 2001, this pleasant member of the Comfort Inn chain has taken a bold step by officially declaring itself a nonsmoking hotel. Rates can climb in autumn or at Christmas, but low-season rates can make the rooms one of Midtown's best bargains. A mahogany-and-marble lobby leads to the petite but comfortable and nicely outfitted guest rooms, which boast neo-Shaker furnishings, coffeemakers, blackout drapes, and marble-and-tile bathrooms; all rooms have tub/shower combinations. Don't expect much in the way of service, but the location is excellent—steps from Times Square, Rockefeller Center, Broadway theaters, and a wealth of dining options.

129 W. 46th St. (btwn Sixth Ave. and Broadway), New York, NY 10036. $\textcircled{C}$ 800/567-7720 or 212/221-2600. Fax 212/790-2760. www.applecorehotels.com or www.comfortinn.com. 79 units. $89–$329 double. Rates include continental breakfast. Ask about senior, AAA, corporate, and other discounts; check www.comfortinn.com for online discounts. Extra person $10. Children under 14 stay free in parents' room. AE, DC, DISC, MC, V. Parking $20 nearby. Subway: 1, 2, 3, 9 to 42nd St./Times Sq.; N, R to 49th St.; B, D, F, V to 47th–50th sts./Rockefeller Center. **Amenities:** Small fitness room; self-serve business center; dry cleaning/laundry. *In room:* A/C, TV, dataport, coffeemaker, hair dryer, iron.

Hotel Edison *Kids*
The Edison is no longer one of the Theater District's best bargains, but it's still a reasonably good deal. A grand, block-long Art Deco–style lobby leads to nicely renovated rooms. You will find a firm bed, decor that's more attractive than most in this category, and a clean tile bathroom. Most double rooms feature two twins or a full bed, but there are some queens; request one at booking and show up early for your best chance at one. The larger quad rooms, with two doubles, are the best reason to consider the

Edison, especially if you're traveling with the kids. Off the lobby is the **Cafe Edison,** a Polish deli that's a favorite among theater types and down-market ladies who lunch; **Sofia's,** a just-fine Italian restaurant; and the **Rum House** tavern, which has a Caribbean flair and live entertainment most nights.

228 W. 47th St. (btwn Broadway and Eighth Ave.), New York, NY 10036. ℂ **800/ 637-7070** or 212/840-5000. Fax 212/596-6850. www.edisonhotelnyc.com. 850 units. $150–$170 single; $170–$200 double; $185–$230 triple or quad; $225–$275 suite. Extra person $15. AE, DC, DISC, MC, V. Parking $35. Subway: N, R to 49th St.; 1, 9 to 50th St. **Amenities:** 2 restaurants; cocktail lounge; exercise room; tour desk; dry cleaning/laundry. *In room:* A/C, TV, dataport.

Hotel Metro ⭐⭐ (Kids)   One of my all-time favorites, the Metro is the best choice in Midtown for those who don't want to sacrifice style or comfort for affordability. This Art Deco–style jewel has larger rooms than you'd expect. They're outfitted with retro furnishings, fluffy pillows, alarm clocks, and small but beautiful marble bathrooms. Only about half the bathrooms have tubs, but the others have huge shower stalls (junior suites have whirlpool tubs). The family room—a two-room suite with a second bedroom in lieu of a sitting area—is an ingenious invention, while families on tighter budgets can opt for a roomy double/double. There's a fire-lit library/ lounge area, where complimentary buffet breakfast is laid out and the coffeepot's on all day. The rooftop terrace boasts a breathtaking view of the Empire State Building, and makes a great place to order room service from the very good **Metro Grill.**

Prices skyrocket in fall, but it's relatively easy to score a rate between $150 and $180 through August, as long as you book well ahead; also check with airlines and other package operators for great-value package deals.

45 W. 35th St. (btwn Fifth and Sixth aves.), New York, NY 10001. ℂ **800/356-3870** or 212/947-2500. Fax 212/279-1310. www.hotelmetronyc.com. 179 units. $150– $250 double; $165–$300 triple or quad; $200–$350 family room; $225–$400 suite. Rates include continental breakfast. Check with airlines and other package operators for great-value package deals. Extra person $25. 1 child under 14 stays free in parents' room. AE, DC, MC, V. Parking $17 nearby. Subway: B, D, F, V, N, R to 34th St. **Amenities:** Restaurant; rooftop bar in summer; fitness room; salon; limited room service; dry cleaning/laundry. *In room:* A/C, TV, dataport, fridge, hair dryer, iron.

Hudson ⭐   If you're a style hound on a budget, it's never too early to book one of the handful of the cheapest rooms at celebrity hotelier Ian Schrager's newest hotel. Hudson attracts an adoring crowd and star-studded events to its Philippe Starck–designed digs. The ivy-draped lobby and the second-level "Private Park" deck—the best outdoor space in any Big Apple hotel—serve as the quad from

which everything radiates, including the hot **Hudson Bar,** the classic-goes-Warhol **Library,** and the surprisingly affordable cafeteria-style restaurant.

It's a good thing about the public spaces, because the handful of budget-friendly guest rooms are miniscule. There's no arguing with their beauty or comforts, though: They were designed on the retro-romantic ocean liner model, with African Makore paneling, hardwood floors, white-on-white beds, clever bedside lamps featuring translucent art by Francesco Clemente, a petite steel desk, and studded white-leather steamer trunk upholstery. Ultra-efficient appointments make even the smallest feel like a treat, but anybody who values space over style should *definitely* book elsewhere.

356 W. 58th St. (btwn Eighth and Ninth aves.), New York, NY 10019. ℂ **800/ 444-4786** or 212/554-6000. Fax 212/554-6001. www.ianschragerhotels.com. 1,000 units. $95–$295 double; $350–$450 studio. AE, DC, DISC, MC, V. Parking $46. Subway: 1, 9, A, B, C, D to 59th St./Columbus Circle. **Amenities:** Restaurant; 2 bars; 24-hr. fitness center; 24-hr. concierge; business center; room service (6:30am–midnight); dry cleaning/laundry; CD library. *In room:* A/C, TV w/pay movies, CD player, dataport and high-speed connectivity, minibar, hair dryer, safe.

Red Roof Inn 𝓴𝓴 Manhattan's first Red Roof Inn offers relief from Midtown's high-priced hotel scene. The hotel occupies a building that was gutted and laid out fresh, allowing for more spacious rooms and bathrooms than you'll usually find at this price. The lobby feels smart, and elevators are quiet and efficient. In-room amenities—including coffeemakers and TVs with on-screen Web access—are better than most competitors', and furnishings are new and comfortable. It's on a bustling block lined with nice hotels and Korean restaurants, just a stone's throw from the Empire State Building and Herald Square.

The rack-rate range is ridiculous, but it's usually easy to score a room for less than $150 if you book well in advance. Be sure to compare the rates offered by Apple Core Hotel's reservation line and those quoted on Red Roof's reservation line and website, as they can vary. Complimentary continental breakfast adds to the good value.

6 W. 32nd St. (btwn Broadway and Fifth Ave.), New York, NY 10001. ℂ **800/567-7720,** 800/RED-ROOF, or 212/643-7100. Fax 212/643-7101. www.applecorehotels. com or www.redroof.com. 171 units. $89–$329 double (usually less than $159). Rates include continental breakfast. Children under 14 stay free in parents' room. AE, DC, DISC, MC, V. Parking $22. Subway: B, D, F, V, N, R to 34th St. **Amenities:** Breakfast room; wine-and-beer lounge; exercise room; concierge; business center; dry cleaning/laundry. *In room:* A/C, TV w/pay movies, dataport, fridge, coffeemaker, hair dryer, iron; video games, Internet access.

Skyline Hotel *(Kids)* This recently renovated motor hotel offers predictable comforts and some uncommon extras—free storage parking and an indoor pool—that make it an excellent value. A pleasant lobby leads to motel-standard rooms that are bigger than most in this price range. They boast decent-size closets, small work desks (in most), and double-paned windows that open to let fresh air in, and shut out a lot of street noise. Some rooms have brand-new bathrooms, but the older ones are fine. Each junior suite is basically one large room with a pullout sofa bed, while each full suite has a sitting room with a pullout sofa and a separate room with two double beds and an extra TV, making them great for families. Everything is well kept. On the downside, some closets are open to the room, there are no bedside alarm clocks, and hair dryers and irons must be requested from housekeeping. The pool has a tiled deck and deck chairs, but it's only open limited hours, so call ahead if it matters.

725 Tenth Ave. (at 49th St.), New York, NY 10019. © 800/433-1982 or 212/586-3400. Fax 212/582-4604. www.skylinehotelny.com. 230 units. $109–$209 double or suite. Check website or inquire about special rates (as low as $89 at press time). Extra person $15. Children 14 and under stay free in parents' room. AE, DC, DISC, MC, V. Free storage parking (charge for in/out privileges). Subway: A, C, E to 50th St. Pets accepted with $200 deposit. **Amenities:** Restaurant; bar with live entertainment; indoor pool; Gray Line tour desk; Internet-access machine in lobby. *In room:* A/C, TV w/pay movies, hair dryer, iron, safe; video games, Internet access.

Super 8 Hotel Times Square *(★★)* *(Value)* This lodging is my favorite new budget hotel of the year. It's a bright, attractive hotel in a heart-of-Midtown location. The Wentworth was built in 1902 as a hotel for women, so it boasts extra-large rooms (by New York standards), outfitted with a king or two doubles, and all-new bathrooms. Decor isn't stylish, but it's attractive, with woods, pastel wallpaper, green carpeting, and floral spreads. Everything is new, and all rooms are outfitted with fridges, coffeemakers, small work desks, hair dryers, irons, and alarm clocks, plus Nintendo and on-screen e-mail access. The family suite features a king in one room and two twins (in lieu of a sitting area) in the other; you may be able to snare this suite for as little as $129.

The lobby is bright and elegant, and service is professional. Perks include a state-of-the-art exercise room and a breakfast room serving a continental meal that's included in the rate—for as little as $89 double! Even in high seasons, when Super 8 rates can climb into the mid-$100s, you'll still get your money's worth.

59 W. 46th St. (btwn Fifth and Sixth aves.), New York, NY 10036. ℂ 800/567-7720 or 212/719-2300. Fax 212/790-2760. www.applecorehotels.com or www.super8. com. 160 units. $89–$329 double (usually less than $179); family suite from $129. Rates include continental breakfast. Check for AAA, AARP, and other discounts. Children under 14 stay free in parents' room. AE, DC, DISC, MC, V. Parking $20 next door. Subway: B, D, F, V to 42nd St. **Amenities:** Breakfast room; exercise room; business center with computer, fax, copier; dry cleaning/laundry. *In room:* A/C, TV w/pay movies, dataport, fridge, coffeemaker, hair dryer, iron, video games, Internet access.

Travel Inn *Kids* Extras like a huge outdoor pool and sun deck, a sunny, up-to-date fitness room, and free parking make the Travel Inn another good deal. Like the Skyline (see above), the Travel Inn may not be loaded with personality, but it offers the clean, bright regularity of a good chain hotel. Rooms are oversize and comfortable, furnished with extra-firm beds and desks; even the smallest double is sizable and has a roomy bathroom, and double/doubles make affordable shares for families. A renovation has made everything feel like new, even the tiled bathrooms. The neighborhood has gentrified; Off-Broadway theaters and good restaurants are nearby, and it's a 10-minute walk to the Theater District. It's a good bet even if you don't have a car.

515 W. 42nd St. (just west of Tenth Ave.), New York, NY 10036. ℂ 888/HOTEL58 (468-3558), 800/869-4630, or 212/695-7171. Fax 212/967-5025. www.newyork hotel.com. 160 units. $125–$200 double. Check website for Internet deals (as low as $105 at press time). Extra person $10. Children under 16 stay free in parents' room. AE, DC, DISC, MC, V. Free self-parking. Subway: A, C, E to 42nd St./Port Authority. **Amenities:** Coffee shop; outdoor pool; fitness center; tour desk; 24-hr. room service. *In room:* A/C, TV, dataport, hair dryer, iron.

SUPERCHEAP SLEEPS

Big Apple Hostel *value* This is the nicest hostel in Midtown. It's not fancy, but it's well run, spotlessly clean, and in the heart of the Theater District. All dorm rooms are four-bedded; they're well spaced and well kept, with metal bunks and good mattresses with blankets and linens. Only guests in private rooms get towels, so dormers should bring their own. Private rooms are basic but better than most in hostels; all have phones (free local calls!), radio, and alarm, and some have a table and chairs. The shared bathrooms are better than average. There's a stocked kitchen with microwave, a backyard patio with barbecue, and a luggage storage room. It's popular with Japanese and other international travelers who like the location. It doesn't get much better at these prices—much better than the more well-known Aladdin Hostel farther west on 45th Street.

119 W. 45th St. (btwn Sixth and Seventh aves.), New York, NY 10036. © **212/302-
2603.** Fax 212/302-2605. www.bigapplehostel.com. 112 dorm beds; 11 private
doubles. $28–$38.50 dorm bed; $78–$109 double. MC, V. Subway: N, R, S, 1, 2, 3,
7, 9 to Times Sq./42nd St. **Amenities:** Common kitchen. *In room:* Fans, no phone
in dorm units.

9 Midtown East & Murray Hill

Hotel Grand Union   This hotel is big with budget-minded international travelers. A white-on-white lobby leads to clean, spacious
rooms with nice extras that are uncommon at this price, like hair
dryers and free HBO. Bad lighting, unattractive furniture, and a
lack of natural light dampen the mood—but considering the roomi-
ness, rates, and location, the Grand Union is a deal. A nicely con-
figured quad with two twins and a queen in a separate alcove, no.
309 is a great bet for families. Most bathrooms have been outfitted
in granite or tile; ask for a newly renovated one. The staff is helpful,
there's a pleasant sitting room off the lobby, and an adjacent coffee
shop is convenient for morning coffee or a quickie burger.

34 E. 32nd St. (btwn Madison and Park aves.), New York, NY 10016. © **212/683-
5890.** Fax 212/689-7397. www.hotelgrandunion.com. 95 units. $116–$138 single
or double; $132–$158 twin or triple; $158–$190 quad. Call or check website for
special rates (as low as $90 at press time). AE, DC, DISC, MC, V. Parking $22 nearby.
Subway: 6 to 33rd St. **Amenities:** Coffee shop; tour desk; fax service. *In room:*
A/C, TV, dataport, fridge, hair dryer.

Murray Hill Inn 🐾 *(Value)*   In a five-story walk-up in a pleasant
neighborhood, the Murray Hill Inn is shoestring-basic—but there's
no arguing with its cleanliness, key in judging accommodations in
this price range. Rooms are tiny and outfitted with one or two beds
with motel-standard bedspread and furnishings, a wall rack, a
phone, and small TV; most rooms with shared bathroom also have
private sinks (request one when booking). These Euro-style rooms
share the new, spotless in-hall bathrooms. Some of the doubles have
an alcove that can accommodate a third traveler on a cot if you're on
an extra-tight budget. Rooms with private bathrooms are the nicest;
they're spacious, with new bathrooms and dataports on the telephones. Most have pullout sofas that can accommodate an extra
traveler. Don't expect much in terms of facilities beyond a pleasant
(if tiny) lobby, a sitting area with a vending machine, an ATM, and
a luggage-storage area. The rooms with private bathrooms go fast, so
book early.

143 E. 30th St. (btwn Lexington and Third aves.), New York, NY 10016. © **888/
996-6376** or 212/683-6900. Fax 212/545-0103. www.murrayhillinn.com. 50 units

(10 with shared bathroom). $60–$65 single with shared bathroom; $75–$80 double with shared bathroom, $125 double with private bathroom. Ask about discounts and special rates (as low as $95 with private bathroom at press time). Extra person $20. Children under 12 stay free in parents' room. AE, MC, V. Parking about $25 nearby. Subway: 6 to 28th St. *In room:* A/C, TV.

Ramada Inn Eastside   The most affordable of the Apple Core Hotels fell under the Ramada banner in 2002. It's nothing special— small, basic rooms with older bathrooms—but a complete renovation has given them a fresh look. Its other features are the location, in Murray Hill, which abounds with affordable restaurants; the value-added amenities, which include free continental breakfast, free local phone calls, business center, and fitness room; and the usually low rates. Don't expect anything in the way of service, but considering how expensive an average room has become, this hotel is a value. It's quite easy to score a room for $139 or less most of the year.

161 Lexington Ave. (at 30th St.), New York, NY 10016. ☎ **800/567-7720** or 212/ 545-1800. Fax 212/790-2760. www.applecorehotels.com. 96 units. $89–$209 double. Rates include continental breakfast. Inquire about seasonal/weekend discounts (as low as $79 at press time). Children under 13 stay free in parents' room. AE, DC, DISC, MC, V. Parking $20 nearby. Subway: 6 to 33rd St. **Amenities:** Coffee shop; exercise room; business center; (both under renovation at press time). *In room:* A/C, TV w/pay movies, dataport, coffeemaker, hair dryer, iron, video games, Internet access.

Thirty Thirty ★★ *Value*   This new-in-2001 hotel is just right for bargain-hunting travelers looking for a splash of style. The building (which formerly housed a women's hotel and a nightclub) has been gutted, renovated, and redone. The design-conscious tone is set in the loftlike industrial-modern lobby. Pretty hallways lead to rooms that are on the smallish side but do the trick for those who intend to spend their days out on the town. They're done in a natural palette with a creative edge—purplish carpet, khaki bedspread, woven wallpaper—that comes together more attractively than you might expect. Configurations are split between twin/twins (great for friends), queens, and queen/queens (great for triples, budget-minded quads, or shares that want more spreading-out room). Features include cushioned headboards, firm mattresses, stylish bedside lamps, two-line phones, built-in wardrobes, and spacious tiled bathrooms. A few larger units have kitchenettes. There's no room service, but delivery is available from nearby restaurants.

30 E. 30th St. (btwn Madison and Park aves.), New York, NY 10016. ☎ **800/497-6028** or 212/689-1900. Fax 212/689-0023. www.thirtythirty-nyc.com. 240 units. $125–$175 double, $145–$195 double with kitchenette; $185–$245 quad. Call for

last-minute deals, or check website for special promotions (as low as $99 at press time). AE, DC, DISC, MC, V. Parking $35, 1 block away. Subway: 6 to 28th St. Pets accepted with advance approval. **Amenities:** Concierge; dry cleaning/laundry. *In room:* A/C, TV, dataport, hair dryer.

10 The Upper West Side

Amsterdam Inn *🎐 Value*   This renovated five-story walk-up offers basic accommodations for a great value in a terrific neighborhood. The private bathrooms are better at the Murray Hill Inn (p. 69), but you might be able to get a better rate here, and I prefer this property if you're going to share a bathroom. The inn's biggest assets are its Upper West Side location—where one-bedroom apartments rent for $2,000 or more per month—its newness, its consistent cleanliness, and its professional management.

The rooms are small and narrow, with a bed, a rack to hang your clothes on, a set of drawers with a TV on top, a table with a lamp and a phone that requires a deposit to activate, and a sink if there's no private bathroom. The Euro-style rooms share the in-hall bathrooms at a ratio of about 2½ to 1. The bathrooms are new but have showers only. If you book a double, make sure it's a *real* double, with a double bed. The singles with trundles can (theoretically) accommodate two, but don't expect to have any space left over. Management seems willing to negotiate, so ask for a lower rate.

340 Amsterdam Ave. (at 76th St.), New York, NY 10023. © **212/579-7500.** Fax 212/579-6127. www.amsterdaminn.com. 25 units (12 with private bathroom). $60–$75 single with shared bathroom; $75–$95 bunk-bed twin or double with shared bathroom, $95–$115 double with private bathroom. Extra person $20. Children under 12 stay free in parents' room. AE, MC, V. Parking $20–$25 nearby. Subway: 1, 9 to 79th St. *In room:* A/C, TV.

Comfort Inn–Central Park West *🎐 Value*   This chain hotel is a great place to stay if you can snag a good rate. It's fabulously located, tucked in the Upper West Side's best residential territory, steps from Central Park—the hotel is so understated and attractive that most locals don't even realize it's there. Everything is fresh, new, and professionally done. Rooms aren't huge or stylish, but there's no arguing with the quality. Layout is smart; bedding, fabrics, and window treatments are good; and blackout drapes let you sleep till noon. Closets are on the small side, but you'll have a new bathroom, some with hair dryers. Most rooms have desks, too. Executive rooms are outfitted in a more modern, less chain-standard style, with mahogany built-ins and individual climate controls.

An extended continental breakfast is served in the breakfast room (with free newspapers), which ups the ante on the value. Rates are seasonal, but low $80 deals are common in the slowest seasons and for AAA cardholders and seniors.

31 W. 71st St. (btwn Columbus Ave. and Central Park W.), New York, NY 10023. ℂ 800/228-5150 (worldwide reservations), 877/727-5236 (direct), or 212/721-4770. Fax 212/579-8544. www.comfortinn.com or www.bestnyhotels.com. 96 units. $119–$209 standard double, $179–$299 executive double. Rates include continental breakfast. Ask about senior, AAA, corporate, and promotional discounts; check www.hotelchoice.com for excellent rates (often as low as $80–$90). Extra person $15. Children under 13 stay free in parents' room. AE, DC, DISC, MC, V. Parking $25 nearby. Subway: B, C to 72nd St. **Amenities:** Exercise room; concierge; business center; dry cleaning/laundry; executive-level units. *In room:* A/C, TV, dataport, iron.

Hotel Newton ⟨ *Value* Finally—an inexpensive hotel that's *nice.*
As you enter the pretty lobby, a uniformed staff that's attentive and professional greets you. The rooms are large, with good, firm beds, work desks, and new bathrooms, plus roomy closets in most (a few have wall racks only). Some are big enough to accommodate families with two doubles or two queen beds. Each suite features two queen beds in the bedroom, a sofa in the sitting room, plus niceties like a microwave, minifridge, and iron, making them worth the few extra dollars. The bigger rooms and suites have been upgraded with cherrywood furnishings. The AAA-approved hotel is impeccably kept, and there was lots of sprucing up going on during my last visit.

The 96th Street subway stop is just a block away. It's a nice bet all the way around. The neighborhood boasts lots of affordable restaurants, and a cute diner in the same block provides room service.

2528 Broadway (btwn 94th and 95th sts.), New York, NY 10025. ℂ 888/HOTEL-58 (468-3558) or 212/678-6500. Fax 212/678-6758. www.newyorkhotel.com. 110 units. $85–$160 double or junior suite. AAA, corporate, senior, and group rates available; check website for Internet deals (from $75 double at press time). Extra person $10. Children under 15 stay free in parents' room. AE, DC, DISC, MC, V. Parking $20 nearby. Subway: 1, 2, 3, 9 to 96th St. **Amenities:** 24-hr. room service. *In room:* A/C, TV, hair dryer.

Hotel Olcott *Value* *Kids* The old dowager remains one of New York's best budget bargains. About half of this residential hotel houses permanent and long-term residents, but the rest is open to out-of-towners. The studios and suites are a steal. The apartments are about as stylish as Aunt Edna's house, but they're maintained with care, and even the studios are bigger than most NYC apartments (the suites are enormous). The discount furnishings are not pretty, but they're comfortable. Every apartment has a big bathroom and a kitchenette with minifridge, hot plate with kettle, toaster, and

basic dishes and utensils; studios generally have dining tables for two and suites have four-tops. Phones have voice mail. Suites have TV in the living room and sofas don't pull out, but the friendly management will lend you a cot (or even an additional bed) if you're bringing the family or sharing with friends. Ask for a renovated room when you book; most of the suites and about half of the studios have brand-new, bright-white kitchenettes and freshly laid tile in the bathroom.

The Olcott is steps from Central Park (the Dakota apartment building is just doors way). Nearby Columbus Avenue bustles with boutiques and restaurants, and just off the lobby is **Dallas BBQ** for cheap eats and bathtub-size cocktails.

27 W. 72nd St. (btwn Columbus Ave. and Central Park W.), New York, NY 10023. © 212/877-4200. Fax 212/580-0511. www.hotelolcott.com. 200 units. $130 studio double ($840 weekly); $150 suite ($980 weekly), $1,600 weekly 2-bedroom suite (sleeps up to 4). Extra person $15. MC, V (check or money order deposit required to guarantee room). Parking $35, 4 blocks away. Subway: B, C to 72nd St. **Amenities:** Restaurant; bar. *In room:* A/C, TV, dataport, kitchenette with fridge.

The Milburn 𝓡 (Kids)

On a quiet street a block from the Beacon, the Milburn offers reasonably priced rooms and suites with kitchenettes—at about half the price. Every suite is rife with amenities, including a dining area; a newish bathroom and kitchenette (with free coffee); two-line phones; and more. Junior and one-bedroom suites boast a pullout queen sofa, an extra TV, a CD player, and a desk. Don't expect much from the decor, but everything is attractive and in good shape. The conscientious management keeps the whole place spotless and in good order. In fact, what makes the Milburn a find is that it's more service-oriented than most hotels in this price range: The friendly staff will do everything from providing free copy, fax, and e-mail services to picking up your laundry at the dry cleaner next door. This is a great choice for bargain hunters—especially families, for whom rollaways and cribs are on hand.

242 W. 76th St. (btwn Broadway and West End Ave.), New York, NY 10023. © 800/833-9622 or 212/362-1006. Fax 212/721-5476. www.milburnhotel.com. 114 units. $129–$179 studio double; $149–$185 junior suite, $169–$205 1-bedroom suite. Extra person $10. Children under 13 stay free in parents' room. AE, DC, MC, V. Parking $20–$29. Subway: 1, 9 to 79th St. **Amenities:** Fitness room; access to nearby health club; business services; coin-op laundry; free video library. *In room:* A/C, TV/VCR (Sony PlayStation on request), dataport, kitchenette with fridge and coffeemaker, hair dryer, iron, safe, CD player in suites.

Quality Hotel on Broadway (Value)

Stay at this reliable, freshly renovated hotel if you like lots of space; some rooms are large enough for two doubles or a king bed. Rooms feature hotel-standard furnishings that include a work desk with a good ergonomic chair; an armoire holds the TV and good drawer space. Each room has an alarm clock, two phones with voice mail and free local calls, and a makeup mirror in the bathroom. Some also have a minifridge or a kitchenette; request one when you book. Most bathrooms have granite countertops. A library-style sitting room is off the lobby. The location is terrific—cheaper than staying on the Upper West Side in the 70s and 80s, but just as nice neighborhood-wise, surrounded by affordable restaurants and 2 blocks from a subway station that will whisk you to Times Square in two stops. Best of all, the online discount deals can be stellar (as low as $70 at press time).

215 W. 94th St. (at Broadway), New York, NY 10025. ℂ **800/228-5151** or 212/866-6400. Fax 212/866-1357. www.bestnyhotels.com. 350 units. $119–$149 single or double; $179–$219 junior suite (sleeps 2 or 3). Ask about senior, AAA, corporate, and promotional discounts; check www.hotelchoice.com for online-booking discounts (as low as $70 at press time). Extra person $15. Children under 18 stay free in parents' room. AE, DC, DISC, MC, V. Parking $20. Subway: 1, 2, 3, 9 to 96th St. **Amenities:** Restaurant; fax service; coin-op laundry; dry cleaning/laundry. *In room:* A/C, TV, dataport, coffeemaker, hair dryer, iron.

SUPERCHEAP SLEEPS

Hostelling International–New York   Staying here is like going back to college—an international college, with clocks set for six different time zones behind the front desk and a clientele from around the globe. Beds are cheap, but expect to bunk it (upper or lower?) with people you don't know in rooms of 4, 6, 8, or 12. Everything is basic, but the mattresses are firm and the shared bathrooms are nicely kept. There are four rooms with one double and two bunk beds that have private bathrooms. The well-managed hostel feels like a student union, with bulletin boards and listings of events posted; a coffee bar with an ample menu and pleasant seating; two TV rooms; a game room; and a library with bill- and credit-card-operated Internet access computers. There's also a common kitchen, vending machines, a coin-op laundry, a terrace, and a yard with picnic tables and barbecues in summer. The neighborhood has improved over the years, but it's still a little sketchy; 1 block over is much nicer Broadway, lined with affordable restaurants and shops.

891 Amsterdam Ave. (at 103rd St.), New York, NY 10025. ℂ **800/909-4776** or 212/932-2300. Fax 212/932-2574. www.hinewyork.org. 624 beds; 4 units with private bathroom. $29–$38 dorm bed; $120–$135 for family room (sleeps up to 4) or private quad. Travelers must be 18 or older. AE, DC, MC, V. Subway: 1, 9 to 103rd St. **Amenities:** Coffee bar; access to nearby health club; game room; activities desk; coin-op laundry. *In room:* A/C, locker (BYO lock), no phone.

4

Great Deals on Dining

New York is the best restaurant town in the country. Other cities might have particular specialties—Paris has better bistros, Hong Kong better Chinese, Los Angeles better Mexican—but no culinary capital spans the globe as successfully as NYC. Wherever you're from, city restaurants will seem *expensive*. But as you peruse this chapter, you'll see that values abound—especially if you eat ethnic and venture into the neighborhoods where real New Yorkers eat.

RESERVATIONS Reservations are always a good idea. If you're booking dinner on a weekend night, call a few days to a week in advance; farther in advance never hurts.

But lots of restaurants, especially at the affordable end of the spectrum, don't take reservations. This means that the best cheap and midpriced restaurants often have a wait. Your best bet is to go early or late. Often, you can get in more quickly on a weeknight.

THE LOWDOWN ON SMOKING The majority of the city's dining rooms are smoke-free. At press time, the City Council was considering a resolution to ban smoking in all bars and restaurants. At the moment, you can smoke in bars, lounges, and alfresco areas.

TIPPING Tipping is easy in New York. Double the 8.25% sales tax and voilà! Happy waitperson. If you check your coat, leave a dollar per item for the checkroom attendant.

1 The Financial District

Burritoville 🍴🍴 *Value* TEX-MEX This bright, cheerful minichain serves up fare that doesn't deserve to be called fast food. It's Mexican, prepared with healthy ingredients—fresh produce, brown rice, and black beans—using no lard, preservatives, or canned goods. Even the tortillas are pressed every day. Options range from well-stuffed tacos and quesadillas to only-at-Burritoville creations such as a spicy white chicken chili with cumin, salad burritos, and a number of wraps. The extensive menu offers a wealth of options for vegetarians. Another nice thing is their flexibility—you can make substitutions and special requests easily, and usually without an extra charge. In addition to this location (close to Battery Park and the Statue of Liberty and Staten Island ferry), a second lower Manhattan location is at 20 John St., between Broadway and Nassau (© **212/766-2020**).

36 Water St. (just north of Broad St.). © **212/747-1100**. www.burritoville.com. Reservations not accepted. Main courses $4.50–$9. AE, DISC, MC, V. Daily 11am–10pm. Subway: 2, 3 to Wall St.; 1, 9 to South Ferry.

Mangia MEDITERRANEAN CAFE   This gourmet cafeteria is an ideal place to take a break while sightseeing. Between the giant salad and soup bars, the sandwich and hot-entree counters, and expansive cappuccino-and-pastry counter, even the most finicky eater will have a hard time deciding what to eat. Everything is freshly prepared and beautifully presented. The soups and stews are particularly good, and a cup goes well with a fresh-baked pizzette (a minipizza). Pay-by-the-pound salad bars don't get any better than this, hot-meal choices (such as cumin-marinated lamb kebab) are cooked to order, and sandwiches made as you watch. It's packed with Wall Streeters between noon and 2pm, but things move quickly. Come in for a late breakfast or an afternoon snack and you'll virtually have the place to yourself.

40 Wall St. (btwn Nassau and William sts.). © **212/425-4040**. www.mangianet. com. Reservations not accepted. Soups and salads $3.50–$5; sandwiches and main courses $6–$14 (most less than $10). AE, DC, DISC, MC, V. Mon–Fri 7am–5pm (waiter service available 11:30am–4pm). Subway: 2, 3, 4, 5 to Wall St.; J, M, Z to Broad St. Also at 50 W. 57th St. (btwn Fifth and Sixth aves.; © **212/582-5554**; Mon–Fri 7am–8pm; Sat 8:30am–6pm; subway: B, Q to 57th St.); 16 E. 48th St. (btwn Fifth and Madison aves.; © **212/754-0637**; Mon–Fri 7am–6pm; subway: B, D, F, Q to 47th–50th sts./Rockefeller Center.).

2 TriBeCa

In addition to the choices below, **Burritoville** (p. 75) is at 144 Chambers St., at Hudson Street (© **212/964-5048**).

Franklin Station Cafe FRENCH-MALAYSIAN   This brick-walled cafe is a winner for Malaysian noodle and curry bowls and French-inspired sandwiches. The dishes on the handwritten-and-illustrated menu are prepared with all-natural ingredients. Sandwiches are simple but satisfying creations such as home-baked ham with honey mustard, lettuce, and tomato; mozzarella with basil, vine-ripened tomato, and extra-virgin olive oil; smoked salmon with mascarpone and chives. For warm and cozy, you can't do better than one of the noodle bowls, such as tom yum shrimp,

Where to Dine in the Financial District, TriBeCa, Chinatown & Little Italy

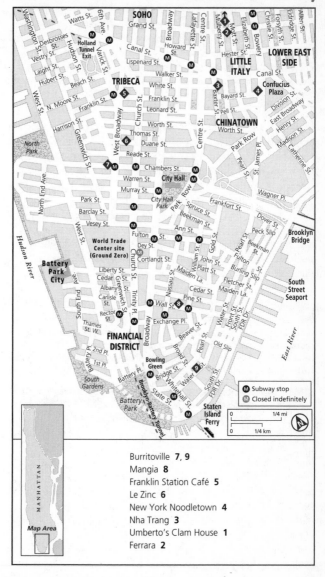

Burritoville **7, 9**
Mangia **8**
Franklin Station Café **5**
Le Zinc **6**
New York Noodletown **4**
Nha Trang **3**
Umberto's Clam House **1**
Ferrara **2**

with sprouts, pineapple, and cucumber in a hot-and-sour broth. For a more substantial meal, check the blackboard for such specials as Chilean sea bass in cardamom sauce. Service is friendly and efficient, wine and beer is available, and the desserts are well priced and pleasing. It's a great choice for a casual meal.

222 W. Broadway (at Franklin St.). ℂ 212/274-8525. Reservations not accepted. Breakfast $4.50–$7.50; sandwiches $6.50–$7; Malaysian specialties and noodle bowls $7–$13.50; house specials $10.50–$16.50. AE, DC, MC, V. Daily 8am–11pm. Subway: 1, 9 to Franklin St.; 2, 3 to Chambers St.

Le Zinc 🟥🟥🟥 *Value* FRENCH BISTRO David and Karen Waltuck (who run big-ticket Chanterelle) also have this affordable, authentic bistro. Despite its TriBeCa address, Le Zinc is unfussy and unpretentious, boasting genuine warmth and creative bistro cuisine. The space is open and comfortable, with soft, sexy lighting.

The menu features bistro favorites with gentle accents, some of which reach beyond France to Eastern Europe, Asia, and even New Orleans. Winning choices include a skate wing browned in butter and capers; Grandma Gaby's Hungarian stuffed cabbage; mussels in snail butter; an excellent duck, foie gras, and pistachio terrine from the charcuterie; rib steak and frites; and a thick, juicy bacon cheeseburger. Reservations aren't taken, but any wait is worth it; put yourself in the competent hands of the bartenders at the mahogany bar. This is a real winner—and reason enough to visit TriBeCa.

139 Duane St. (btwn W. Broadway and Church St.). ℂ 212/513-0001. www.lezinc nyc.com. Reservations not accepted. Main courses $2–$7 at breakfast, $7–$16 at lunch, $10–$21 at dinner. AE, DISC, MC, V. Sun–Thurs 8am–1am; Fri–Sat 8am–3am. Subway: 1, 2, 3, 9 to Chambers St.

3 Chinatown & Little Italy

New York Noodletown 🟥🟥 CHINESE/SEAFOOD This just may be the best Chinese food in the city. So what if the fluorescent-lit room has the ambience of a school cafeteria? The food is fabulous. The mushroom soup is a lunch in itself, thick with chunks of shiitakes, vegetables, and noodles. Another appetizer that can serve as a meal is the hacked roast duck in noodle soup. The kitchen excels at seafood, so be sure to try some: Looking like a snow-dusted plate of meaty fish, the salt-baked squid is sublime. The quick-woked Chinese broccoli or the crisp sautéed baby *bok choy* are great accompaniments. New York Noodletown keeps long hours, which makes it the best late-night bet in the neighborhood.

28½ Bowery (at Bayard St.). ℂ 212/349-0923. Reservations accepted. Main courses $4–$13. No credit cards. Daily 9am–3:30am. Subway: N, R, 6 to Canal St.

Nha Trang ✺ *(Finds)* VIETNAMESE   The decor may be standard-issue, Chinatown (glass-topped tables, linoleum floors, mirrored walls), but this place serves up the best Vietnamese fare in Chinatown. A plate of six crispy, finger-size spring rolls is a nice way to start; the slightly spicy pork-and-shrimp filling is offset by the wrapping of lettuce, cucumber, and mint. The *pho* noodle soup comes in a quart-size bowl brimming with bright vegetables and meats and seafood. My favorite dish is the barbecued pork chops—sliced paper-thin, soaked in a soy/sugarcane marinade, and grilled to perfection. Your waiter will be glad to help you design a meal to suit your tastes. If there's a line, and you don't want to wait, head over to the second location, **Nha Trang Centre,** which accepts credit cards.

87 Baxter St. (btwn Canal and Bayard sts.). ℰ **212/233-5948.** Reservations accepted. Main courses $4–$12.50. No credit cards. Daily 11am–9:30pm. Subway: N, R, 6 to Canal St. Also at 148 Centre St. (at Walker St.; ℰ **212/941-9292;** MC, V; subway: N, R, 6 to Canal St.).

Umberto's Clam House ITALIAN/SEAFOOD   Umberto's is where, in 1973, reputed Mafioso Joey Gallo was assassinated while savoring a plate of scungilli. Umberto's moved here a few years back, leaving those famed bullet holes behind, but it still brims with classic Little Italy ambience. The traditional, seafood-heavy menu is pleasing. I found the *scungilli* (conch) to be a bit chewy, but the baked clams were divine. You can also expect al dente linguine with a generous helping of fresh shelled clams in red sauce or extra-virgin olive oil; and lobster ravioli stuffed with chunks of lobster (a steal at $15). Plenty of meat and pasta dishes are on hand. The wine list is decent and affordable. The atmosphere is old-world nautical, with comfortably spaced tables and a small outdoor patio. Autographed pictures on the walls run the gamut from Sinatra to never-beens with big dreams. The restaurant is staffed with career waiters who are friendly and attentive. It's a bit pricey, but a very good bet.

386 Broome St. (btwn Mulberry and Mott sts.). ℰ **212/431-7545.** www.umbertos clamhouse.com. Reservations required for Fri–Sat dinner, and for parties of 5 or more. Pastas $10–$19.50; main courses $7–$30 (most $10–$20). AE, DISC, MC, V. Daily 11am–4am. Subway: N, R to Prince St.; 6 to Spring St.

QUICK BITES

America's first espresso bar was **Ferrara** ✺, 195 Grand St., between Mott and Mulberry streets (ℰ **212/226-6150**), founded in 1892. This pleasant Little Italy *pasticceria* is still the place for Italian treats like cannoli (fresh-squeezed in the pastry shell as you watch), zeppoles, *sfogliatelle* (a flaky shell stuffed with baked ricotta), napoleons, and more. Cafe seating is available. Open Sunday to Friday from 8am to midnight, Saturday from 8am to 1am.

4 The Lower East Side

Bereket ✦ (Value) TURKISH   This popular kebab house has undergone an expansion that has more than doubled the number of tables and upgraded its hole-in-the-wall ambience to shiny diner-style decor—and the quality of their grilled meats is as excellent as ever. Order at the counter, where you'll see the kebabs displayed behind glass waiting to hit the grill, and then snare a table. The *kofte,* ground lamb with spices, is a favorite, but you won't go wrong with any of the choices. Complete dinners—two skewers of your choice, rice, and salad—are a steal for a 10 spot, especially the mixed grill, which features chicken, *shish* (beef), and *doner* (lamb) kebabs. Vegetarians have a lot to choose from, including excellently herbed hummus, falafel, great *piyaz* (white-bean salad with chopped onions and parsley), and babaganoush. Everything is freshly prepared in-house, and the counter staff is friendly and accommodating. No alcohol is served, but Turkish coffee should provide the necessary jolt.

187 Houston St. (at Orchard St.). © 212/475-7700. Reservations not accepted. Main courses $3.50–$13.50. No credit cards. Open daily 24 hr. Subway: F to Second Ave.

Katz's Delicatessen ✦✦ (Value) JEWISH DELI   The motto here is, "There's Nothing More New York than Katz's," and it's spot-on. Founded in 1888, this brightly lit place is suitably Noo Yawk, with dill pickles, Dr. Brown's cream soda, and old-world attitude to spare. The Lower East Side institution draws everybody from housewives in for a day of shopping to tattooed club-goers looking for after-hours nutrition. Half of the space is dedicated to cafeteria-style counter service—perfect for budget-minded travelers who'd rather save on tip money—the other half offers waiter service (though it's considered appropriate to tip the carver who slices the meat for your sandwich if you get it at the counter).

All of Katz's traditional eats are first-rate: matzo ball and chicken noodle soups, potato knishes, cheese blintzes, egg creams (made with Katz's very own seltzer), and all-beef hot dogs. There's no faulting the pastrami—smoked to perfection and piled high on rye—or the dry-cured roast beef, either. All of the well-stuffed sandwiches are substantially cheaper than you'll find at any other deli in town.

Where to Dine on the Lower East Side, SoHo, Nolita, the East Village and NoHo

A Salt & Battery **9**

Angelica Kitchen **3**

Bereket **11**

Bulgin' Waffles **10**

Burritoville **5**

Cafe Habana **14**

Emerald Planet **15**

Fanelli's Café **16**

Frank **8**

Katz's Delicatessen **12**

Le Pain Quotidien **19**

Le Pere Pinard **13**

Lombardi's **18**

Moustache **7**

Paul's **6**

Snack **17**

Soba-Ya **2**

Veselka **4**

Village Yokocho **1**

What's more, Katz's is the only deli cool enough to let you split one with your travel partner without adding a bogus $2 to $3 "sharing" charge.

205 E. Houston St. (at Ludlow St.). ℂ **212/254-2246.** Reservations not accepted. Sandwiches $2.15–$10; other main courses $5–$17.50. AE, MC, V ($20 minimum). Sun–Tues 8am–10pm; Wed–Thurs 8am–11pm; Fri–Sat 8am–2:30am. Subway: F to Second Ave.

Le Pere Pinard ℛ *Finds* FRENCH BISTRO/WINE BAR This French wine bar and bistro is a charming slice of Le Marais, with high ceilings, brick walls, well-spaced tables with mix-and-match chairs, and a come-as-you-are air. The kitchen specializes in the Gallic version of comfort food: steak frites, shell steak with Roquefort sauce, shepherd's pie with a cheesy crust, a terrific *brandade* (a dish of salt fish puréed with olive oil, milk and garlic) and a charcuterie and cheese plate—the perfect match for the sublime bread that accompanies every meal. Greens are fresh and well prepared; even a simple mesclun salad wears a just-right vinaigrette.

There's a wonderful and affordable wine selection by the bottle, carafe, and glass; I like the restaurant's protocol, which allows you to taste first even if you're ordering by the glass. Service is attentive in an easygoing way. There's also a pleasant garden in warm weather. Attention diners happy to eat on the early side (before 7pm): The pre-theater meal—three courses for $14—is a stellar deal.

175 Ludlow St. (south of Houston St.). ℂ **212/777-4917.** Reservations recommended. Main courses $11.50–$19.50; pre-theater menu daily 5–7pm, $14 for 3 courses. AE. Mon–Thurs 5pm–midnight; Fri 5pm–1am; Sat 11am–1am; Sat–Sun 11am–midnight. Subway: F to Second Ave.

5 SoHo & Nolita

Cafe Habana ℛ LATIN AMERICAN I love this update on a typical Hispanic luncheonette. It's hip without being pretentious, and what the food may lack in authenticity it makes up for in quality and flavor: Shrimps are big and hearty; pork is moist and flavorful; cilantro and other spices fresh and aromatic. Starters include *pozole*, hominy corn stew with shredded chicken or pork in a clear broth that you season to taste with oregano, chili, and lime. Main courses include the moist roast pork and *camarones al ajillo*, shrimp in spicy garlic sauce. Most everything comes with your choice of red or black beans and rice; go with the yellow rice. Wine and Mexican beers are served, but I enjoyed the not-too-sweet red hibiscus tea.

The room is narrow and tables are petite, but a middle aisle keeps the place from feeling too crowded, and service is easygoing and friendly. If you're too hungry to wait for a table, stop into the adjacent storefront sandwich shop on Elizabeth Street for a pressed sandwich, burrito, or other takeout treat (open daily noon–10pm).

17 Prince St. (at Elizabeth St.). ℰ 212/625-2001. Reservations not accepted. Main courses $5–$15. AE, MC, V. Daily 9am–midnight. Subway: F, S to Broadway/Lafayette St.; 6 to Spring St.

Fanelli's Cafe AMERICAN Once, SoHo consisted of a few galleries, artists living in loft space no one wanted, a few Italian bakeries, and Fanelli's. It couldn't be more different now; but, Fanelli's remains the same. This is a classic New York pub, with a long bar propped up by regulars, and a corner door and pressed-tin ceiling that have locked in the 1847 atmosphere. If smoke bothers you, ask to be seated in the back. The burgers are great, the pastas fresh, the beer served in pint glasses. The Bloody Marys are a godsend for a hangover (white wine is the secret ingredient). If you're coming for dinner, your best bet is to arrive before 7pm.

94 Prince St. (at Mercer St.). ℰ 212/226-9412. Reservations not accepted. Main courses $6–$15 (most less than $12). AE, MC, V. Sun–Thurs 10am–12:30am; Fri–Sat 10am–1am. Subway: N, R to Prince St.

Le Pain Quotidien ✿✿ FRENCH-BELGIAN/BAKERY CAFÉ
This airy neoclassical-goes-farmhouse cafe is one of my favorites for a sophisticated casual meal at a bargain-basement price. Take a seat at a table for two or cozy up to one of the generous and comfy common tables (the one in the sunlit front room is best). The light menu is comprised mostly of beautiful sandwiches and salads. Excellent choices include the open-faced beef carpaccio sandwich dressed with basil, Parmesan, and virgin olive oil on dark country bread. All are garnished with seasonal greens and fresh herbs. Salads are a good value because they come piled high and accompanied by a plate of French bread. Soups are homemade, hearty, and warming. Breads are baked five times daily. Save room for dessert—fruit tarts, pies, brownies, cookies, brioches—or stop just for a sweet and a cappuccino; the warm Belgian waffle sprinkled with powdered sugar and fresh blueberries makes a light-as-air choice. Tables are waiter-serviced, but an up-front counter serves walk-ins and takeout.

100 Grand St. (between Mercer and Greene sts.). ℰ 212/625-9009. www.pain quotidien.com. Reservations not accepted. Breakfast $3–$7.50; sandwiches and salads $7.50–$18 (most less than $12). No credit cards. Daily 8am–7pm. Subway: N, R to Canal St. Also at ABC Carpet & Home, 38 E. 19th St. (btwn Broadway and Park Ave. S.; ℰ 212/625-9009; subway: 4, 5, 6, N, R, L to 14th St./Union Sq.); 50 W. 72nd St. (btwn Columbus Ave. and Central Park W.; ℰ 212/712-9700; subway: B, C to 72nd St.); 833 Lexington Ave. (btwn 63rd and 64th sts.; ℰ 212/755-5810;

subway: 4, 5, 6 to 59th St.; N, R to Lexington Ave.); 1336 First Ave. (btwn 71st and 72nd sts.; ✆ **212/717-4800**; subway: 6 to 68th St.); 1131 Madison Ave. (btwn 84th and 85th sts.; ✆ **212/327-4900**; subway: 4, 5, 6 to 86th St.).

Lombardi's ⭐⭐ (Kids) PIZZA   Lombardi's makes the best pizza in Manhattan. First opened in 1905, "America's first licensed pizzeria" cooks its delectable pies in its original coal brick oven. The smoky crust (a generations-old family recipe) is topped with fresh mozzarella, basil, pecorino Romano, and San Marzano tomato sauce. From there, the choice is yours. Topping options are suitably old-world (Citterio pancetta, kalamata olives, Esposito sweet Italian sausage and the like), but Lombardi's specialty is the fresh clam pie, with hand-shucked clams, oregano, fresh garlic, Romano, extra-virgin olive oil, and fresh-ground pepper (no sauce). A big draw is the back garden. Another plus: In a city where rudeness is a badge of honor, Lombardi's wait staff is extremely affable.

32 Spring St. (btwn Mott and Mulberry sts.). ✆ **212/941-7994**. Reservations accepted for parties of 6 or more. Pies $11.50–$21; extra charge for additional toppings. No credit cards. Mon–Thurs 11:30am–11pm; Fri–Sat 11:30am–midnight; Sun 11:30am–10pm. Subway: 6 to Spring St.; N, R to Prince St.

Snack GREEK   This SoHo nook draws a hip crowd with its beautifully prepared Hellenic eats. Tables are tiny and seating is tight, but a tin ceiling, Art Nouveau light fixtures, and shelves lined with Greek grocery goods transform the storefront dining room into a charmer. Even with paper plates and plastic utensils, this place is atmospheric enough to enjoy a wallet-friendly date (BYO wine or beer). The menu is traditional Greek, and the kitchen usually strikes gold. The *taramosalata* (carp roe dip) is the best I've had, and the *spanikopitakia* (spinach squares) come close. Dressed with fresh tomatoes, roasted red onions, and a roasted tomato aioli and served on fresh, crusty *ciabatta,* the braised lamb sandwich was terrific. If the wait is too long at lunch and the weather's nice, order to go and head down the block to the park. Come after 6pm for yummy entrees like *saganaki* (fried cheese), vegetarian moussaka, grilled octopus, and chicken slow-roasted with lemon, rosemary, and garlic.

105 Thompson St. (btwn Prince and Spring sts.). ✆ **212/925-1040**. Reservations not accepted. Main courses $6–$14. No credit cards. Sun–Mon 11am–8:30pm; Tues–Sat 11am–10:30pm. Subway: C, E to Spring St.

6 The East Village & NoHo

In addition to the choices below, a great choice for wallet-friendly Middle Eastern fare is **Moustache** (p. 91), at 265 E. 10th St., between First Avenue and Avenue A (✆ **212/228-2022**).

Burritoville (p. 75) is at 141 Second Ave., between St. Marks Place and 9th Street (℃ **212/260-3300**). Additionally, a second location of British chippery **A Salt & Battery** (p. 89) is at 80 Second Ave., between 4th and 5th streets (℃ **212/254 6610**).

Angelica Kitchen ORGANIC VEGETARIAN   This cheerful restaurant is serious about vegan cuisine. The kitchen prepares everything fresh daily; at least 95% of ingredients are organically grown. But good-for-you doesn't have to mean boring—this is flavorful, beautifully prepared cuisine. Salads spill over with sprouts and crisp veggies and are crowned with homemade dressings. The Dragon Bowls, a specialty, are heaping portions of rice, beans, tofu, and steamed vegetables. The daily specials feature the best of what's fresh and in season in such dishes as fiery three-bean chili, slow-simmered with sun-dried tomatoes and a blend of chili peppers. Breads and desserts are fresh-baked and similarly wholesome (and made without eggs). If you like the eats, you can take home *The Angelica Home Kitchen* cookbook.

300 E. 12th St. (just east of Second Ave.). ℃ 212/228-2909. Reservations accepted for parties of 6 or more. Main courses $6–$14.50. No credit cards. Daily 11:30am–10:30pm. Subway: L, N, R, 4, 5, 6 to 14th St./Union Sq.

Bulgin' Waffles *(Finds* WAFFLES   This joint does one thing—waffles—and does them very well. The waffles come in two sizes—normal, or "wafflette," and extra-thick, or "bulgin'." You have a number of varieties, from plain to hazelnut to pumpkin, and a full slate of toppings. Everybody else will love the fab food, low prices, and ambience. It's great for breakfast, brunch, dinner, or dessert! The "Dream Machine" is the ultimate ice-cream sandwich—made with waffles. The room is comprised of a bustling order counter and a collection of rough-hewn tables; your food is delivered to your table on paper plates. There's also an ice cream and Italian ice counter.

49½ First Ave. (at 3rd St.). ℃ 212/477-6555. Main courses $2–$8. MC, V ($10 minimum). Sun 10am–10pm; Mon–Thurs 8am–10pm; Fri 8am–2am; Sat 10am–2am. Subway: F to Second Ave.

Emerald Planet *(ℛ* INTERNATIONAL WRAPS   This San Francisco import has buried the sandwich and replaced it with the wrap. The Emerald Planet ideology is simple: You can eat wraps at every meal, from bacon and eggs (the Omaha) in the morning to grilled veggies with goat cheese (the Sonoma) at noon to jerk chicken, mango salsa, and jasmine rice (the Kingston) at dinner.

Dining Zone: Little India

East 6th Street between First and Second avenues in the East Village is called "Little India," thanks to the dozen or more Indian restaurants that line the block (Subway: F to Second Ave.). Dining here isn't exactly high style, its restaurants offer decent food at discount prices, sometimes accompanied by live sitar music. It's fun to grab a bottle of wine or a six-pack (many of Little India's restaurants don't serve alcohol, but even those that do will often let you bring in your own) and cruise the strip. In warm weather, each usually stations a hawker out front.

Some people speculate that there's one big kitchen behind East 6th, but a few of Little India's restaurants deserve special attention. **Bombay Dining**, at 320 E. 6th St. (© 212/260-8229), is a standout, serving excellent *samosa* (vegetable-and-meat patties), *pakora* (banana fritters), and *papadum* (crispy bean wafers with coarse peppercorns). Also try **Gandhi**, 345 E. 6th St. (© 212/614-9718), for a touch of low-light romance; **Mitali East**, 334 E. 6th St. (© 212/533-2508), the king of curry; and **Rose of India**, 308 E. 6th St. (© 212/533-5011), most notable for the pure spectacle of its every-day-is-Christmas decor.

The tortilla-like wrapping changes depending on the ingredients, from flour to whole wheat to tomato to spinach. All ingredients are fresh, and the emphasis is on healthy. Supplement your wrap with one of the smoothies, or opt for a margarita, iced tea, a latte, sangria, or one of the international bottled beers on offer. The decor is downtown stylish—wee dangling halogen lights, clean woody surfaces, rainforest-green walls. This is one of downtown's best stops for quick, quality chow—just ask Madonna, an Emerald Planet regular.

2 Great Jones St. (at Broadway). © 212/353-9727. www.emeraldplanet.city search.com. Wraps $1.50–$3.50 at breakfast, $6–$8 at lunch/dinner; smoothies $4–$5. AE, MC, V. Mon–Fri 9am–10pm; Sat noon–10pm; Sun noon–8pm. Subway: 6 to Bleecker St.; N, R to 8th St. Also at 30 Rockefeller Plaza, lower concourse level (down the hall from the skating rink; © 212/218-1133; subway: B, D, F, Q to 47th–50th sts./Rockefeller Center).

Frank 🟊🟊 *Value* ITALIAN   This home-style restaurant serves straight-from-the-boot cuisine. The menu is small but satisfying, focusing on what the kitchen does well: Rigatoni al ragu wears a meat-and-tomato "gravy" slow-cooked to perfection. It appears again on the house specialty, the *polpettone*—literally "the big meatball"—a beautifully seasoned mound of beef with a potato-and-pancetta gratin that's better than dessert in my book. There's homemade gnocchi and ravioli, plus spiced meat loaf. The wine list is well priced, with a good selection by the glass.

The young wait staff is easygoing and earnest, and the brick-walled room is dimly lit and attractive. On the downside, the tables are so close together that you can't help but overhear your neighbors' conversation; the open kitchen can make the dining room rather smoky at times; and there's often a wait (Vera, Frank's bar, offers a place to unwind with a glass of wine). But these inconveniences are well worth it for the marvelous payoff that is Frank fare.

88 Second Ave. (btwn 5th and 6th sts.). © 212/420-0202. Reservations accepted only for parties of 8 or more. Main courses $9–$14. No credit cards. Mon–Thurs 10:30am–4pm and 5pm–12:45am; Fri–Sat 10:30am–4pm and 5pm–1:45am; Sun 10:30am–11:45pm. Subway: 6 to Astor Place.

Paul's ⋒⋒ *Value* BURGERS/DINER   This neighborhood diner serves the best burgers in town—period. Every burger is a half-pounder, made from 100% pure beef or turkey. Both versions are thick, juicy, and delicious. Variations run the gamut from a slate of cheeseburgers (American, Swiss, mozzarella, cheddar, Monterey Jack, blue) to concoctions like the Texas (topped with a fried egg) and the Eastsider (a bacon cheeseburger with ham, mushrooms, tomatoes, and onions). If you're in the mood for something else, consider a Philly cheese steak, a tuna melt, or any one of a dozen omelets. Fries are crisp and yummy. A better-than-average selection of beers is on hand, while egg creams, milk shakes, and root-beer floats offer old-fashioned comfort.

131 Second Ave. (btwn 7th St. and St. Marks Place). © 212/529-3033 or 212/529-3097. Reservations not accepted. Burgers and main courses $2.30–$10.60. No credit cards. Sun–Thurs 11am–midnight; Fri–Sat 11am–1am. Subway: 6 to Astor Place.

Soba-Ya ⋒⋒ *Finds* JAPANESE NOODLES   *Shhh*—don't tell anybody about Soba-Ya. It has a loyal following, but the masses haven't discovered it yet. That makes it easy to walk in and enjoy an affordable Japanese meal without a wait. Go with one of the special starters, which might be grilled shiitakes or luscious *toro* (tuna belly) sashimi, and then move on to one of the house specialties: generous, steaming noodle bowls. They come with *soba* (thin buckwheat) or *udon* (a very thick noodle much like pasta) and in a number of combinations. A menu with descriptions and pictures makes it easy for noodle novices to order. I love the *nabeyaki,* an udon bowl with shrimp tempura. Cold soba dishes topped with your choice of ingredients are also available. Everything is beautifully presented on Japanese dishware, and there's a lengthy list of sakes. The lovely dining room is blessed with a Zen-like vibe and attentive service.

229 E. 9th St. (btwn Second and Third aves.). ✆ **212/533-6966.** Reservations not accepted. Main courses $6.50–$14. AE, DC, DISC, MC, V. Daily noon–4pm and 5:30–10:30pm. Subway: 6 to Astor Place.

Veselka ✿ UKRAINIAN DINER   Whenever the craving hits for eastern European fare at old-world prices, Veselka fits the bill with *pirogi* (dumplings filled with potatoes, cheese, or sauerkraut), *kasha varnishkes* (cracked buckwheat and noodles with mushroom sauce), stuffed cabbage, Polish kielbasa, potato pancakes, and classic soups like a borscht, voted best in the city by the *New York Times* and *New York* magazine. Try the buckwheat pancakes or cheese blintzes; the Christmas borscht, which hits the menu in early December and stays through January, is a simple but divine rendering of the eastern European classic.

Despite the authentic fare, the diner is comfortable, modern, and appealing, with an artsy slant and house-made desserts. Regional beers from the Ukraine and Poland and a nice selection of wines from California and South America add a sophisticated touch. No wonder Veselka surpasses its status as a popular after-hours hangout with club kids and other night owls to be a favorite at any hour.

144 Second Ave. (at 9th St.). ✆ **212/228-9682.** Reservations not accepted. Main courses $5–$13. AE, DC, DISC, MC, V. Daily 24 hr. Subway: 6 to Astor Place.

Village Yokocho ✿*Value* JAPANESE/KOREAN BARBECUE Entering this second-floor spot feels like stepping into a Tokyo yakitori bar, complete with a hip clientele that's a mix of Japanese and in-the-know Americans. Between the regular menu and the handwritten specials on the wall, the choices are vast. Dishes run the gamut from dumplings and yakisoba noodles to exotica such as deep-fried squid eggs. The broiled-eel bowl is finer quality than you'll get at many restaurants and a deal at $8. Korean dishes include oxtail soup and *bibinbop,* a rice bowl topped with veggies, ground beef, and a fried egg. The specials change depending on the season, but you might find soft-shell crab in ponzu sauce, broiled yellowtail with teriyaki sauce, and any number of sashimi appetizers. There's a big, affordable sake menu as well as several beers.

8 Stuyvesant St. (at Third Ave. and E. 9th St.), 2nd floor. ℂ **212/598-3041.**
Reservations not accepted. Main courses $4–$12. AE, MC, V. Sun–Wed 5pm–3am;
Thurs–Sat 5pm–4am. Subway: 6 to Astor Place.

7 Greenwich Village & the Meat-Packing District

In addition to the choices below, there's a **Burritoville** (p. 75) at 298
Bleecker St., near Seventh Avenue (ℂ **212/633-9249**). The ultra-
fresh, supercheap **Go Sushi** (p. 106) is at 3 Greenwich Ave. (Sixth
Ave. at 8th St.; ℂ **212/366-9272**).

A Salt & Battery BRITISH   This straight-outta-London fish-
and-chippery is so genuine that they serve the goods wrapped in
newspaper. Stick with the traditional varieties (halibut, cod) and
you'll enjoy the real thing (crisp-battered outside, flaky and grease-
less inside). The room is tiny, with no more than six or eight seats,
so come at an off hour or be prepared for a wait—but it's worth it.
Word is that the deep-fried Mars Bar makes a divine dessert. English
beers are available, of course.

112 Greenwich Ave. (btwn 12th and 13th sts.). ℂ **212/691-2713.** www.asalt
andbattery.com. Reservations not accepted. Main courses $5–$13. AE, MC, V. Daily
noon–10pm. Subway: A, C, E, 1, 2, 3, 9 to 14th St. Also at 80 Second Ave. (btwn 4th
and 5th sts.; ℂ **212/254-6610**; subway: F to Second Ave.).

Bar Pitti ☆ *Value* TUSCAN ITALIAN   This indoor/outdoor
trattoria is a hip sidewalk scene, and one of downtown's best dining
bargains. Waiting for a table can be a chore, but all is forgiven once
you take a seat, thanks to authentic, affordably priced cuisine and
some of the friendliest waiters in town. Bar Pitti wins you over with
Italian charm—it's the kind of place where the waiter brings over
the list of daily specials on a blackboard, and if you want more
cheese, a block of Parmesan and a grater suddenly appear. Peruse the
menu, but don't get your heart set on anything until you see the
board, which boasts the best of what the kitchen has to offer; on my
last visit, they wowed me with fabulous veal meatballs. Winners off
the regular menu, which focuses heavily on pastas and panini,
include excellent beef carpaccio; and grilled country bread with pro-
sciutto, garlic, and olive oil. The all-Italian wine list is high-priced
compared to the menu, but you'll find a few good-value choices.

268 Sixth Ave. (btwn Bleecker and Houston sts.). ℂ **212/982-3300.** Reservations
accepted for parties of 4 or more. Main courses $7.50–$13 (some specials may be
higher). No credit cards. Daily noon–midnight. Subway: A, C, E, F, V to W. 4th St. (use
3rd St. exit).

Florent (Kids) DINER/FRENCH BISTRO So you get a craving at 3am for *rillettes, boudin noir,* or steak frites and can't decide whether you'd like to eat with club kids, celebrities, transvestites, truckers, or the odd stockbroker? Then get thee down to Florent, the nearly 24-hour French bistro dressed up as a '50s-style diner, where you can have it all. Florent is a hot spot no matter what time of day; a children's menu makes this the perfect place to bring the kids for lunch or early dinner. But it's after the clubs close when the joint really jumps. Tables are packed, but it's all part of the late-night festivities. This place has a sense of humor (check out the menu boards) and a CD catalog full of the latest indie sounds. The food's good, too: The grilled chicken with herbs and mustard sauce is a winner, as is the French onion soup with Gruyère. There are always faves like burgers and chili in addition to Gallic standards like *moules frites* (fried mussels). The fries are light, crispy, and addictive. The fixed-price lunches and dinners are excellent deals.

69 Gansevoort St. (2 blocks south of 14th St. and 1 block west of Ninth Ave., btwn Greenwich and Washington sts.). ℂ 212/989-5779. www.restaurantflorent.com. Reservations recommended for dinner. Main courses $4.50–$14.50 at brunch and lunch, $8–$20.50 at dinner (most less than $15); 2-course fixed-price lunches $8.25–$11.95; 3-course fixed-price dinner $18.95 before 7:30pm, $20.95 7:30pm–midnight. No credit cards. Mon–Wed 9am–5am; Thurs–Sun 24 hr. Subway: A, C, E, L to 14th St. L to 8th Ave.

Lupa (Kids) (Value) CENTRAL ITALIAN God bless Mario Batali, New York's big-name chef who thinks you shouldn't have to spend a fortune to eat like a king. The man behind the acclaimed and expensive Babbo, the Food Network's "Molto Mario" operates this Roman-style trattoria. Reservations are taken for the back room only, and I advise you to get them, as it's quieter and more civilized. The front room is for walk-ins; it's loud and cramped and you'll probably have to wait unless you come early, but the food is worth it.

(Tips) **Pizza! Pizza!**

In the mood for a slice or two? The original **John's Pizzeria** (p. 101), 278 Bleecker St. between Sixth and Seventh avenues (ℂ 212/243-1680), is a New York classic and still one of the city's best. The pies are thin-crusted, properly sauced, and served in an authentic old-world setting. Sorry, no slices.

A Salt & Battery **2**
Bar Pitti **6**
Florent **1**
Gray's Papaya **3**
John's Pizzeria **5**
Lupa **7**
Moustache **4**

Don't be scared off by the all-Italian menu; the waiter will steer you through the language and preparations. It's a short list, but one that boasts lots of treats. As always with Mario, the pastas stand out: The *bucatini all'amatriciana,* a classic Italian tube pasta in a smoky tomato sauce made from hog jowl (bacon), is divine, as is the ricotta gnocchi with Italian sausage and fennel. Don't miss an opportunity to start with the *prosciutto di carpegna* with roasted figs; it's easy to build a value-packed meal from the list of antipasti. Among the main courses the oven-roasted littleneck clams with sweet *soppressata* (salami) were a joy. The wine list is massive and super affordable.

170 Thompson St. (btwn Houston and Bleecker sts.). ℰ 212/982-5089. www.luparestaurant.com. Reservations highly recommended. Antipasti $5–$12; main courses $9–$17; 4-course prix fixe $30 at lunch, $45 at dinner (only for parties of 7 or more). AE, DC, MC, V. Daily noon–2:45pm and 5:30–11:30pm. Subway: 1, 9 to Houston St.

Moustache *Value* MIDDLE EASTERN   Moustache (pronounced moo-*stahsh*) is a charming hole-in-the-wall that boasts a Middle Eastern vibe and fare that's both palate-pleasing and wallet-friendly.

Delicately seasoned dishes bear little resemblance to the food at your average falafel joint. Expect subtly flavored hummus, tabbouleh, and spinach-chickpea-tomato salad (or a plate of all three); oven-roasted "pitzas," thin, matzolike pita crusts topped with spicy minced lamb and other ingredients; and—best of all—homemade pita bread, which puts any of those store-bought Frisbees to shame. Moustache is hugely popular, so there may be a line—but it's worth the wait.

90 Bedford St. (btwn Barrow and Grove sts.). ✆ 212/229-2220. Reservations not accepted. Main courses $5–$12. No credit cards. Daily noon–midnight (last order at 11pm). Subway: 1, 9 to Christopher St. Also at 265 E. 10th St. (btwn First Ave. and Ave. A; ✆ 212/228-2022; L to First Ave.).

QUICK BITES

Ask any New Yorker—one of the cheapest, most satisfying meals in the city is the $2.45 two-dogs-and-drink deal from **Gray's Papaya,** 402 Sixth Ave., at 8th Street (✆ **212/260-3532**). This legendary hot-dog stand hawks nothing but all-beef dogs, fries, and your choice of tropical-flavored fruit drinks ranging from piña colada to Orange Julius–style OJ. Best of all, they never close.

8 Chelsea

In addition to the choices below, **Burritoville** (p. 76) is at 264 W. 23rd St., between Seventh and Eighth avenues (✆ **212/367-9844**).

Antique Cafe ⭐ CAFE   I love the atmosphere and the beautifully prepared food at this brick-walled cafe, named for the flea markets that fill the nearby Sixth Avenue parking lots on weekends, always fragrant with the aroma of fresh-baked goods. There's no printed menu; instead, the day's bill of fare features whatever's fresh, including homemade soups, bounteous salads, gourmet sandwiches that run the gamut from roast beef to peanut butter and jelly, quiche, and pastries and cappuccino. Making regular appearances are a terrific bruschetta with melted Swiss, mushroom, and onion ($3.50); a dynamite haddock chowder ($3.75); a London broil salad boasting a beautiful cut, tomatoes, red onions, and cilantro over mixed greens ($6.25). Order at the counter and take a seat at one of the small cafe tables indoors or out, or take your food over to Madison Square Park.

101 W. 25th St. (just west of Sixth Ave.). ✆ 212/675-1663. All items less than $8. No credit cards. Daily 7:30am–6:30pm. Subway: F to 23rd St.

F&B ⭐ *Finds* INTERNATIONAL   Budget-minded New Yorkers rejoiced at the arrival of F&B, which serves a global menu of

European street food (Danish and German hot dogs, Swedish meat-balls, Belgian frites) in a stylish powder-blue space. The signature dog comes in a variety of styles, from the Great Dane, a Danish dog dressed with rémoulade, roast onions, marinated cucumber slices, Danish mustard and ketchup on a toasted bun, to Pups in a Blanket, adorable minidogs in puff pastry served with honey mustard. A veggie dog is also available. The warm New Orleans beignets come brushed with powdered sugar and your choice of dips, including chocolate, maple syrup, and crème anglaise. The twice-cooked frites come accompanied with your choice of a range of flavored butters, oils, and dips, including a yummy garlic aioli. You can wash it down with Belgian-style beers, ciders, wine, and even champagne. Delivery is available if you're staying in the area.

269 W. 23rd St. (btwn Seventh and Eighth Aves.). ℂ **646/486-4441**. Reservations not accepted. Main courses $1.50–$10. AE, MC, V. Daily 11am–11pm. Subway: C, E to 23rd St.

Grand Sichuan International ℛ *Value* SICHUAN CHINESE

They serve up real Chinese here in Chelsea. This comfortable spot has garnered raves for its authentic Sichuan cuisine. Spicy-food lovers will be thrilled, as the kitchen excels at dishes that are intensely spiced without being numbing—a balance that few Chinatown kitchens can achieve. The flavors are complex and strong, especially in such top choices as Sichuan wontons in red oil, Chairman Mao's pork with chestnuts, and my favorite, boneless whole fish with pine nuts in a modified sweet-and-sour sauce. The staff will be more than happy to recommend milder dishes.

229 Ninth Ave. (at 24th St.). ℂ **212/620-5200**. Reservations accepted for parties of 3 or more. Main courses $3.25–$14. AE, DC, MC, V. Daily 11:30am–11pm. Subway: C, E to 23rd St. Also at 745 Ninth Ave. (btwn 50th and 51st sts.; ℂ **212/582-2288**; subway: C, E to 50th St.).

The Half King ℛ IRISH

Author Sebastian Junger took his earnings from *The Perfect Storm,* and opened the perfect pub in west Chelsea. It's the spitting image of an upscale Dublin watering hole, complete with long wooden bar and an adjacent dining room with a mix of standard dining tables and larger-party booths with low-slung tables and well-stuffed leather sofas; there's also a garden out back for warm-weather dining. The crowd is easygoing, as is service.

Each menu—breakfast, brunch, lunch, dinner, late-night—features versions of Irish classics and more nouveau fare. Morning starts with a traditional Irish breakfast (bacon, eggs, sausage, black and white pudding, mushrooms, tomatoes, baked beans, and home

Where to Dine in Midtown, Chelsea & Union Square

Antique Café **42**
Brazil Grill **26**
Burritoville **8, 29, 33, 40**
Canova Market **12**
Chanpen **22**
Chat 'n' Chew **44**
Emerald Planet **9**
ESPN Zone **16**
Ess-A-Bagel **11**
F&B **39**
44 Southwest **31**
Go Sushi **10, 21, 34**
Grand Central Terminal **14**
  •Cafe Spice Express
  •Christer's
  •Junior's
  •Knödel
  •Little Pie Company
  •Mike's Take-Away
  •Two Boots
Grand Sichuan International **24, 37**
The Half King **38**
Hallo! Berlin **23, 30**
Hard Rock Café **5**
Joe Allen **27**
John's Pizzeria **1, 3, 28**
La Bonne Soupe **7**
Le Pain Quotidien **2, 45**
L'Express **48**
Mandoo Bar **35**
Mangia **4, 13**
Manhattan Chili Co. **5, 17**
Mars 2112 **19**
Old Town Bar & Restaurant **46**
Papaya King **32**
Pigalle **25**
Planet Hollywood **18**
Pongal **36**
Republic **43**
Rue des Crepes **41**
Via Emilia **47**
Virgil's Real BBQ **15**
Vynl **20**

Ⓜ Subway stop

UPPER EAST
SIDE

E. 66th St.
E. 65th St.
E. 64th St.
E. 63rd St.
E. 62nd St.
E. 61st St.
E. 60th St.
E. 59th St.
E. 58th St.
E. 57th St.
E. 56th St.
E. 55th St.
E. 54th St.
E. 53rd St.
E. 52nd St.
E. 51st St.
E. 50th St.
E. 49th St.
E. 48th St.
E. 47th St.
E. 46th St.
E. 45th St.
E. 44th St.
E. 43rd St.
E. 42nd St.
E. 41st St.
E. 40th St.
E. 39th St.
E. 38th St.
E. 37th St.
E. 36th St.
E. 35th St.
E. 34th St.
E. 33rd St.
E. 32nd St.
E. 31st St.
E. 30th St.
E. 29th St.
E. 28th St.
E. 27th St.
E. 26th St.
E. 25th St.
E. 24th St.
E. 23rd St.
E. 22nd St.
E. 21st St.
E. 20th St.
E. 19th St.
E. 18th St.
E. 17th St.
E. 16th St.
E. 15th St.
E. 14th St.
E. 13th St.

Transverse

PARK

The
Pond

Central Park S.

Fifth Ave.

Madison Ave.

MIDTOWN
EAST

Rockefeller
Center

Fifth Ave.

Madison Ave.

Park Ave.

Vanderbilt Ave.

Lexington Ave.

Third Ave.

Second Ave.

First Ave.

Grand
Central
Terminal

Sixth Ave. (Ave. of the Americas)

Bryant
Park

New York
Public Library

MURRAY
HILL

Tunnel
Exit

Tunnel
Entrance

Empire
State Bldg.

Broadway

Fifth Ave.

Madison Ave.

Park Ave. S.

Lexington Ave.

Madison
Square
Park

FLATIRON
DISTRICT

GRAMERCY
PARK

Gramercy
Park

Union
Square

Sixth Ave. (Ave. of the Americas)

Fifth Ave.

Union Sq. W.

Union Sq. E.

Irving Pl.

From Lower
Level

Roosevelt Island Tram
Queensboro Bridge

To Upper
Level

Sutton Pl.

Sutton Pl. South

Beekman
Place

Mitchell
Place

ROOSEVELT
ISLAND

QUEENS

United
Nations

Queens-Midtown Tunnel

FDR Drive

Queens-Midtown
Tunnel

East River

Asser Levy Pl.

Ave. C

Peter
Cooper
Village

Stuyvesant
Town

N.D. Perlman Pl.

fries), a smoked-salmon scramble if you're in the mood for something lighter, or a bowl of Weetabix and fruit. Daytime and evening bring bounteous salads; a rich, creamy seafood chowder; gorgeous realizations of pub standards, including fish and chips made with fresh Chatham cod, pork roast with parsnip hash and capers, and a beef-and-Guinness pie with a flaky crust; and well-prepared pastas, chicken, and burgers. The food isn't cheap, but it's well priced considering the quality, Look for readings on Monday nights, plus art events some Tuesdays.

505 W. 23rd St. (just west of Tenth Ave.). ℂ **212/462-4300.** www.thehalfking.com. Breakfast and brunch $3–$12; lunch $6–$12; dinner $9–$18 (most less than $15); late night $6–$16. AE, DC, DISC, MC, V. Sun–Thurs 9am–2am; Fri–Sat 9am–4am. Subway: C, E to 23rd St.

Rue des Crepes 🐾🐾 *(Finds* FRENCH   This *creperie* is a real find. Seldom do decor, quality, and service come together so well in such an affordable restaurant. Evoking a Parisian cafe with muraled walls, tiled floors, Art Nouveau lamps, and petite tables, the dining room is comfortable and romantic. Chef Michael Kalajian whips up light-as-air buckwheat (and cholesterol-free) crepes and folds them around a host of fillings, from classics like turkey and brie to spicy Moroccan *merguez* sausage accompanied by white beans and roasted garlic. Vegetarian options are available, including homemade hummus and roasted veggies. Soups and salads are also served; sandwiches are prepared on fresh baguettes, and pre-prepared ones are ready to go in the takeout case. Dessert crepes come with your choice of fillings; my favorite is the "Sidewalk," a classic preparation with butter, sugar, lemon, and chocolate. You'll order at the counter, but a server takes over from there. Beer and wine are available. *Money-saving tip:* Check the website for a 10% off coupon.

104 Eighth Ave. (btwn 15th and 16th sts.). ℂ **212/242-9900.** www.ruedescrepes. com. Reservations not accepted. Main courses $6–$9. AE, MC, V. Sun–Thurs 11am– 11pm; Fri–Sat 11am–1am. Subway: A, C, E to 14th St.

9 The Flatiron District, Union Square & Gramercy Park

For lovely baked goods and sandwiches and salads, try **Le Pain Quotidien** 🐾🐾 (p. 83) at ABC Carpet & Home, 38 E. 19th St., between Broadway and Park Avenue South (ℂ **212/625-9009**).

Chat 'n' Chew AMERICAN   Looking for a place to get a square meal that won't break the bank or leave you hungry? Then head to this cute hole-in-the-wall that excels at down-home American cooking. The space is so down-homey that it's on the brink of becoming a theme restaurant, but the chow's the real thing. Look for honey-dipped fried chicken, roast turkey with all the fixin's, BBQ pork chops with skin-on mashed potatoes. There are a few unnecessary nods to contemporary tastes—if you're looking for grilled tuna, you don't belong here!—but the only real misstep is the meat loaf, which is a disappointment. Weekend brunch sees such standards as oatmeal with brown sugar and omelets with honey-baked ham on the side. Portions are all Hungry Man–size, service is snappy, and beer's available. Desserts are of the Duncan Hines layer-cake variety, and the soda fountain serves up everything from egg creams to Häagen-Dazs shakes. The crowd mainly consists of the young and hip, but everyone will feel perfectly welcome.

10 E. 16th St. (btwn Fifth Ave. and Union Sq. W.). ✆ 212/243-1616. www.chatn chew.citysearch.com. Reservations not accepted. Sandwiches and salads $6–$11; main courses $7–$14. AE, MC, V. Mon–Fri 11:30am–midnight; Sat 10:30am–midnight; Sun 10:30am–11pm. Subway: L, N, R, Q, W, 4, 5, 6 to 14th St./Union Sq.

L'Express FRENCH This round-the-clock French bistro is a favorite of New Yorkers. The service is friendly and attentive, and the mood-lit room comfortable and romantic in the evening; the food is respectable, if not fabulous. I like the appetizers best, especially the escargots in butter and herbs, the onion tart, and *boudin noir* (blood sausage) with caramelized apples and mashed potato. Among the mains are a roasted half-chicken, a juicy lamb burger, and roasted rabbit in Dijon mustard sauce; skip the boeuf bourguignon. Wines are somewhat pricey, averaging $7 a glass, but a large selection of imported beers is on hand, including Trappist ales. The dense, gooey French bread that comes with every meal is alone worth the price of a meal. Daytime diners will feel perfectly welcome to camp out for a couple of hours, nursing a cup of tea and delving into a good book.

249 Park Ave. S. (at 20th St.). ✆ 212/254-5858. Reservations accepted for parties of 5 or more only. Main courses $2–$7.50 at breakfast, $5–$15 at lunch, $9–$18 at dinner (most less than $15). AE, MC, V. Open daily 24 hr. Subway: 6 to 23rd St.

Old Town Bar & Restaurant ✪ AMERICAN If you've watched TV at all the last couple of decades, this place should look familiar: It was featured in the old *Late Night with David Letterman* intro and starred as Riff's Bar in *Mad About You*. But this is no stage set—it's a genuine tin-ceilinged 19th-century bar serving up good pub grub, lots of beers on tap, and a sense of New York history. Sure, there are salads on the menu, but everybody comes for the burgers. Whether you go low-fat turkey or bacon-chili-cheddar, they're perfect every time. You have your choice of sides, but go with the shoestring fries. Other good choices include spicy Buffalo wings, fiery bowls of chili with cheddar cheese and dolloped with sour cream, and a Herculean Caesar salad. Food comes up from the basement kitchen courtesy of ancient dumbwaiters behind the bar, where equally crusty bartenders would rather *not* make you a Cosmopolitan. If you want to escape the cigarettes and the predatory singles scene, head upstairs to the blissfully smoke-free dining room.

45 E. 18th St. (btwn Broadway and Park Ave. S.). ℂ **212/529-6732.** Reservations not accepted. Main courses $6–$12. AE, MC, V. Mon–Fri 11:30am–midnight; Sat–Sun 12:30pm–midnight. Subway: L, N, R, Q, W, 4, 5, 6 to 14th St./Union Sq.

Republic PAN-ASIAN NOODLES   Proving once and for all that you don't have to sacrifice style for value, this chic noodle joint serves up affordable food in a neighborhood where it's getting harder to find an affordable meal. Cushionless, backless benches pulled up to pine-and-steel tables don't encourage lingering, but that's the point: This is the kind of place that knows how to make you feel happy and get you out the door quickly. The Chinese, Vietnamese-, and Thai-inspired noodle menu attracts a stream of on-the-go customers. For a one-bowl meal, try the spicy coconut chicken (chicken slices in coconut milk, lime juice, lemongrass, and galangal) or spicy beef (rare beef with wheat noodles spiced with chilies, garlic, and lemongrass). The long, curving bar is perfect for solitary diners in the daytime and during the early-dinner hour; later, it livens up with a crowd who come to enjoy such libations as the Sake Dragon (sake and Chambord) and Fuji apple Cosmopolitan.

37 Union Sq. W. (btwn 16th and 17th sts.). ℂ **212/627-7172** or 212/627-7168. Reservations accepted for parties of 10 or more. Main courses $7–$9. AE, DISC, MC, V. Sun–Wed 11:30am–11pm; Thurs–Sat 11:30am–11:30pm. Subway: L, N, R, Q, W, 4, 5, 6 to 14th St./Union Sq.

Via Emilia ⓡ ⓥ*alue*EMILIA-ROMAGNA ITALIAN   This candlelit, brick-walled trattoria is a haven for budget diners in the high-priced Park Avenue South area. The menu is simple but satisfying, with an emphasis on house-made pastas. The specialty is tortellini; the *tortellini in brodo,* meat-stuffed tortellini in a chicken broth, is a great way to start your meal. Other starters include fresh-grilled squid or thin-sliced tenderloin carpaccio, served with shaved Parmesan and leafy arugula. There's not a dud among the pastas, all of which are oversize, none exceeding $12; I love the tortellini filled with chicken and wild mushrooms in truffle oil. There's also a handful of nonpasta entrees, including the *cosciotto d'agnello,* a thinly sliced leg of lamb with mushrooms, cannelloni beans, and tomatoes, like a lighter, Italian cassoulet. Wines are well priced, too, and service better than you'd expect at a restaurant this affordable.

240 Park Ave. S. (btwn 19th and 20th sts.). ✆ 212/505-3072. Reservations not accepted. Main courses $7.50–$15. No credit cards. Mon–Sat 5–11pm. Subway: N, R, 6 to 23rd St.

10 Times Square & Midtown West

An outpost of **Grand Sichuan International** (p. 93) is at 745 Ninth Ave., between 50th and 51st streets (✆ **212/582-2288**). A new branch of the ultrafresh, supercheap sushi joint, **Go Sushi** (p. 106), is at 756 Ninth Ave., at 51st Street (✆ **212/459-2288**).

There's a cafeteria-style **Mangia** (p. 76) at 50 W. 57th St., between Fifth and Sixth avenues (✆ 212/582-5882). Two branches of **Burritoville** (p. 75) are at 352 W. 39th St., at Ninth Avenue (✆ **212/563-9088**), and 625 Ninth Ave., at 44th Street (✆ **212/333-5352**). Also consider **Emerald Planet** (p. 85), on the lower concourse at 30 Rockefeller Plaza, near the skating rink (✆ **212/218-1133**), for wraps and yummy smoothies.

Brazil Grill ✿ BRAZILIAN   The Theater District is loaded with tourist traps, and many affordable restaurants feel dowdy or downscale. So where can you go for a pre- (or post-) theater dinner that won't break the bank? Make a beeline for Brazil Grill, where the tables are spacious, the staff is charming, cobalt-blue accents add a touch of elegance, and the menu showcases the sunny flavors of Brazil. The prix-fixe is an incredible deal: Three courses for $19.95 will have you mamboing all the way to the theater. The menu offers lots of country cooking to satisfy the meat-and-potatoes crowd (sizzling beef skewers with peppers and onions), while diners with more adventurous palates might try the spicy *camarao baiana* (shrimp sautéed with palm oil and served in a sauce of coconut milk, tomatoes, and garlic). Portions are generous, and main courses come with sides of rice and beans. The wine list offers affordable choices, including an array of wines by the glass for only $5 to $6. Don't miss the incredible *doce de leite* for dessert—if you've never tasted this rich and creamy caramel confection of the gods, you'll thank me.

787 Eighth Ave. (at 48th St.). ✆ **212/307-9449.** www.brazilgrill.citysearch.com. Reservations recommended, especially pre-theater. Main courses $10.95–$21.95; 3-course prix-fixe dinner $19.95. AE, DC, MC, V. Daily noon–midnight. Subway: 1, 2 to 50th St.; C, E to 50th St.

Chanpen THAI   This charming restaurant serves Thai food at Chinatown prices. It's a very good value, especially at lunch. In addition to the prices, you'll be pleased by the bright dining room, the pleasant and attentive service, and the classic preparations of familiar Thai favorites.

761 Ninth Ave. (at 51st St.). ℂ **212/586-6808.** AE, MC, V. Reservations accepted for dinner Sun–Thurs only. Main courses $8–$15; lunch special (Mon–Fri 11:30am–3pm) $7–$8. AE, MC, V. Sun–Thurs 11:30am–11pm; Fri–Sat 11:30am–midnight. Subway: C, E to 50th St.

44 Southwest ⭐ *Finds* ITALIAN   This mom-and-pop restaurant serves up the best Italian food in Midtown for the money. It's simple but charming, with an original tin ceiling, red-checkered tablecloths, and soft lighting; the result is a romantic first-date ambience. The dishes are generously portioned and satisfying. Pastas are perfectly al dente; I especially love the thick and hearty meat sauce on the linguine Bolognese. The chicken Parmesan is classically yummy, and personal pizzas arrive with wonderfully chewy crusts. The wine list is affordable and the service attentive, making 44 Southwest a winner on all fronts for wallet-watching visitors.

621 Ninth Ave. (at 44th St.). ℂ **212/315-4582** or 212/315-4681. Reservations accepted (recommended for pre-theater dining). Main courses $8–$14. AE, DC, DISC, MC, V. Sun–Thurs noon–11pm; Fri–Sat noon–midnight. Subway: A, C, E to 42nd St.

Hallo! Berlin ⭐ GERMAN   Hallo! Berlin bills itself as "New York's Wurst Restaurant"—and indeed it is. If wurst is best in your book, don't miss it. Hallo! Berlin is straight outta Deutschland, serving up eight varieties of sausage, from boiled beef-and-pork knockwurst to pan-fried veal bavarianwurst and beef currywurst. Sandwiches come with all the fixings, including red cabbage, sauerkraut, onions, and mustard, but I prefer the combo, which lets me choose two kinds of sausage (substitute spaetzle for German fries for maximum satisfaction). There's also a terrific Wiener schnitzel. The potato pancakes make a great starter. A big bowl of lentil, split pea, or potato soup with cut-up wurst and bread and butter makes a satisfying lunch for just $5. The main location is petite and pleasant, with efficient service and a couple of taps pouring German brews, while the Tenth Avenue location is a full-scale beer hall.

402 W. 51st St. (just west of Ninth Ave.). ℂ **212/541-6248.** Reservations not accepted. Sandwiches $3–$3.75; main courses (with soup) $6.50–$15; lunch specials (until 5pm) $5.25–$6.50. MC, V. Mon–Sat 11am–11pm; Sun 4–11pm. Subway: C, E to 50th St. Also at 626 Tenth Ave. (at 44th St.; ℂ **212/977-1944;** subway: A, C, E to 42nd St./Port Authority).

Joe Allen AMERICAN PUB This Restaurant Row pub is a glorious throwback to yesteryear, when theater types went to places like Sardi's and Lüchow's—and yep, Joe Allen. Joe Allen is still going strong; don't be surprised if you spot a stage star or two. The pub food is reliable and well priced, and served at big, comfortable tables covered with red-checked cloths. The meatloaf is terrific, but you can't go wrong with the chili, the Greek salad, the burgers, or anything that comes with mashed potatoes. More than 30 beers are available, and some good wines by the glass. The staff is a congenial and neighborhood-appropriate mix of career waiters and aspiring thespians. You'll enjoy perusing the walls covered with posters and other memorabilia from legendary Broadway flops.

326 W. 46th St. (btwn Eighth and Ninth aves.). ℂ 212/581-6464. Reservations recommended (a must for pre-theater dining). Main courses $9–$22 (most less than $17). MC, V. Mon–Tues and Thurs–Fri noon–11:45pm; Wed and Sat–Sun 11:30am–11:45pm. Subway: A, C, E to 42nd St./Port Authority.

John's Pizzeria *Kids* PIZZA Thin-crusted, properly sauced, and fresh, the pizza at John's has long been one of New York's best. Housed in the century-old Gospel Tabernacle Church, the split-level dining room is vast and pretty, featuring a stained-glass ceiling and chefs working at classic brick ovens. More important, it's big enough to hold pre-theater crowds, so the wait's never too long. At John's you order a whole made-to-order pie rather than ordering by the slice as at most New York pizzerias, so come with friends or family. There's also a good selection of traditional pastas.

This Theater District location is my favorite, but the original Bleecker Street location is loaded with old-world atmosphere; the Lincoln Center branch makes for a good, affordable pre-theater meal.

260 W. 44th St. (btwn Broadway and Eighth Ave.). ℂ 212/391-7560. Reservations accepted for 10 or more. Pizzas $11–$16 (plus toppings); pastas $7–$13. AE, DISC, MC, V. Daily 11:30am–11:30pm. Subway: A, C, E to 42nd St.; N, R, S, 1, 2, 3, 7, 9 to 42nd St./Times Sq. Also at 278 Bleecker St. (btwn Sixth and Seventh aves.; ℂ 212/243-1680; subway: 1, 9 to Houston St.); 48 W. 65th St. (btwn Broadway and Central Park W.; ℂ 212/721-7001; subway: 1, 9 to 66th St.); 408 E. 64th St. (btwn First and York aves.; ℂ 212/935-2895; subway: 6 to 68th St.).

La Bonne Soupe *Kids* FRENCH BISTRO This slice of Paris has been around forever; I remember discovering the magic of fondue here on a high school field trip more years ago than I care to think about. You'll even see French natives elbow-to-elbow in the newly renovated dining room. "Les bonnes soupes" are satisfying noontime meals of salad, bread, a bowl of soup (mushroom and barley with lamb is a favorite), dessert (chocolate mousse, crème caramel, or ice cream), and wine or coffee—a great bargain at just $13.95. The menu also features entree-size salads (including a good niçoise), steak burgers, and bistro fare like omelets, quiche Lorraine, croque monsieur, and fancier fare like steak frites and filet mignon au poivre. Rounding out the menu are French fondues: Emmethal cheese, beef, and creamy chocolate; the silky smooth chocolate mousse is yummy. A kids' menu is available, offering a burger or chicken and fries, plus dessert, for $10.25. Bon appétit!

48 W. 55th St. (btwn Fifth and Sixth aves.). ℂ 212/586-7650. www.labonnesoupe. com. Reservations recommended for parties of 3 or more. Main courses $9–$19.25 (most less than $15); "les bonnes soupes" fixed price $13.95; 3-course fixed price $20 at lunch and dinner. AE, DC, MC, V. Mon–Sat 11:30am–midnight; Sun 11:30am–11pm. Subway: E, F to Fifth Ave.; B, Q to 57th St.

Mandoo Bar *Finds* KOREAN   This bustling block of 32nd Street has grown into a bright, neon-lit haven for lovers of zesty, cheap Korean food. My favorite is this dumpling house, which specializes in all manner of fresh dumplings. I love the *mool mandoo,* broiled dumplings stuffed with vegetables and meat, and the baby mandoo, bite-size dumplings of beef, pork, and leek. The menu also offers fried-noodle dishes, including great pad Thai and Korean-style noodle soups; fried rice and bibimbob with veggies and beef; and *pajeon,* a Korean pancake with seafood. Plenty of meatless options are on hand. The room is pleasant, with a long blond-wood tables and benches that speak to Mandoo Bar as a quick-bite kind of place. Service is brisk and efficient. Beer and wine are available. Don't be surprised if there's a lunchtime wait, but the line moves quickly.

2 W. 32nd St. (just west of Fifth Ave.). ℂ 212/279-3075. Reservations not accepted. Main courses $6–$14. AE, DC, MC, V. Daily 11:30am–11pm. Subway: B, D, F, N, Q, R, V, W to 34th St./Herald Sq.

Manhattan Chili Co. *Kids* SOUTHWESTERN/AMERICAN This big, festive Theater District restaurant adjacent to Dave Letterman's Ed Sullivan Theater is a great choice for a casual, affordable meal, especially if you have kids. The hearty chili bowls are geared to young palates. The extensive list of chili choices is clearly marked by spice level, from traditional Abilene with ground beef, tomatoes, basil, and red wine (mild enough for tenderfeet) to the Texas Chain Gang, which adds jalapeños to the mix for those who prefer hot. In addition, expect favorites like nachos, chicken wings, big salads, and generous burritos and burgers. Even vegetarians have lots to choose from. A fun place to eat!

1697 Broadway (53rd and 54th sts.). © **212/246-6555.** www.manhattanchilico. com. Reservations accepted. Chili bowls $10; main courses $11–$16; Sat–Sun brunch $10.95. AE, DISC, MC, V. Sun–Mon 11:30am–11pm; Tues–Sat 11:30am– midnight. Subway: B, D, E to Seventh Ave.; 1, 9 to 50th St. Also at 1500 Broadway (entrance on 43rd St.; © **212/730-8666;** subway: N, R, S, 1, 2, 3, 7, 9 to 42nd St./ Times Sq.).

Pigalle FRENCH BRASSERIE   This French brasserie is a wonderful addition to the Theater District, with high-quality fare, low prices, and convenient-to-Broadway location—not to mention a we-never-close policy. The room boasts the trimmings of a traditional brasserie—zinc bar, rattan, soft ochre lighting—with a designer edge. The room is airy and comfortable, great for couples and larger parties alike. The menu offers classic brasserie fare, including an onion soup gratinée, a *classique* cassoulet, duck confit, and steak au poivre. The food isn't groundbreaking, but it's satisfying. I love the cocktail menu. The Violet Martini is perfectly shaken with Grey Goose and a hint of violet essence, then dressed with a single purple petal. The New Yorker is my husband's new favorite: gin, dry vermouth, dill pickle, and garlic, straight up. The only downside was the service on our last visit; if you're going pre-theater, make it clear the moment you arrive.

790 Eighth Ave. (at 48th St.), adjacent to the Days Hotel. © 212/489-2233. Reservations recommended. Main courses $6.50–$14 at breakfast and lunch, $8–$18 at dinner. AE, DC, DISC, MC, V. Daily 24 hr. Subway: A, C, E to 50th St.

Virgil's Real BBQ ★★ *Kids* BARBECUE/SOUTHERN   Virgil's may look like a theme-park version of a barbecue joint, but they take their barbecue seriously. The meat is house-smoked with a blend of hickory, oak, and fruitwood chips, and most every regional school is represented, from Carolina pulled pork to Texas beef brisket to Memphis ribs. You may not consider this contest-winning chow if you're from barbecue country, but we Yankees are thrilled to have it. I love to start with the barbecued shrimp, with mustard slaw, and a plate of buttermilk onion rings with blue cheese for dipping. The ribs are good and the chicken is moist and tender—go for a combo if you can't choose. Burgers, sandwiches, and other entrees (chicken-fried steak, anyone?) are also available. And cast that cornbread aside for an order of buttermilk biscuits, which come with maple butter so good it's like dessert. Kids will enjoy the atmosphere and friendly staff. The bar offers a huge selection of on-tap and bottled brews.

Theme Restaurant Thrills!

ESPN Zone ✈, 1472 Broadway, at 42nd Street (☎ **212/921-3776;** www.espnzone.com) is a nonstop party palace for sports fans. This 42,000-square-foot space houses the Studio Grill, with continuous ESPN programming; the Screening Room, with two giant screens and a dozen 36-inchers, audio and video touch screens, and reclining leather chairs with built-in speakers; the Sports Arena, a full floor of sports-related arcade games; set replicas from ESPN's shows; and much more.

New York's **Hard Rock Cafe** ✈, 221 W. 57th St., between Broadway and Seventh Avenue (☎ **212/489-6565;** www. hardrockcafe.com), is one of the originals, and a wonderful realization of the concept. The memorabilia collection is terrific, with lots of John Lennon items. The menu boasts the Hard Rock standards, including a good burger and fajitas, and the bar mixes up great cocktails.

The subterranean red planet–themed **Mars 2112,** 1633 Broadway, at 51st Street (☎ **212/582-2112;** www.mars2112. com), is a hoot, from the simulated red-rock rooms to the Martian-costumed wait staff to the silly "Man Eats on Mars!" newspaper-style menu. The food is better than you might expect, but skip the Star Tours–style simulated spacecraft ride at the entrance if you don't want to lose your appetite before you get to your table. The kids won't mind—they'll love it, along with the video arcade.

Planet Hollywood got a jolt of much-needed energy in 2000, thanks to a new circle of celebrity investors and a move to the heart of Times Square at 1540 Broadway, at 45th Street (☎ **212/333-7827**). JC and Justin do not stop in for Cap'n Crunch fried chicken, and the movie memorabilia doesn't hold the same excitement as the rock-and-roll goods at the Hard Rock.

152 W. 44th St. (btwn Sixth and Seventh aves.). ☎ **212/921-9494.** www.virgils bbq.com. Reservations recommended. Sandwiches $6–$11; main courses and barbecue platters $13–$26 (most less than $19). AE, DC, DISC, MC, V. Sun–Mon 11:30am–11pm; Tues–Sat 11:30am–midnight. Subway: 1, 2, 3, 7, 9, N, R to 42nd St./Times Sq.

Vynl ✦ AMERICAN DINER   Vynl adds a hip quotient to the traditional diner formula with Lucite and Bakelite decor, a collection of action figures through the ages (from Captain and Tenille to Tyson Beckford), a 1970s-to-now soundtrack, and an affordable menu in a gatefold album cover. But Vynl isn't all veneer—the food is terrific. The brioche French toast with sautéed apples and caramel sauce is a great way to launch a weekend. For daytime and evening, the fare runs the gamut from diner fare to Asian-accented dishes including Thai curries, a veggie stir-fry, and Chinese chicken salad. Service is friendly and attentive. Pay with a credit card so you can sign the bill with the coolest pen in town (yours to purchase, if you wish).

824 Ninth Ave. (at 54th St.). ℂ **212/974-2003.** Reservations not accepted. Main courses $4.50–$11. AE, MC, V. Mon–Tues 11:30am–11pm; Wed–Fri 11:30am–midnight; Sat 9:30am–midnight; Sun 9:30am–11pm. Subway: C, E to 50th St.

QUICK BITES

Canova Market, 134 W. 51st St., between Sixth and Seventh avenues (ℂ **212/969-9200**), is a 24-hour gourmet deli where your choices are only limited by your imagination. There's a salad bar, a deli counter, a soup bar, a sushi bar, and the lunchtime-only pay-per-pound Mongolian grill, where you assemble your own veggies, meats, seafood, rice, noodles, and seasonings and watch the chefs do their stuff ($5.30 per lb.). There's a dining area in the back where you can eat. This place really bustles at lunch, but lines move fast.

   Papaya King (p. 111) is at 255 W. 43rd St., just off Eighth Ave. (ℂ **212/944-4590**). The two-all-beef-franks-and-an-all-natural-fruit-drink combo is a bargain at $4.30.

11 Midtown East & Murray Hill

In addition to the listings below, there's a cafeteria-style branch of **Mangia** (p. 76) at 16 E. 48th St., east of Fifth Avenue (ℂ **212/754-0637**); and a **Burritoville** (p. 75) at 866 Third Ave. (really on 52nd St. between Lexington and Third aves.; ℂ **212/980-4111**).

   There's a Midtown East outpost of **Le Pain Quotidien,** at 833 Lexington Ave. (between 63rd and 64th sts.; ℂ **212/755-5810**).

Ess-A-Bagel ✦ BAGEL SANDWICHES   Ess-A-Bagel turns out the city's best bagel, edging out rival H&H, which won't make you a sandwich. Baked daily, the hand-rolled delicacies come in 12 flavors—plain, sesame, poppy, onion, garlic, salt, whole wheat, pumpernickel, pumpernickel raisin, cinnamon raisin, oat bran, and everything. They're so plump, chewy, and satisfying it's hard to believe they have no fat, cholesterol, or preservatives. Head to the back counter for a baker's dozen or line up for a sandwich stuffed with salads and spreads. Fillings can range from a schmear of cream cheese to Nova salmon or sun-dried tomato tofu spread. There also are lots of deli-style meats, plus a range of cheeses, salads, and vegetarian items. Homemade soups and salads round out the menu. The dining room has plenty of bistro-style tables.

831 Third Ave. (at 51st St.). © **212/980-1010.** Reservations not accepted. Sandwiches $1.50–$8.50. AE, DC, DISC, MC, V. Mon–Fri 6am–10pm; Sat–Sun 7am–5pm. Subway: E, F to Lexington Ave.; 6 to 51st St. Also at 359 First Ave. (at 21st St.; © **212/260-2252;** subway: L to First Ave.; 6 to 23rd St.).

Go Sushi *Value* SUSHI This bright, attractive chain of eat-in/ takeout joints serves up excellent sushi for wallet-watching fans. It's boxed in bento-style containers, but everything is prepared fresh, so you never have to worry about quality; you can also place orders if what you desire is not ready-made. In addition to sashimi, nigiri,

 Grand Dining at Grand Central

The lower concourse of **Grand Central Terminal** 🕰🕰, 42nd Street at Park Avenue, is a haven of cheap eats—and the setting is an architecture-lover's delight. Head downstairs and choose among the outlets offering everything from bratwurst to sushi. Standouts include **Junior's,** a branch of the Brooklyn stalwart, serving deli sandwiches, burgers, and their world-famous cheesecake in a waiter-serviced dining area. (Most of the outlets are takeout counters; there's abundant, seating at the center of the concourse.) **Mike's Take-Away** serves up soups, salads, and sandwiches, including a warming mushroom stew in winter. **Little Pie Company** serves up the Big Apple's best pies, plus fresh-baked muffins and the concourse's best coffee. **Cafe Spice Express,** serves terrific Indian fare, while **Christer's** and **Knödel** specialize, respectively, in fish 'n' chips and German-style brats, wieners, and sausages. There's also an outpost of pizzeria **Two Boots.** If you want beer or wine, visit one of the two **bar cars,** near tracks 105 and 112. For a complete list of vendors, check out www.grandcentral terminal.com.

and cut-roll choices, you can choose from a selection of fresh-made noodle bowls as well as bentos with teriyaki or tempura. I know locals who eat at Go Sushi three times a week. All in all, it's a wallet-friendly choice for a quick, healthy meal. No alcohol is served.

982 Second Ave. (at 52nd St.). ✆ 212/593-3883. Reservations not accepted. A la carte sushi $1.50–$2; rolls $3.80–$9 (most less than $6); sushi combos and bentos $5–$17 (most less than $10); noodle soups $5.50–$6.50. AE, MC, V. Daily 11:30am–11:10pm. Subway: 6 to 51st St. Also at 511 Third Ave. (btwn 34th and 35th sts.; ✆ 212/679-1999; subway: 6 to 33rd St.); 756 Ninth Ave. (at 51st St.; ✆ 212/459-2288; subway: C, E to 50th St.); 3 Greenwich Ave. (Sixth Ave. at 8th St.; ✆ 212/366-9272; subway: A, C, E, F, V, S to W. 4th St.).

Pongal 🏟🏟 VEGETARIAN INDIAN My favorite Indian food is served at this standout on Curry Hill, the stretch of Lexington that's home to a number of Indian restaurants. Pongal specializes in the vegetarian cuisine of southern India, and also happens to be kosher. You don't have to be a vegetarian to love it. The dishes are prepared to order (no vats of *saag paneer* sitting around getting stale). Ingredients are top-quality, vegetables and legume dishes never overcooked, and the sauces are divine. The specialty is *dosai*, a large golden crepe filled with onions, potatoes, and other goodies, accompanied by coconut chutney and flavorful sauce. The food is very cheap, with almost nothing over $10. The restaurant is low-lit and attractive, with professional service and a pleasing ambience, making it a nice choice for a special night on the town.

110 Lexington Ave. (btwn 27th and 28th sts.). ✆ 212/696-9458. www.pongal.org. Reservations not accepted. Main courses $6–$11 (most less than $9). DC, DISC, MC, V. Mon–Fri noon–3pm and 5–10pm; Sat–Sun noon–10pm. Subway: 6 to 28th St.

12 The Upper West Side

Artie's Delicatessen JEWISH DELI Yay for Artie's, which opened in 1999 but already has the vibe of an institution. It's as good as many of the best delis in Manhattan (I prefer it over tourist traps like the Carnegie and the Stage), and far more cheery. All of your favorites are here—from corned beef to chopped liver to tongue on rye—and arrive at your table in top form. The pastrami is everything it should be, and the chicken soup with kreplach is a sore throat's worst nightmare. Artie's chilidogs deserve special note—they may be the best in town. Burgers, omelets, and salads are also on hand. Nostalgia-inducing desserts include New York black-and-white cookies, homemade ruggelach, and sliced birthday cake every day.

2290 Broadway (btwn 82nd and 83rd sts.). ℂ 212/579-5959. www.arties.com. Reservations not accepted. Main courses $6–$12 at breakfast, $6–$17 at lunch and dinner. AE, DISC, MC, V. Sun–Thurs 9am–11pm; Fri–Sat 9am–11:30pm. Subway: 1, 9 to 86th St.

Blondie's ⭐ AMERICAN

This sports bar is the place for the best Buffalo wings in town. They're big and meaty; even my husband, who can eat 20 anywhere else, can only manage an order of 10 ($6.50) here. Choose your heat level, from plain to ouch!—the kitchen will get it right. Additional flavors include honey mustard, barbecue, or honey barbecue. All the standard fixings are on hand: celery, carrots, and blue cheese. Standard sports-bar fare rounds out the menu: burgers, fries, mozzarella sticks, with most food served in baskets. There's a huge selection of on-tap and bottled beers, but beware—this is where they make their money.

212 W. 79th St. (btwn Amsterdam Ave. and Broadway). ℂ 212/362-3311. Reservations not accepted. Main courses $5.50–$13. AE, DC, DISC, MC, V. Sun–Mon 11:30am–midnight; Tues 11:30am–12:30am; Wed 11:30am–1am; Thurs 11:30am–2am; Fri–Sat 11:30am–3am. Subway: 1, 9 to 79th St.

Flor de Mayo (Finds) SPANISH/CHINESE

This hybrid Latin/Chinese restaurant far surpasses the more famous La Caridad 78 for quality. The kitchen excels at both sides of the menu. The best dish on the menu is the half *la brasa* chicken lunch special, beautifully spiced and slow-roasted until it's falling off the bone, served with a giant pile of fried rice, bounteous with roast pork, shrimp, and veggies. Offered Monday through Saturday until 4:30pm, the whole meal is just $6.95, and it's enough to fortify you for the day. Expect nothing in the way of decor and you won't be disappointed. Service is reminiscent of Chinatown: efficient and lightning-quick.

2651 Broadway (btwn 100th and 101st sts.). ℂ 212/663-5520 or 212/595-2525. Reservations not accepted. Main courses $4.50–$19 (most under $10); lunch specials $5–$7 (Mon–Sat to 4:30pm). AE, MC, V ($15 minimum). Daily noon–midnight. Subway: 1, 9 to 103rd St.

Gabriela's ⭐⭐ (Value) MEXICAN

If you love roast chicken, Gabriela's is the best. A blend of Yucatán spices and a slow-roasting rotisserie results in some of the most tender, juicy chicken in town—and at $7 for a half chicken with two sides and $13 for a whole, it's a great value. The Mexican specialties are well prepared, generously portioned, and satisfying, from the monster tacos to the enchiladas. The dining room is bright and pretty, and the service is quick and attentive. Try one of Gabriela's fruit shakes (mango and papaya are good bets) or *aguas frescas* (fresh-fruit drinks), which come in a variety of flavors; beer, wine, and margaritas are served, too.

315 Amsterdam Ave. (at 75th St.). ℭ **212/875-8532**. www.gabrielas.com. Reservations accepted for parties of 6 or more. Main courses $5–$9 at lunch, $7–$20 at brunch and dinner (most less than $15); early dinner specials $9.95, includes glass of wine or frozen margarita (Mon–Fri 4–7pm, Sat–Sun 3:30–6:30pm). AE, DC, MC, V. Mon–Thurs 11:30am–11pm; Fri–Sat 11:30am–midnight; Sun 11:30am–10pm. Subway: 1, 2, 3, 9 to 96th St. Also at 685 Amsterdam Ave. (at 93rd St.; ℭ **212/961-0574**; subway: 1, 2, 3, 9 to 96th St.).

Josie's Restaurant & Juice Bar HEALTH-CONSCIOUS NEW AMERICAN   You have to admire the sincerity of an organic restaurant that uses chemical-free milk paint on its walls. Chef/owner Louis Lanza doesn't stop there: His menu shuns dairy, preservatives, and concentrated fats. Free-range and farm-raised meats and poultry augment vegetarian choices like baked sweet potato with tofu, tamari brown rice, broccoli, roasted beets, and lemon-tahini sauce; and a sautéed three-grain vegetable burger made from quinoa, bulghur wheat, and couscous with homemade ketchup and barbecued onions. Latin and Asian accents are copious, as in citrus-marinated skirt-steak fajita, accompanied by chipotle corn salsa, guacamole, and whole-wheat tortillas. Everything is made with organic grains, beans, and flour and produce when possible. If beet or arugula juice isn't your thing, a full wine and beer list is served in this pleasing modern space, which boasts enough colorful Jetsons-style touches to give the room a playful, relaxed feel.

300 Amsterdam Ave. (at 74th St.). ℭ **212/769-1212**. www.josiesnyc.com. Reservations recommended. Main courses $7.50–$13.50 at brunch, $8–$13.75 at lunch, $8.75–$18.50 at dinner (most less than $15). AE, DC, MC, V. Mon–Wed noon–11pm; Thurs–Fri noon–midnight; Sat 11:30am–midnight; Sun 11am–11pm. Subway: 1, 2, 3, 9 to 72nd St. Also at 565 Third Ave. (at 37th St.; ℭ **212/490-1558**; subway: 6 to 33rd St.).

Sarabeth's Kitchen ⭐⭐ CONTEMPORARY AMERICAN Sarabeth's fresh-baked goods, preserves, and American cooking with a European touch keep a loyal following. This country restaurant with a Hamptons feel is best known for its breakfast and weekend brunch, when the menu features porridge with wheatberries, fresh cream, butter, and brown sugar; pumpkin waffles topped with sour cream, raisins, pumpkin seeds, and honey; and a host of farm-fresh omelets. Expect a *long* wait for weekend brunch; weekday breakfast and lunch are just as good, and a lot less crowded. Lunch might be a Caesar salad with Parmesan, brioche croutons, and anchovy dressing, accompanied by cream of tomato soup; or old-fashioned chicken potpie. Dinner is more sophisticated and splurge-priced, with such specialties as hazelnut-crusted halibut in a seven-vegetable

---

Tips **Pizza! Pizza!**

The Upper West Side does not lack for good pizza. Near Lincoln Center, **John's Pizzeria** (p. 101), 48 W. 65th St., between Broadway and Central Park West (© **212/721-7001**), serves up one of the city's best pies.

Farther uptown, the place to go is **V&T Pizzeria** ☆, 1024 Amsterdam Ave., between 110th and 111th streets (© **212/ 666-8051** or 212/663-1708). This is a sit-down (or carry-out) restaurant with red-checked tablecloths, and traditional pies with red sauce and a chewy crust. V&T caters to a Columbia University crowd, so prices stay low—how can you *not* splurge on a cannoli for dessert, right?

---

broth and oven-roasted lamb crusted in black mushrooms, with grilled leeks and Vidalia onion rings. Leave room for the luscious desserts—or stop by just for dessert!

423 Amsterdam Ave. (btwn 80th and 81st sts.). © 212/496-6280. Reservations accepted for dinner only. Main courses $4.50–$13 at breakfast and brunch, $10.50–$17.50 at lunch, $10.50–$15.50 afternoon tea (Mon–Fri 3:30–5:30pm), $13–$26 at dinner. AE, DC, DISC, MC, V. Mon–Sat 8am–10:30pm; Sun 8am–9:30pm. Subway: 1, 9 to 79th St. Also at 1295 Madison Ave. (at 92nd St.; © 212/410-7335; subway: 4, 5, 6 to 96th St.); Cafe inside the Whitney Museum, 945 Madison Ave. (at 75th St.; © 212/570-3670; subway: 6 to 77th St.); Bakery location at Chelsea Market, 75 Ninth Ave. (btwn 15th and 16th sts.; © 212/989-2424; subway: A, C, E, L to 14th St.).

QUICK BITES

For one of the most satisfying meal deals in the city, head for **Gray's Papaya** (p. 92), 2090 Broadway, at 72nd Street (© **212/799-0243**), where all-beef dogs are available around the clock. Add some crispy fries and a tropical juice drink.

13 The Upper East Side

Sarabeth's Kitchen (p. 109) has two Upper East Side locations for breakfasts or sweet treats: a full-service outpost at 1295 Madison Ave., at 92nd Street (© **212/410-7335**), and a cafe inside the Whitney Museum, 945 Madison Ave., at 75th Street (© **212/606-0218**). **Burritoville** (p. 75) is at 1489 First Ave., between 77th and 78th streets (© **212/472-8800**), and 1606 Third Ave., between 90th and 91st (© **212/410-2255**).

Bardolino *(Value)* ITALIAN   This trattoria prepares terrific pastas in a romantic atmosphere. On my last visit, I enjoyed a traditional Caesar, followed by a fantastic penne alla vodka with peas and pro-sciutto in a lightly creamy pink sauce so good I dream about it when I'm hungry. Other choices include fusilli *norcia,* in a tomato sauce with hot and sweet Italian sausage. The wine list is well priced and pleasing. This is the kind of solicitous service you usually have to pay twice as much to enjoy. The fixed-price meal deals at weekend brunch, lunch, and early dinner make an excellent value even better.

1496 Second Ave. (at 78th St.). (✆ 212/734-9050 or 212/734-9395. Reservations accepted. Pastas $7–$11; main courses $11–$13 (specials may be slightly higher); 2-course fixed-price lunch $5.95 (daily to 3:45pm); weekend brunch $7.95 (with mimosa or juice); 2-course fixed-price dinner $9.95 (daily 4–7pm). AE, DC, MC, V. Mon–Fri noon–11:30pm; Sat–Sun 11am–11:30pm. Subway: 6 to 77th St.

Serendipity 3 *(Kids)* AMERICAN   You'd never guess that this whimsical place was once a top stop on Andy Warhol's agenda. Serendipity's small front-room curiosity shop overflows with odd objects, from jigsaw puzzles to silly jewelry. But the real action is behind the shop, where the quintessential American soda fountain reigns supreme. Happy people gather at marble-topped ice-cream parlor tables for burgers and foot-long hot dogs, meat loaf with mashed potatoes and gravy, and salads and sandwiches with cute names like "The Catcher in the Rye" (their own twist on the BLT, with chicken and Russian dressing—on rye, of course). What they're really there for are the desserts. The restaurant's signature is Frozen Hot Chocolate, a slushie version of everybody's cold-weather favorite; other crowd pleasers include dark double devil mousse, celestial carrot cake, lemon icebox pie, and anything with hot fudge. Serendipity is a charmer to be appreciated by adults and kids alike.

225 E. 60th St. (btwn Second and Third aves.). (✆ 212/838-3531. www.seren dipity3.com. Reservations accepted for lunch and dinner (not just dessert). Main courses $7–$18; sweets and sundaes $5–$17 (most under $10). AE, DC, DISC, MC, V. Sun–Thurs 11:30am–midnight; Fri 11:30am–1am; Sat 11:30am–2am. Subway: N, R to Lexington Ave.; 4, 5, 6 to 59th St.

QUICK BITES

In business since 1932, **Papaya King,** 179 E. 86th St., at Third Avenue (✆ 212/369-0648; www.papayaking.com), is the origina-tor of the two-franks-and-a-fruit-drink combo that Gray's Papaya (p. 92) has popularized. Papaya King isn't as inexpensive as Gray's—the combo is $4.30 here—but the quality is high.

14 Harlem

Miss Mamie's Spoonbread Too ★ (Finds) SOUTHERN
Entering this strawberry-curtained charmer is like stepping straight
into South Carolina. Take a seat at one of the Formica-topped tables
and nibble from the plate of cornbread as you peruse the menu of
Southern classics: fried chicken, barbecue shrimp (great sauce!),
short ribs falling off the bone and topped with a perfect gravy. Or
try the sampler plate, a "smorgasbord of Southern delights." Every
entree comes with your choice of two sides, including macaroni and
cheese, collard greens, candied yams, and potato salad. Save room
for dessert, which follows the traditional line with sweet-potato pie,
banana pudding, and home-baked cobblers and cakes. Service is
charming and attentive, beer and wine are available.

366 W. 110th St. (btwn Columbus and Manhattan aves.). © **212/865-6744.**
Reservations not accepted. Main courses $7–$15. MC, V. Mon–Sat noon–10:30pm;
Sun 11am–10:30pm. Subway: 2, 3 to 125th St. Also at 547 Lenox Ave. (btwn 137th
and 138th sts.; © **212/690-3100;** subway: 2, 3 to 135th St.).

Sylvia's ★★ SOUL FOOD   South Carolina–born Sylvia Woods
is the last word in New York soul food. Don't be surprised if you
have a wait for a table, but the food is worth it. Since 1962, this
Harlem institution has dished up Southern fried goods: turkey with
down-home stuffing, smothered chicken and pork chops, fried
chicken and baked ham, collard greens and candied yams, and sweet
tea. And then there's "Sylvia's World Famous, Talked About, Bar-B-
Que Ribs Special"—the sauce is sweet, with a potent afterburn. This
Harlem landmark is still presided over by 73-year-old Sylvia, who's
likely to greet you at the door. Eating here is still a one-of-a-kind
New York experience. Sunday gospel brunch is a joyous time to go.

328 Lenox Ave. (btwn 126th and 127th sts.). © **212/996-0660.** www.sylviassoul
food.com. Reservations only accepted for parties of 10 or more. Main courses
$2.50–$8.25 at breakfast, $8–$19 at lunch and dinner; lunch special Mon–Fri
11am–3pm $3.75–$9.25; Sun gospel brunch $17 (includes a cocktail). AE, DISC,
MC, V. Mon–Thurs 8am–10:30pm; Fri–Sat 7:30am–10:30pm; Sun 11am–8pm.
Subway: 2, 3 to 125th St.

5

Exploring New York City

If this is your first trip to New York, face facts: It will be impossible to take in the entire city. Because New York is almost unfathomably big and constantly changing, you could live your whole life here and still make fascinating daily discoveries.

So decide on a few must-see attractions, and then let the city take you on its own ride. Inevitably, you'll be blown off course by unplanned diversions that are as much fun as what you meant to see.

1 The Top Attractions

In addition to the choices below, don't forget **Central Park** &&&, the great green swath that is, by virtue of its existence, New York City's greatest marvel. Central Park is so big and multifaceted that it earns its own section (p. 135).

American Museum of Natural History &&& This is one of the hottest museum tickets in town, thanks to the $210 million **Rose Center for Earth and Space** &, whose planetarium sphere hosts the Harrison Ford–narrated show "Are We Alone?" The show is short—less than a half-hour—but phenomenal. **Buy your tickets in advance** in order to guarantee admission (they're available online); you can also buy tickets in advance for a specific IMAX film or exhibition, which I recommend, especially during peak seasons and for weekend visits; otherwise, you might miss out.

Start your tour with the Space Show. Afterwards, follow the Cosmic Pathway, which spirals around the sphere and down to the main level, chronicling the 15-billion-year evolution of the universe. Other must-sees include the Big Bang Theater, which re-creates the birth of the universe; the Hall of the Universe, with its very own 15½-ton meteorite; and the Hall of Planet Earth, which focuses on the geologic processes of our home planet (great volcano display!). All in all, you'll need at least 2 hours to fully explore the Rose Center. The rest of the 4-square-block museum is nothing to sneeze at. Founded in 1869, it houses the world's greatest natural-science collection in a group of buildings made of towers and turrets, pink granite, and red brick. The diversity is astounding: some 36 million specimens ranging from microscopic organisms to the world's largest cut gem, the Brazilian Princess Topaz (21,005 carats). If you don't have a lot of time, you can see the best of the best on free **Highlights Tours** offered daily every hour at 15 minutes after the hour from 10:15am to 3:15pm. **Audio Expeditions,** high-tech audio tours that allow you to access narration in the order you choose, are available to help you make sense of it all.

If you only see one exhibit, see the **dinosaurs** 𝆏, on the fourth floor. Start in the **Orientation Room,** where a video gives an overview of the 500 million years of evolutionary history that led to you. Continue to the **Vertebrate Origins Room,** where models of ancient fish and turtles hang overhead, with plenty of interactive exhibits and kid-level displays to keep young minds fascinated. Next come the great **dinosaur halls,** with mammoth, spectacularly reconstructed skeletons and more interactive displays. **Mammals and Their Extinct Relatives** brings what you've learned in the previous halls home.

The **Hall of Biodiversity** is a multimedia exhibit, but its doom-and-gloom story about the future of rain forests and other natural habitats might be too much for the little ones. Kids 5 and older should head to the **Discovery Room,** with lots of hands-on exhibits and experiments. The museum excels at **special exhibitions,** so check to see what's on. The **Butterfly Conservatory** 𝆏, a walk-in enclosure housing nearly 500 free-flying tropical butterflies, has developed into a can't-miss fixture from October through May.

Central Park W. (btwn 77th and 81st sts.). ℭ **212/769-5100** for information, or 212/769-5200 for tickets (tickets can also be ordered online). www.amnh.org. Suggested admission $10 adults, $7.50 seniors and students, $6 children 2–12. Space Show and museum admission $19 adults, $14 seniors and students, $11.50 children under 12. Additional charges for IMAX movies and some special exhibitions. Daily 10am–5:45pm; Rose Center open Fri to 8:45pm. Subway: B, C to 81st St.; 1, 9 to 79th St.

Brooklyn Bridge 𝆏𝆏 *(Moments)*   Its Gothic-inspired stone pylons and steel-cable webs have moved poets like Walt Whitman and Hart Crane to sing the praises of this great span, the first to connect Manhattan to Brooklyn. Begun in 1867 and completed in 1883, the Brooklyn Bridge is the city's best-known symbol of the age of growth that seized the city during the late 19th century. Walk across it and imagine the awe that New Yorkers felt at seeing two boroughs joined by this monumental span. It's still astounding.

Walking the Bridge: This is one of my all-time favorite New York activities, although there's no doubt that the Lower Manhattan views from the bridge now have a painful resonance. A wide wood-plank pedestrian walkway is elevated above the traffic, making it a relatively peaceful, and popular, walk. It's a great vantage point from which to contemplate the New York skyline.

There's a sidewalk entrance on Park Row, just across from City Hall Park (take the 4, 5, or 6 train to Brooklyn Bridge/City Hall). But why do this walk *away* from Manhattan? For Manhattan sky-line views, take an A or C train to High Street, one stop into Brooklyn. From there, you'll be on the bridge in no time: Come above ground, then walk through the park to Cadman Plaza East and head down (left) to the stairwell that will take you up to the footpath. (Following Prospect Place under the bridge, turning right onto Cadman Plaza E., will also take you directly to the stairwell.) It's about a 20- to 40-minute stroll over the bridge to Manhattan (there are benches along the way). The footpath will deposit you right at City Hall Park.

Subway: A, C to High St.; 4, 5, 6 to Brooklyn Bridge–City Hall.

Ellis Island 🎩🎩 The restored Ellis Island opened in 1990, north of Liberty Island. Roughly 40% of Americans can trace their her-itage back to an ancestor who came through here. For the 62 years when it was America's main entry point for immigrants (1892–1954), Ellis Island processed some 12 million people. The **Immigration Museum** tells the story of Ellis Island and immigra-tion in America by placing the emphasis on personal experience.

It's difficult to leave unmoved. You enter the Main Building's baggage room, just as the immigrants did, and then climb the stairs to the **Registry Room,** with its vaulted tiled ceiling, where millions waited for medical and legal processing. A step-by-step account of the immigrants' voyage is detailed with haunting photos and oral histories. What might be the most poignant exhibit is **"Treasures from Home,"** 1,000 objects and photos donated by descendants of immigrants, including family heirlooms, religious articles, and clothing and jewelry. Outside, the **American Immigrant Wall of Honor** commemorates the names of more than 500,000 immi-grants and their families, from Myles Standish to Jay Leno. You can research your family history at the **American Family Immigration History Center;** start at home at www.ellisislandrecords.org.

Touring Tips: Ferries run daily to Ellis Island and Liberty Island from Battery Park and Liberty State Park (in New Jersey) at frequent intervals; see the Statue of Liberty listing (p. 121) for details.

In New York Harbor. ℂ **212/363-3200** (general info), or 212/269-5755 (ticket/ferry info). www.nps.gov/elis or www.ellisisland.org. Free admission (ferry ticket charge). Daily 9:30am–5pm (last ferry departs around 3:30pm). For subway and ferry details, see the Statue of Liberty listing on p. 121 (ferry trip includes stops at both sights).

Empire State Building ⟡⟡⟡   It took 60,000 tons of steel, 10 million bricks, 2½ million feet of electrical wire, 120 miles of pipe, and 7 million man-hours to build. King Kong climbed it in 1933. A plane slammed into it in 1945. The World Trade Center superseded it in 1970 as the island's tallest building. On September 11, 2001, it regained its status as New York City's tallest building. And through it all, the Empire State Building has remained one of the city's favorite landmarks. Completed in 1931, the limestone-and-stainless-steel streamline deco dazzler climbs 102 stories (1,454 ft./ 436m) and now harbors the offices of fashion firms, and, in its upper reaches, a jumble of broadcast equipment.

Always a conversation piece, the Empire State Building glows every night, bathed in colored floodlights to commemorate events of significance—red, white, and blue for Independence Day; green for St. Patrick's Day; red, black, and green for Martin Luther King Day; blue and white for Hanukkah; even lavender and white for Gay Pride Day. The silver spire can be seen from all over the city. My favorite view is from 23rd Street, where Fifth Avenue and Broadway converge. On a lovely day, stand at the base of the Flatiron Building and gaze up Fifth; the crisp, gleaming deco tower jumps out, soaring above the sooty office buildings that surround it.

But the views that keep nearly three million visitors coming every year are the ones from the 86th- and 102nd-floor **observatories.** The lower one is best—you can walk out on a deck and look through coin-operated viewers (bring quarters!) over what, on a clear day, can be as much as an 80-mile (129km) radius. The higher observation deck is glass-enclosed and cramped.

Light fog can create an admirably moody effect, but a clear day is best. Dusk brings the most remarkable views and the biggest crowds. Consider going in the morning, when the light is still low on the horizon, keeping glare to a minimum. Starry nights are pure magic.

350 Fifth Ave. (at 34th St.). © 212/736-3100. www.esbnyc.com. Observatory admission $10 adults, $9 seniors and children 12–17, $4 children 5–11, free for children under 5. Mon–Fri 10am–midnight; Sat–Sun 9:30am–midnight; tickets sold until 11:25pm. Subway: B, D, F, N, R, V, Q, W to 34th St.; 6 to 33rd St.

Grand Central Terminal ✶   The triumphant restoration of this 1913 landmark has put the "grand" back into Grand Central.

Come and visit, even if you're not catching the subway or train. Even if you arrive and leave by subway, be sure to exit the station, walking a couple of blocks south, to about 40th Street, before you turn to admire Jules-Alexis Coutan's neoclassical sculpture *Transportation* over the south entrance, with a majestic Mercury, the Roman god of commerce and travel, as its central figure.

The greatest visual impact comes when you enter the vast **main concourse.** Cleaned of decades of grime and cheesy advertisements, it boasts renewed majesty. The high windows again allow sunlight to penetrate the space, glinting off the half-acre Tennessee marble floor. The brass clock over the central kiosk gleams, as do the gold- and nickel-plated chandeliers piercing the side archways. The **sky ceiling,** again a brilliant greenish blue, depicts the constellations of the winter sky above New York. They're lit with 59 stars, surrounded by 24-carat gold and emitting light through fiber-optic cables. On the east end of the main concourse is a **marble staircase** where there had never been one before, but as the original plans had always intended.

New retail shops and restaurants have taken over the mezzanine and lower levels. Off the main concourse at street level, there's a mix of specialty shops and national retailers, as well as the **Grand Central Market** for gourmet foods. The **New York Transit Museum Gallery Annex & Store,** in the shuttle passage, houses city transit-related exhibitions and a gift shop that's worth a look. The **lower concourse** houses a food court that's a budget diner's delight, as well as the **Oyster Bar & Restaurant** (© 212/490-6650).

42nd St. at Park Ave. © 212/340-2210 (events hot line). www.grandcentralterminal. com. Subway: S, 4, 5, 6, 7 to 42nd St./Grand Central.

Metropolitan Museum of Art ✶✶✶   The Metropolitan Museum of Art draws some five million people a year, more than any other attraction in the city. At 1.6 million square feet (480,000 sq. m), this is the largest museum in the Western Hemisphere. Nearly all the world's cultures through the ages are on display—from Egyptian mummies to ancient Greek statuary to Islamic carvings to Renaissance paintings to Native American masks to 20th-century decorative arts—and masterpieces are the rule. You could go once a week for a lifetime and find something new on each visit.

So unless you plan on spending your entire vacation here (some do), you cannot see the entire collection. My recommendation is to give it one good, long day. One way to get an overview is to take the **Museum Highlights Tour,** offered every day (usually 10:15am–3:15pm). Visit the museum's website for a schedule of this and subject-specific walking tours (Old Master Paintings, American Period Rooms, and so on); you can also get a schedule of the day's tours and gallery talks at the Visitor Services desk.

The least overwhelming way to see the Met on your own is to pick up a map at the round desk in the entry hall and concentrate on what you like, whether it's 17th-century paintings, American furniture, or the art of the South Pacific. Highlights include the American Wing's **Garden Court,** with its 19th-century sculpture; the ground-level **Costume Hall;** and the **Frank Lloyd Wright room.** The **Roman and Greek galleries** are overwhelming, but in a marvelous way, as is the collection of later **Chinese art.** The highlight of the **Egyptian collection** is the **Temple of Dendur.** The **Greek Galleries,** which at last fully realize McKim, Mead & White's grand neoclassical plans of 1917, and the **Ancient Near East Galleries** are particularly of note. Marvelous **special exhibitions** can range from "Jade in Ancient Costa Rica" to "Cubism and Fashion."

Money-saving tip: The Met's medieval collections are housed in Upper Manhattan at the **Cloisters** 🐾 (p. 126); admission is included with your Met ticket purchase, but seeing both satisfactorily in a single day is more than only the most die-hard budget travelers should try to accomplish. If you're committed to seeing both on one ticket, start at the Cloisters at opening time on a Friday or Saturday (the Met's extended-hour days, so you can maximize your time), then move downtown to the main museum in the afternoon.

Fifth Ave. at 82nd St. ✆ 212/535-7710. www.metmuseum.org. Admission (includes same-day entrance to the Cloisters) $10 adults, $5 seniors and students, free for children under 12 when accompanied by an adult. Sun and Tues–Thurs 9:30am–5:30pm; Fri–Sat 9:30am–9pm. No strollers allowed Sun (back carriers available at 81st St. entrance coat-check area). Subway: 4, 5, 6 to 86th St.

Museum of Modern Art/MoMA QNS 🐾 The Museum of

Modern Art (or MoMA) boasts the world's greatest collection of painting and sculpture from the late 19th century to the present, from Monet's *Water Lilies* and Klimt's *The Kiss* to masterworks by Frida Kahlo, Edward Hopper, Andy Warhol, Robert Rauschenberg, and others. Top that off with an extensive collection of drawings, photography, architectural models and furniture, design objects ranging from tableware to sports cars, and film and video (including the world's largest collection of D. W. Griffith films), and you have quite a museum. If you're into modernism, this is the place to be.

Here's the Bad News: MoMA is undergoing a $650 million renovation of its West 53rd Street building under the guidance of Japanese architect Yoshio Taniguchi that will double the exhibit space when the project is complete, which won't be until 2005.

Here's the Good News: The museum has opened temporary exhibit space called **MoMA QNS** in the old Swingline stapler factory in Long Island City. The spectacularly renovated 45,000-square-foot gallery will exhibit highlights of the collection, among them van Gogh's *Starry Night,* Picasso's *Les Demoiselles d'Avignon,* and Warhol's *Gold Marilyn Monroe.* Workshops, a limited program schedule, and special exhibitions will also be part of the fun: Spring 2003 will showcase masterworks by Matisse and Picasso, while summer visitors can expect an exhibit of Ansel Adams photographs.

Yes—it's definitely worth a short subway ride to Queens. Getting there is quick and easy; in fact, from Midtown, you can be here quicker than you can get to the Village.

45-20 33rd St., Long Island City, Queens. ✆ **212/708-9400.** www.moma.org. Admission $12 adults, $8.50 seniors and students, free for children under 16 accompanied by an adult; pay what you wish Fri 4:30–8:15pm. Sat–Tues and Thurs 10:30am–5:45pm; Fri 10:30am–8:15pm. Subway: 7 to 33rd St. (MoMA QNS is across the st.).

Rockefeller Center ✦✦ *Moments*   A streamline masterpiece, Rockefeller Center is one of New York's central gathering spots. It was erected in the 1930s, when the city was deep in the Depression as well as its most passionate Art Deco phase. Designated a National Historic Landmark in 1988, it's the world's largest privately owned business-and-entertainment center, with 18 buildings on 21 acres.

For a dramatic approach to the entire complex, start at Fifth Avenue between 49th and 50th streets. The builders purposely created the gentle slope of the Promenade, known here as the **Channel Gardens** because it's flanked to the south by La Maison Française and to the north by the British Building. The Promenade leads to the **Lower Plaza,** home to the famous ice-skating rink and alfresco dining in summer in the shadow of Paul Manship's gilded bronze statue *Prometheus.* All around the flags of the United Nations' member countries flap in the breeze. Just behind *Prometheus,* in December and early January, the city's majestic official Christmas tree towers over the ice rink.

The **Rink at Rockefeller Center** ✿ (✆ **212/332-7654;** www. rockefellercenter.com) is tiny but romantic. It's open mid-October to mid-March, and you'll skate under the tree from early December through the holiday season.

The focal point of this "city within a city" is the **GE Building** ✿, at 30 Rockefeller Plaza, a 70-story showpiece. It's still one of the city's most impressive buildings; walk through for a look at the granite-and-marble lobby, lined with sepia-toned murals by José Maria Sert. **NBC** maintains studios throughout the complex. Shows like *Saturday Night Live, Dateline NBC,* and *Late Night with Conan O'Brien* originate in the GE Building (see "Talk of the Town: Free TV Tapings," on p. 144, for tips on getting tickets). NBC's ***Today* show** is broadcast live on weekdays from 7 to 10am from the glass-enclosed studio on the corner of 49th Street and Rockefeller Plaza.

Designed by Donald Deskey, **Radio City Music Hall** ✿, 1260 Sixth Ave., at 50th Street (✆ **212/247-4777;** www.radiocity.com), is one of the city's largest indoor theaters, with 6,200 seats, but its true grandeur derives from its Art Deco appointments.

Btwn 48th and 50th sts., from Fifth to Sixth aves. ✆ **212/332-6868.** www.rocke fellercenter.com. Subway: B, D, F, V to 47th–50th sts./Rockefeller Center.

Solomon R. Guggenheim Museum ✿

It's been called a bun, a snail, a concrete tornado, and a giant wedding cake. Whatever descriptive you choose, Frank Lloyd Wright's only New York building, completed in 1959, is best summed up as a brilliant work of architecture—so brilliant it competes with the art for your attention.

It's easy to see the bulk of what's on display in 2 to 4 hours. Inside, a spiraling rotunda circles over a slowly inclined ramp that leads you past changing exhibits. Usually the progression is counterintuitive: from the first floor up, rather than from the sixth floor down. Permanent exhibits of 19th- and 20th-century art, including Kandinsky, Klee, Picasso, and French Impressionists, occupy a stark annex called the **Tower Galleries.**

1071 Fifth Ave. (at 88th St.). ✆ **212/423-3500.** www.guggenheim.org. Admission $12 adults, $8 seniors and students, free for children under 12; pay as you wish Fri 6–8pm. Sun–Wed 9am–6pm; Fri–Sat 9am–8pm. Subway: 4, 5, 6 to 86th St.

Staten Island Ferry ✿✿ *Value*

Here's New York's best freebie. You get an hour-long excursion (round-trip) into the world's biggest harbor. This is not strictly a sightseeing ride but commuter transportation to and from Staten Island. During business hours you'll share the boat with working stiffs reading papers and drinking coffee, blissfully unaware of the sights outside.

You, however, should go on deck and enjoy the harbor traffic. The old orange-and-green boats usually have open decks along the sides or at the bow and stern; try to catch one of these if you can, because the newer white boats don't have decks. Grab a seat on the right side of the boat for the best view. On the way out of Manhattan, you'll pass the Statue of Liberty, Ellis Island, and from the left side of the boat, Governor's Island; you'll see the Verrazano Narrows Bridge spanning the distance from Brooklyn to Staten Island in the distance.

When the boat arrives at St. George, Staten Island, if you are required to disembark, follow the boat-loading sign on your right as you get off; you'll circle around to the next loading dock, where there's usually another boat waiting to depart.

Departs from the Whitehall Ferry Terminal at the southern tip of Manhattan. ℂ 718/815-BOAT. www.ci.nyc.ny.us/html/dot. Free admission ($3 for car transport on select ferries). 24 hr.; every 20–30 min. weekdays, less frequently off-peak and weekend hours. Subway: N, R to Whitehall St.; 4, 5 to Bowling Green; 1, 9 to South Ferry (ride in 1 of the 1st 5 cars).

Statue of Liberty ✶✶✶ (Kids)

For the millions who came by ship to America in the last century—as tourists or immigrants—Lady Liberty was their first glimpse of America. Even if you don't make it to Liberty Island, you can get a glimpse from Battery Park, from the New Jersey side of the bay, or from the Staten Island Ferry.

Touring Tips: Ferries leave daily every half hour to 45 minutes from 9am to about 3:30pm (their clock), with more frequent ferries in the morning and extended hours in summer. Try to go early on a weekday to avoid the crowds that swarm in the afternoon, on weekends, and on holidays.

A stop at **Ellis Island** ✶✶ (p. 115) is included in the fare, but on the last ferry, you can only visit the statue or Ellis Island, not both.

Buy ferry tickets in advance via www.statueoflibertyferry.com, which will allow you to board without standing in the ticket line; however, there is a service charge. Even if you've purchased tickets, arrive as much as 30 minutes before your desired ferry time to allow for security procedures. The ferry ride takes about 20 minutes.

Once on Liberty Island, you'll start to get an idea of the statue's immensity: She weighs 225 tons and measures 152 feet (46m) from

Tips **Lady Liberty Touring Updates**

At press time, **only the grounds of Liberty Island were open to the public.** Whether and when the pedestal, museum, and/or the body of the statue itself will reopen was unknown at this writing.

If the statue does reopen, be sure to arrive by noon if your heart's set on experiencing everything. And keep in mind that, for the last few years, the National Park Service has instituted a "crown" policy during the peak **summer** season: Visitors who want to walk up to the crown must be on one of the **first two ferries of the day.** At other times, you must be on line to climb to the crown by 2pm; otherwise, you will not be allowed up.

Please call or check the website (**www.nps.gov/stli**) for the latest access information.

foot to flame. Her nose alone is 4½ feet (1.5m) long, and her index finger is 8 feet (2.5m) long.

Note that access to the statue itself was severely restricted at this writing; see "Lady Liberty Touring Updates" (below) for details.

If the statue does reopen to the public, you may have to wait as long as 3 hours to walk up into the crown. If it's summer, or you're not in shape, you may want to skip it: It's a grueling 354 steps (the equivalent of 22 stories) to the crown, or you can take the elevator the first 10 stories up (a shortcut I endorse). You don't have to go all the way up to the crown; there are **observation decks** at different levels, including one at the top of the pedestal that's reachable by elevator. Even if you don't go in, a stroll around the base is an extraordinary experience, and the views of the Manhattan skyline are stellar.

On Liberty Island in New York Harbor. © **212/363-3200** (general info), or 212/269-5755 (ticket/ferry info). www.nps.gov/stli or www.statueoflibertyferry. com. Free admission; ferry ticket to Statue of Liberty and Ellis Island $8 adults, $6 seniors, $3 children 3–17. Daily 9am–5pm (last ferry departs around 3:30pm); extended hours in summer. Subway: 4, 5 to Bowling Green; 1, 9 to South Ferry (note that 1, 9 had not resumed service to Lower Manhattan at press time). Walk south through Battery Park to Castle Clinton, the fort housing the ferry ticket booth.

Wall Street & the New York Stock Exchange ✦✦ *Value*   Wall Street: this 18th-century lane (you'll be surprised at how little it is) is appropriately monumental, lined with neoclassical towers that

What's Happening in Times Square

The dust has finally settled on the epic renewal where Broadway meets 42nd Street; what was once the city's gritty heart is now the hub of its tourist-friendly rebirth.

The neon lights of Broadway are more dazzling than ever, now that ABC's *Good Morning America* has set up a street-facing studio at Broadway and 44th Street; **NASDAQ**'s eight-story billboard at Broadway and 43rd has joined the landscape, and World Wrestling Entertainment spent a mint restoring the Paramount Building and installing a 47,500-square-foot entertainment complex, **WWE New York.** (Take note of the WWE's marquee: Between the restored historic scrollwork is a full-color sign that incorporates the latest in LED and fiber-optic technology.) A handful of upper-end new hotels means that thousands more visitors can stay right on (or just off) the Great White Way—as long as they're willing to shell out big-time to do it.

Along with WWE New York, **ESPN Zone,** the freshly *NSync-funded **Planet Hollywood,** and **B.B. King Blues Club & Grill** all joined the Times Square pack in the 21st century, reinvigorating the notion of themed dining and nightlife. The **Virgin Megastore** has a major presence, as does **MTV,** which draws busloads of fans to Broadway and 45th Street every weekday afternoon for Total Request Live.

Forty-Second Street between Seventh and Eighth avenues, the former porn paradise, has been rebuilt as a family-oriented entertainment mecca. The neon-bright block is chock-full with retail and amusements, including the multilevel, **Broadway City** 🎯 video arcade; two 20-plus-screen movie complexes; and plenty of mall-familiar shopping and dining, including the **Museum Company,** and a **Yankees Clubhouse Shop** (where you can purchase tickets).

reach as far skyward as the dreams of investors who built it into the world's most famous financial market.

At the heart of the action is the **New York Stock Exchange** (NYSE), where you can watch the billions change hands and get an idea of how the money merchants work. NYSE came into being in 1792, when merchants met daily under a buttonwood tree to pass off to each other the U.S. bonds that had been sold to fund the Revolutionary War. By 1903, they were trading stocks of publicly held companies in this Corinthian-columned beaux-arts "temple" designed by George Post. Until September 11, 2001, visitors could acquire free tickets to tour a small interactive museum and watch the action on the trading floor from the glass-lined, mezzanine-level

Moments   Paying Your Respects at Ground Zero

The World Trade Center dominated Lower Manhattan. The complex occupied 16 acres. About 50,000 people worked there, some 70,000 others (tourists and businesspeople) visited each day. The complex included, in addition to two 110-story towers, five additional buildings (including a hotel), a plaza rich with outdoor sculpture, a shopping mall, and a full slate of restaurants, including Windows on the World, the city's ultimate special-occasion restaurant.

Then the first plane hit Tower 1, at 8:45am on Tuesday, September 11, 2001. By 10:30am, it was all gone, along with nearly 3,000 people.

The former Trade Center is now a vast crater. Cleanup was scheduled to be complete by the end of 2002, but no decisions had yet been finalized as to what will come next.

At press time, a **temporary viewing platform** was in place at Broadway and Liberty Street, open daily from 9am to 9pm; tickets are not required. *Please check the sources listed below for the latest viewing and access information.*

As of March 11, 2002, a victims' memorial was in place at **Battery Park:** The bronze sphere that once stood on the World Trade Center plaza between the Twin Towers now stands witness, bearing its war wounds, until a permanent one can be erected.

Ground Zero is bounded by Church, Barclay, Liberty, and West streets. Call © **212/484-1222** or visit www.nycvisit.com or www.southstseaport.org for viewing info; www.downtowny.com for information and updates. Subway: C, E to World Trade Center; N, R to Cortlandt St.

observation gallery. However, the facility has been closed to the public since the terrorist attack. It was scheduled to reopen to the public sometime in 2002, but no date could be confirmed at this writing. Your best bet is to call to check the status—as well as the updated ticket procedure—before you arrive.

20 Broad St. (between Wall St. and Exchange Place). ℂ 212/656-5165. www.nyse. com. Free admission. Mon–Fri 9am–4:30pm (ticket booth opens 8:45am). *Note that information may change when the facility reopens in 2002.* Subway: J, M, Z to Broad St.; 2, 3, 4, 5 to Wall St.

Whitney Museum of American Art ⭐⭐   The world's finest museum of 20th-century American art is an imposing presence on Madison Avenue—an inverted three-tiered pyramid of concrete and gray granite with seven seemingly random windows. The rotating permanent collection consists of a selection of major works by Edward Hopper, Georgia O'Keeffe, Roy Lichtenstein, Jasper Johns, and other significant artists. The second floor is devoted to works from its permanent collection from 1900 to 1950, while the rest is dedicated to rotating exhibits.

Shows are usually all well curated and more edgy than what you'd see at MoMA or the Guggenheim. Topics range from topical surveys, such as "American Art in the Age of Technology" and "The Warhol Look: Glamour Style Fashion," to in-depth retrospectives of famous or lesser-known movements (such as Fluxus, the movement that spawned Yoko Ono, among others) and artists (Mark Rothko, Keith Haring, Duane Hanson). Free **gallery tours** are offered daily.

945 Madison Ave. (at 75th St.). ℂ **877/WHITNEY** or 212/570-3676. www.whitney. org. Admission $10 adults, $8 seniors and students, free for children under 12; pay as you wish Fri 6–9pm. Tues–Thurs and Sat–Sun 11am–6pm; Fri 1–9pm. Subway: 6 to 77th St.

2 More Manhattan Museums

American Folk Art Museum ⭐⭐   New Yorkers can't stop raving about the brand-new home of the American Folk Art Museum. This ultramodern boutique museum has been called no less than the city's greatest new museum. Not only is it a stunning structure, but it heralds American folk art into the top echelon of museum-worthy art. The modified open-plan interior features a collection of traditional works from the 18th century to those of self-taught artists and craftspeople of the present. A variety of quilts, in particular, make the textiles collection the most popular. The gift-and-book shop is outstanding, filled with one-of-a-kind objects.

45 W. 53rd St. (btwn Fifth and Sixth aves.). © **212/265-1040**. www.folkartmuseum. org. Admission $9 adults, $5 seniors and students, free for children under 12, free to all Fri 6–8pm. Tues–Sun 11:30am–7:30pm. Subway: E or V to 5th Ave. **Eva and Morris Feld Gallery:** 2 Lincoln Sq. (Columbus Ave. between 65th and 66th sts.,). © **212/595-9533**. Free admission. Tues–Sun 11am–7:30pm; Mon 11am–6pm. Subway: 1, 9 to 66th St.

Children's Museum of Manhattan 🌟 Kids

Designed for ages 2 to 12, this museum is strictly hands-on. Interactive exhibits and activity centers encourage self-discovery—and a recent expansion means there's now even more to keep the kids learning. The Time Warner Media Center takes children through the world of animation and helps them produce their own videos. The Body Odyssey is a zany, scientific journey through the body. This isn't just a museum for the 5-and-up set—there are exhibits designed for babies and toddlers, too. The busy schedule also includes daily art classes and storytellers. Look for *Art Inside Out,* an interactive exhibit dedicated to introducing families to art and museums and featuring a video-making installation from photographer and Weimaraner lover William Wegman.

212 W. 83rd St. (btwn Broadway and Amsterdam Ave.). © **212/721-1234**. www. cmom.org. Admission $6 adults and children, $3 seniors. Wed–Sun and school holidays 10am–5pm. Subway: 1, 9 to 86th St.

The Cloisters 🌟

This remote yet lovely branch of the Metropolitan Museum of Art is devoted to the art and architecture of medieval Europe. Atop a cliff overlooking the Hudson River, you'll find a 12th-century chapter house, parts of five cloisters from medieval monasteries, a Romanesque chapel, and a 12th-century Spanish apse brought intact from Europe. Surrounded by gardens, this is the one place on the island that can even approximate the kind of solitude suitable to such a collection. Inside you'll find extraordinary works that include the famed Unicorn tapestries, sculpture, stained glass, ivory, and precious metal work.

The Cloisters are extremely popular, especially in fine weather, so try to schedule your visit on a weekday. A free guided **Highlights Tour** is offered Tuesday through Friday at 3pm and Sunday at noon; gallery talks are also a regular feature.

At the north end of Fort Tryon Park. © **212/923-3700**. www.metmuseum.org. Suggested admission (includes same-day entrance to the Metropolitan Museum of Art) $10 adults, $5 seniors and students, free for children under 12. Nov–Feb Tues–Sun 9:30am–4:45pm; Mar–Oct Tues–Sun 9:30am–5:15pm. Subway: A to 190th St., then a 10-min. walk north along Margaret Corbin Dr., or pick up the M4 bus at the station (1 stop to Cloisters). Bus: M4 Madison Ave. (Fort Tryon Park–The Cloisters).

Cooper-Hewitt National Design Museum 𝄇   Part of the Smithsonian Institution, the Cooper-Hewitt is in the Carnegie Mansion, built by Andrew Carnegie in 1901 and renovated in 1996. Some 11,000 square feet of space is devoted to exhibits that are well conceived, engaging, and educational. Shows are both historic and contemporary in nature, and topics range from "The Work of Charles and Ray Eames: A Legacy of Invention" to "The Architecture of Reassurance: Designing the Disney Theme Parks." Exhibitions scheduled for 2003 include "New Hotels for Global Nomads."

2 E. 91st St. (at Fifth Ave.). 𝄐 212/849-8400. www.si.edu/ndm. Admission $8 adults, $5 seniors and students, free for children under 12, free to all Tues 5–9pm. Tues 10am–9pm; Wed–Sat 10am–5pm; Sun noon–5pm. Subway: 4, 5, 6 to 86th St.

El Museo del Barrio   This is the only museum in America dedicated to Puerto Rican, Caribbean, and Latin American art. The northernmost Museum Mile institution has a permanent exhibit ranging from pre-Columbian artifacts to photographic art and video. The display of *santos de palo,* carved religious figurines, is worth noting, as is "Taíno, Ancient Voyagers of the Caribbean," dedicated to the cultures that Columbus encountered when he landed in the "New World." The changing exhibitions focus on 20th-century artists and contemporary subjects.

1230 Fifth Ave. (at 104th St.). 𝄐 212/831-7272. www.elmuseo.org. Suggested admission $5 adults, $3 seniors and students, free for children under 12. Wed–Sun 11am–5pm. Subway: 6 to 103rd St.

The Frick Collection 𝄇𝄇   Henry Clay Frick could afford to be an avid collector of European art after amassing a fortune in the coke and steel industries at the turn of the 20th century. To house his treasures and himself, he hired Carrère & Hastings to build this 18th-century French-style mansion (1914). This is a living testament to New York's Gilded Age—the interior still feels like a private home graced with beautiful paintings. Come here to see classics by Titian, Rembrandt, Turner, Vermeer, El Greco, and Goya. A highlight is the **Fragonard Room,** graced with the rococo series *The Progress of Love.* The portrait of Montesquieu by Whistler is stunning. Sculpture, furniture, Chinese vases, and French enamels complement the paintings. Included in the admission price, the AcousticGuide audio tour is useful because it allows you to follow your own path rather than a proscribed route. A free 22-minute **video** presentation is screened every half-hour from 10am to 4:30pm (from 1:30 on Sun). In addition to the permanent collection, the Frick mounts temporary exhibitions. Andrea Mantegna's

Descent into Limbo (1468), a magnificent example of Italian Renaissance painting, will be on display in the Enamel Room through August 1, 2003.

1 E. 70th St. (at Fifth Ave.). © **212/288-0700**. www.frick.org. Admission $10 adults, $5 seniors and students. Children under 10 not admitted; children 10–16 must be accompanied by an adult. Tues–Sat 10am–6pm; Sun 1–6pm. Closed all major holidays. Subway: 6 to 68th St./Hunter College.

International Center of Photography ⭐ *Finds*   In late 2000, the ICP—one of the world's premier educators, collectors, and exhibitors of photographic art—relocated from its Museum Mile location to this expanded Midtown facility. The state-of-the-art gallery space is ideal for viewing exhibitions of the museum's 50,000-plus prints as well as visiting shows. The emphasis is on contemporary photographic works, but historically important photographers aren't ignored.

1133 Sixth Ave. (at 43rd St.). © **212/857-0000**. www.icp.org. Admission $9 adults, $6 seniors and students. Tues–Thurs 10am–5pm; Fri 10am–8pm; Sat–Sun 10am–6pm. Subway: B, D, F, V to 42nd St.

Intrepid Sea-Air-Space Museum *Kids*   The most astonishing thing about the aircraft carrier USS *Intrepid* is how it can be simultaneously so big and so small. It's a few football fields long, weighs 40,000 tons, and holds 40 aircraft. In the passageways below, you'll find it isn't quite the roomiest of vessels. Now a National Historic Landmark, the exhibit also includes the destroyer USS *Edson,* and the submarine USS *Growler,* the only intact strategic missile submarine open to the public, as well as a collection of vintage and modern aircraft, including the A-12 Blackbird, the world's fastest spy plane. Kids just love this place. They—and you—can climb inside a replica of a Revolutionary War submarine, sit in an A-6 Intruder cockpit, and follow the progress of America's astronauts as they work in space. There are even navy flight simulators in the Technologies Hall.

New in 2002 is "All Hands on Deck," which teaches kids and adults how things work on ships, plus a new AH-1 Cobra attack helicopter. The action-packed *Intrepid Wings* shows aircraft carrier take-offs and recoveries in the new Allison and Howard Lutnick Theater; the film runs throughout the day. "Remembering 9-11" recalls those lost, both civilians and rescuers. Dress warmly for a winter visit—it's almost impossible to heat an aircraft carrier.

Pier 86 (W. 46th St. at Twelfth Ave.). © **212/245-0072**. www.intrepidmuseum.org. Admission $13 adults; $9 veterans, seniors, and students; $6 children 6–11; $2 children 2–5. $5 extra for flight simulator rides. Apr–Sept Mon–Fri 10am–5pm, Sat–Sun 10am–7pm; Oct–Mar Tues–Sun 10am–5pm. Last admission 1 hr. before closing. Subway: A, C, E to 42nd St./Port Authority. Bus: M42 crosstown.

Lower East Side Tenement Museum 🎭   This museum is a five-story tenement that 10,000 people from 25 countries called home between 1863 and 1935—people who came to the United States looking for the American dream. The museum tells the story of the immigration boom of the late 19th and early 20th centuries, when the Lower East Side was considered the "Gateway to America." The only way to see the museum is by guided tour. Two tenement tours, held on all open days and lasting an hour, offer an exploration of the museum: **Piecing It Together: Immigrants in the Garment Industry,** which focuses on the apartment and the lives of its turn-of-the-century tenants, an immigrant Jewish family named Levine from Poland; and **Getting By: Weathering the Great Depressions of 1873 and 1929,** featuring the homes of the German-Jewish Gumpertz family and the Sicilian-Catholic Baldizzi family, respectively. A guide leads you into each dingy urban time capsule, where several apartments have been restored to their lived-in condition, and recounts the stories of the families who occupied them. Better for kids is the 45-minute, weekends-only **Confino Family Apartment** tour, a living history program geared to families, which allows kids to converse with an interpreter playing teenage immigrant Victoria Confino (ca. 1916); kids can handle whatever they like and try on period clothes.

Tours are limited in number and sell out quickly, so buy tickets in advance online, or over the phone through **Ticketweb** at © **800/965-4827.** The potential acquisition of a neighboring tenement at 99 Orchard St. may change programming, so confirm schedules.

Visitor Center at 90 Orchard St. (at Broome St.). © **212/431-0233**. www.tenement.org. Tenement and walking tours $9 adults, $7 seniors and students; Confino Apartment $8 adults, $6 seniors and students. Tenement tours depart every 40 min. Tues–Fri 1–4pm; Sat–Sun every half hr. 11am–4:45pm. Confino Apartment tour Sat–Sun hourly noon–3pm. Walking tour Apr–Dec Sat–Sun 1 and 2:30pm. Subway: F to Delancey St.; J, M, Z to Essex St.

Morgan Library 🎭🎭 *Finds*   Here's an undiscovered New York treasure, boasting one of the world's most important collections of manuscripts, rare books and bindings, drawings, and personal writings. Among the artifacts on display under glass are illuminated manuscripts (including Gutenberg bibles), a draft of the U.S. Constitution, and handwritten scores by Beethoven, Mozart, and Puccini. The collection of 19th-century drawings—featuring works by Seurat, Degas, Rubens, and others—have an immediacy to them the artists' more well-known paintings often lack.

This rich repository originated as the private collection of turn-of-the-20th-century financier J. Pierpont Morgan and is housed in a Renaissance-style palazzo building (1906) he commissioned from McKim, Mead & White. Morgan's library and study are preserved and worth a look themselves for their architecture (particularly the rotunda) and fittings. The special exhibitions are particularly well chosen and curated.

29 E. 36th St. (at Madison Ave.). ✆ **212/685-0610**. www.morganlibrary.org. Admission $8 adults, $6 students and seniors, free for children 12 and under. Tues–Thurs 10:30am–5pm; Fri 10:30am–8pm; Sat 10:30am–6pm; Sun noon–6pm. Subway: 6 to 33rd St.

Museum of the City of New York   A wide variety of objects—costumes, photographs, prints, maps, dioramas, and memorabilia—trace the history of New York City from its beginnings in the 16th century to its present-day prominence. Two outstanding exhibits are the re-creation of John D. Rockefeller's master bedroom and dressing room, and the space devoted to "Broadway!" a history of New York theater. Kids will love "New York Toy Stories," a permanent exhibit of toys and dolls owned and adored by centuries of New York children. The "Painting the Town: Cityscapes of New York" explores the changing cityscape from 1809 to 1997, and carries new profundity in the wake of September 11, 2001. Check for a schedule of other exhibits as part of the museum's Project September 11.

1220 Fifth Ave. (at 103rd St.). ✆ **212/534-1672**. www.mcny.org. Suggested admission $7 adults; $4 seniors, students, and children; $12 families. Wed–Sat 10am–5pm; Sun noon–5pm. Subway: 6 to 103rd St.

Museum of Jewish Heritage—A Living Memorial to the Holocaust ✩   In the south end of Battery Park City, the Museum of Jewish Heritage occupies a six-sided building designed by architect Kevin Roche, with a six-tier roof alluding to the Star of David and the six million murdered in the Holocaust. The permanent exhibits ("Jewish Life a Century Ago," "The War Against the Jews," and "Jewish Renewal") recount the prewar lives, the horror that destroyed them, and the renewal experienced by European and immigrant Jews in the years from the late 19th century to the present. The museum's power derives from the way it tells that story: through the objects, photographs, documents, and the videotaped testimonies of Holocaust victims, survivors, and their families, all chronicled by Steven Spielberg's Survivors of the Shoah Visual History Foundation. Thursday evenings are dedicated to panel discussions, performances, and music, while Sundays are for family programs and workshops; a film series is also a regular part of the calendar. A new East Wing that will triple the exhibition and events space and add a Family History Center is slated for completion in fall 2003.

While advance tickets are not usually necessary, you may want to buy them to guarantee admission; call ✆ **212/945-0039.** *Money-saving tip:* Check the website for $2-off admission coupon (available at press time), which you'll need to print out and bring with you.

18 First Place (at Battery Place), Battery Park City. ✆ **212/509-6130.** www.mjh nyc.org. Admission $7 adults, $5 seniors and students, free for children under 5. Sun–Wed 10am–5:45pm; Thurs 9am–8pm; Fri and eves of Jewish holidays 10am–3pm. Subway: 4, 5 to Bowling Green.

Neue Galerie New York *(Finds)*

This new museum is dedicated to German and Austrian art and design, with a focus on the early 20th century. The collection features painting, works on paper, decorative arts, and other media from such artists as Klimt, Kokoschka, Kandinsky, Klee, and leaders of the Wiener Werkstätte decorative arts and Bauhaus movements such as Adolf Loos and Mies van der Rohe. Once occupied by Mrs. Cornelius Vanderbilt III, the landmark-designated 1914 Carrère & Hastings building (they built the New York Public Library as well) is worth a look. Cafe Sabarsky is modeled on a Viennese cafe, so museumgoers in need of a snack break can expect a fine linzer torte.

1048 Fifth Ave. (at 86th St.). ✆ **212/628-6200.** www.neuegalerie.org. Admission $10. Fri–Mon 11am–7pm. Subway: 4, 5, 6 to 86th St.

New Museum of Contemporary Art 🖈

This contemporary arts museum has moved closer to the mainstream in recent years, but it's only a safety margin in from the edge as far as most of us are concerned. Expect adventurous and well-curated exhibitions. The **Zenith Media Lounge,** a digital and media arts technology space housing rotating installations, is free to the public.

583 Broadway (btwn Houston and Prince sts.). ✆ **212/219-1222.** www.new museum.org. Admission $6 adults, $3 on Thurs 6–8pm. Free for children 18 and under. Tues–Wed and Fri–Sun noon–6pm (Zenith Media Lounge to 6:30pm); Thurs noon–8pm. Subway: N, R to Prince St.; F, S to Broadway/Lafayette St.

New-York Historical Society ★   Launched in 1804, the New-York Historical Society is a major repository of American history, culture, and art, with a special focus on New York. The grand neoclassical edifice has finally emerged from the renovation tent. Now open on the fourth floor is the Henry Luce III Center for the Study of American Culture, a state-of-the-art study facility and gallery of fine and decorative arts. Also look for paintings from Hudson River School artists Thomas Cole, Asher Durand, and Frederic Church, including Cole's five-part masterpiece, *The Course of Empire.* Also of note are the society's wide-ranging temporary exhibits; a 2002 series of exhibits called "History Responds" were some of the best in the city dealing with the 9/11 terrorist attack and its aftermath. World Trade Center–related exhibits are likely to continue, so interested visitors should check the exhibition schedule.

2 W. 77th St. (at Central Park W.). ✆ 212/873-3400. www.nyhistory.org. Admission $5 adults, $3 seniors and students, free for children 12 and under. Tues–Sun 10am–5pm. Subway: B, C to 81st St.; 1, 9 to 79th St.

South Street Seaport & Museum *Kids*   This landmark district encompasses 11 blocks of historic buildings, a museum, several piers, shops, and restaurants. You can explore most of the Seaport on your own. It's an odd place. The 18th- and 19th-century buildings lining the cobbled streets and alleyways are beautifully restored but have a theme-park air about them, no doubt due to the mall-familiar shops housed within. Pier 17 is a barge converted into a mall, complete with food court and jewelry kiosks.

Despite its commercialism, the Seaport is worth a look. There's a good amount of history to be discovered, most of it around the **South Street Seaport Museum,** a tribute to the sea commerce that once thrived here. In addition to the galleries—which house paintings and prints, ship models, scrimshaw, and nautical designs, as well as exhibitions—there are a number of historic ships berthed at the pier, including the 1911 *Peking* and the 1893 Gloucester fishing schooner *Lettie G. Howard.* The museum also offers a number of guided **walking tours;** call or check **www.southstseaport.org** for details.

At Water and South sts.; museum Visitor Center is at 12 Fulton St. ✆ 212/748-8600 or 212/SEA-PORT. www.southstseaport.org or www.southstreetseaport.com. Museum admission $6 adults, $5 seniors, $4 students, $3 children. Museum Apr–Sept Fri–Wed 10am–6pm, Thurs 10am–8pm; Oct–Mar Wed–Mon 10am–5pm. Subway: 2, 3, 4, 5 to Fulton St. (walk east, or downslope, on Fulton St. to Water St.).

3 Skyscrapers & Other Architectural Highlights

Chrysler Building 🎭🎭   Built as Chrysler Corporation headquarters in 1930, this is perhaps the 20th century's most romantic architectural achievement, especially at night, when the lights in its triangular openings play off its steely crown. As you admire its facade, be sure to note the gargoyles reaching out from the upper floors, looking for all the world like streamline-Gothic hood ornaments. The observation deck closed long ago, but you can visit its lavish ground-floor interior, which is Art Deco to the max.

405 Lexington Ave. (at 42nd St.). Subway: S, 4, 5, 6, 7 to 42nd St./Grand Central.

New York Public Library 🎭🎭 *(Value*   The New York Public Library, adjacent to Bryant Park, and designed by Carrère & Hastings (1911), is one of the country's finest examples of beaux-arts architecture, a majestic structure of white Vermont marble with Corinthian columns and statues. Before climbing the broad flight of steps to the Fifth Avenue entrance, take note of the famous lion sculptures. At Christmastime they don natty wreaths to keep warm.

This library is actually the **Humanities and Social Sciences Library,** one of the research libraries in the New York Public Library system. The interior features **Astor Hall,** with arched marble ceilings and grand staircases. The **Main Reading Rooms** have now reopened after a massive restoration and modernization that brought them back to their stately glory and moved them into the computer age (goodbye, card catalogs!).

You can also check out the **exhibitions;** look for "Drawings by Charles Addams: The Unnatural," "Urban Neighbors: Images of New York City Wildlife," and "New York Eats Out," among other exhibitions in late 2002 to 2003.

Fifth Ave. and 42nd St. ✆ **212/869-8089** (exhibits and events), or 212/661-7220 (library hours). www.nypl.org. Free admission to exhibitions. Mon and Thurs–Sat 10am–6pm; Tues–Wed 11am–7:30pm. Subway: B, D, F, V to 42nd St.; S, 4, 5, 6, 7 to Grand Central/42nd St.

United Nations   The U.N. headquarters occupies 18 acres of international territory along the East River from 42nd to 48th streets. Designed by an international team of architects, the complex along the East River weds the 39-story glass slab Secretariat with the free-form General Assembly on grounds donated by John D. Rockefeller Jr. One hundred eighty nations use the facilities to arbitrate worldwide disputes. **Guided tours** last 45 minutes to an hour and take you to the General Assembly Hall and the Security Council Chamber and introduce the history and activities of the United Nations and its related organizations. Along the tour you'll see donated objects and artwork, including charred artifacts that survived the atomic bombs at Hiroshima and Nagasaki, stained-glass windows by Chagall, a replica of the first *Sputnik,* and a colorful mosaic called *The Golden Rule,* based on a Norman Rockwell drawing, which was a gift from the United States in 1985.

At First Ave. and 46th St. ℂ **212/963-8687.** www.un.org/tours. Guided tours $10.00 adults, $7.50 seniors, $6.50 high school and college students with valid ID, $5 children grades 1-8 $5.50. Children under 5 not permitted. Daily tours every half hr. 9:30am–4:45pm; closed weekends Jan–Feb; limited schedule may be in effect during the general debate (late Sept to mid-Oct). Subway: S, 4, 5, 6, 7 to 42nd St./ Grand Central.

4 Places of Worship

Abyssinian Baptist Church ℛ The most famous of Harlem's more than 400 houses of worship is this Baptist church, founded downtown in 1808 by African-American and Ethiopian merchants. It moved uptown to Harlem in the 1920. Adam Clayton Powell Sr., built it into the largest Protestant congregation in America. His son, Adam Clayton Powell Jr. (for whom the adjoining boulevard was named), carried on his tradition, and also became a U.S. congressman. Abyssinian is now the domain of the Rev. Calvin O. Butts, whom the Chamber of Commerce has declared a "Living Treasure." The Sunday-morning services—at 9 and 11am—offer a wonderful opportunity to experience the Harlem gospel tradition.

132 Odell Clark Place (W. 138th St., btwn Adam Clayton Powell Blvd. and Lenox Ave.). ℂ **212/862-7474.** www.abyssinian.org. Subway: 2, 3, B, C to 135th St.

Cathedral of St. John the Divine ℛ The world's largest Gothic cathedral has been a work in progress since 1892. Its sheer size is amazing enough—a nave that stretches two football fields and a seating capacity of 5,000—but keep in mind that there is no steel structural support. The church is being built using Gothic engineering; blocks of granite and limestone are carved by master masons and their apprentices—which may explain why construction is still ongoing, more than 100 years after it began. Though the seat of the Episcopal Diocese of New York, St. John's embraces an interfaith tradition. Each chapel is dedicated to a different national, ethnic, or social group. You can explore on your own, or on the **Public Tour,** offered 6 days a week; also inquire about periodic (usually twice-monthly) **Vertical Tours,** which take you on a hike up the 11-flight circular staircase to the top, for spectacular views.

1047 Amsterdam Ave. (at 112th St.). 🕿 **212/316-7540,** 212/932-7347 (tour information and reservations), or 212/662-2133 (event information and tickets). www.stjohndivine.org. Suggested admission $2; tour $3; vertical tour $10. Mon–Sat 7am–6pm; Sun 7am–8pm. Tours offered Tues–Sat 11am; Sun 1pm. Worship services Mon–Sat 8 and 8:30am (morning prayer and holy Eucharist), 12:15 and 5:30pm (1st Thurs service 7:15am); Sun 8, 9, and 11am and 6pm; AIDS memorial service 4th Sat of the month at 1pm. Subway: B, C, 1, 9 to Cathedral Pkwy.

St. Patrick's Cathedral   This Gothic white marble–and-stone structure is the largest Catholic cathedral in the United States, as well as the seat of the Archdiocese of New York. Designed by James Renwick, begun in 1859, and consecrated in 1879, St. Patrick's wasn't completed until 1906. The vast cathedral sits a congregation of 2,200; if you don't want to come for Mass, you can pop in between services to get a look at the impressive interior.

Fifth Ave. (btwn 50th and 51st sts.). 🕿 **212/753-2261.** www.ny-archdiocese.org/pastoral/cathedral_about.html. Free admission. Sun–Fri 7am–8:30pm; Sat 8am–8:30pm. Mass Mon–Fri 7, 7:30, 8, and 8:30am, noon, and 12:30, 1, and 5:30pm; Sat 8 and 8:30am, noon, and 12:30 and 5:30pm; Sun 7, 8, 9, and 10:15am (Cardinal's Mass), noon, and 1, 4, and 5:30pm; holy days 7, 7:30, 8, 8:30, 9, 11, and 11:30am, noon, and 12:30, 1, 5:30 and 6:30pm. Subway: B, D, F, V to 47th–50th sts./Rockefeller Center.

Temple Emanu-El   Many of New York's most prominent families are members of this Reform congregation—the first established in New York City. The largest house of Jewish worship in the world is a blend of Moorish and Romanesque styles, symbolizing the mingling of Eastern and Western cultures. The museum houses a collection of Judaica, including Hanukkah lamps ranging from the 14th to the 20th centuries. Three galleries also tell the story of the congregation from 1845 to the present. Free **tours** are given after services Saturday at noon.

1 E. 65th St. (at Fifth Ave.). 🕿 **212/744-1400.** www.emanuelnyc.org. Free admission. Daily 10am–5pm. Services Sun–Thurs 5:30pm; Fri 5:15pm; Sat 10:30am. Subway: N, R to Fifth Ave.; 6 to 68th St.

5 Central Park

In the middle of Gotham, **Central Park** is an 843-acre retreat that provides an escape and tranquilizer for millions of New Yorkers.

While you're here, take advantage of the park's many charms—not the least of which is its layout. Frederick Law Olmsted and Calvert Vaux won a competition with a plan that marries flowing paths with bridges, integrating them into the natural landscape with its rocky outcroppings, man-made lakes, and wooded pockets.

On just about any day, Central Park is crowded with New Yorkers and visitors. On nice days, it's the city's party-central. Families come to play; in-line skaters fly through the crisp air and twirl in front of the band shell; couples stroll or paddle the lake; and just about everybody comes to sunbathe at the first sign of summer. On beautiful days, the crowds are part of the appeal—everybody comes to peel off their urban armor and relax. But even on the most crowded days, there's always somewhere to get away from it all.

ORIENTATION & GETTING THERE   That great green swath in the center of Manhattan is Central Park. It runs from 59th Street (also known as Central Park S.) at the south end to 110th Street at the north end, and from Fifth Avenue on the east side to Central Park West (the equivalent of Eighth Ave.) on the west side. A 6-mile (9.5km) rolling road, **Central Park Drive,** circles the park, and has a lane for bikers, joggers, and in-line skaters. A number of **transverse (crosstown) roads** cross the park at major points—at 65th, 79th, 86th, and 97th streets—but they're built down a level, largely out of view, to minimize intrusion on the bucolic nature of the park.

A number of subway stops and lines serve the park. To reach the southernmost entrance on the west side, take an A, B, C, D, 1, or 9 to 59th Street/Columbus Circle. To reach the southeast corner, take the N, R to Fifth Avenue; from this stop, it's an easy walk to the Information Center in the **Dairy** (© 212/794-6564; open daily 11am–5pm, to 4pm in winter), midpark at about 65th Street. You can ask questions, pick up information, and purchase a park map.

If your time is limited, I suggest entering the park at 72nd or 79th streets (subway: B, C to 72nd St. or 81st St./Museum of Natural History). From here, you can pick up information at the visitor center at **Belvedere Castle** (© 212/772-0210; open Tues–Sun 10am–5pm, to 4pm in winter), midpark at 79th Street. There's also a visitor center at the **Charles A. Dana Discovery Center** (© 212/860-1370; open daily 11am–5pm, to 4pm in winter), at the northeast corner of the park at Harlem Meer, at 110th Street between Fifth and Lenox avenues (subway: 2, 3 to 110th St.).

Food carts and vendors are at all of the park's main gathering points, so finding a bite is never a problem. You'll also find food counters at the **Conservatory,** on the east side of the park, north of the 72nd Street entrance; and at **The Boat House,** on the lake near 72nd Street and Park Drive North (© 212/517-2233).

FOR FURTHER INFORMATION   Call the main number at
℗ **212/360-3444** for recorded info, or 212/310-6600 or 212/628-
1036 to speak to a person. Call ℗ **888/NY-PARKS** for events information. The park also has two websites: The city parks department's
site at **www.centralpark.org**, and the Central Park Conservancy's
site at **www.centralparknyc.org**, each of which features maps and
a listing of attractions and activities. For a park **emergency,** dial
℗ **800/201-PARK,** for park rangers.

SAFETY TIP   Even though the park has the lowest crime rate of
any of the city's precincts, keep your wits about you, especially in the
more remote northern end. It's a good idea to avoid the park entirely
after dark, unless you're heading to one of the restaurants for dinner
or to a SummerStage or Shakespeare in the Park event (see chapter 6), when you should stick with the crowds.

EXPLORING THE PARK

The best way to see Central Park is to wander along its 58 miles
(93km) of pedestrian paths, keeping in mind the following highlights.

Before starting your stroll, stop by the **Information Center** in
the Dairy (℗ **212/794-6464;** open daily 11am–5pm, to 4pm in
winter), midpark in a 19th-century-style building overlooking
Wollman Rink at about 65th Street, to get a good park map and
other information on sights and events.

The southern part of Central Park is more formally designed and
heavily visited than the relatively rugged and remote northern end.
Not far from the Dairy is the **carousel** with 58 hand-carved horses
(℗ **212/879-0244;** open daily 10:30am–6pm, to 5pm in winter;
rides are 90¢); the zoo (see listing for "Central Park Zoo"); and the
Wollman Rink for roller- or ice-skating (see "Activities," below).

The **Mall,** a long walkway lined with elms shading benches and
sculptures, leads to the focal point of Central Park, **Bethesda
Fountain** ✿ (along the 72nd St. transverse road). **Bethesda Terrace**
and its sculpted entryway border a large **lake** where dogs fetch
sticks, boaters glide by, and anglers try their luck. You can rent a
rowboat at or take a gondola ride from **Loeb Boathouse,** on the
eastern end of the lake (see "Activities," below). Boats of another
kind are at **Conservatory Water** (on the east side at 73rd St.), a
stone-walled pond flanked by statues of both **Hans Christian
Andersen** and **Alice in Wonderland.**

Sheep Meadow on the southwestern side of the park is a quiet
zone, where Frisbee throwing and kite flying are as energetic as
things get. Another respite is **Strawberry Fields** ✿, at 72nd Street

on the West Side. This memorial to John Lennon, who was murdered across the street, is a garden centered around an Italian mosaic bearing the title of this Beatle's most famous solo song, and his life-long message: IMAGINE. It's a wonderful place for contemplation.

Bow Bridge, a graceful lacework of cast iron designed by Calvert Vaux, crosses over the lake and leads to the most bucolic area of Central Park, the **Ramble.** This dense 38-acre woodland with spiraling paths, rocky outcroppings, and a stream is the best spot for bird-watching and feeling as if you've discovered an unimaginably leafy forest right in the middle of the city.

North of the Ramble, **Belvedere Castle** 👧 is home to the **Henry Luce Nature Observatory** (✆ 212/772-0210), worth a visit if you're with children. From the castle, set on Vista Rock (the park's highest point at 135 ft.), you can look down on the **Great Lawn,** and the **Delacorte Theater,** home to Shakespeare in the Park (p. 160). The **Shakespeare Garden** south of the theater is scruffy, but it has plants, herbs, and trees mentioned by the playwright. Behind Belvedere Castle is the **Swedish Cottage Marionette Theatre** 👧 (✆ 212/988-9093).

Continue north along the east side of the Great Lawn, parallel to East Drive. Near the glass-enclosed back of the **Metropolitan Museum of Art** 👧👧👧 (p. 117) is **Cleopatra's Needle,** a 69-foot (21m) obelisk erected in Heliopolis around 1475 B.C. It was given to the city by the khedive of Egypt in 1880. North of the 86th Street Transverse Road is the **Jacqueline Kennedy Onassis Reservoir,** named for the former First Lady, who often enjoyed a run along the 1½-mile jogging track that circles the reservoir.

At the northeast end of the park is the **Conservatory Garden** 👧 (at 105th St. and Fifth Ave.), Central Park's formal garden, with a magnificent display of flowers and trees reflected in pools of water. **Harlem Meer** and its boathouse were recently renovated and look beautiful. The boathouse now hosts the **Charles A. Dana Discovery Center,** near 110th Street between Fifth and Lenox avenues (✆ 212/860-1370), where children learn about the environment and borrow fishing poles for catch-and-release at no charge.

GOING TO THE ZOO

Central Park Zoo 👧 *Kids* Because of its small size, the zoo is at its best with its displays of smaller animals. The indoor Tropic Zone is a real highlight, its steamy rain forest home to everything from black-and-white colobus monkeys to emerald tree boa constrictors to a leaf-cutter ant farm; look for the dart poison frog exhibit, which is very cool. So is the large penguin enclosure in the Polar Circle, which is better than the one at San Diego's Sea World. In the Temperate Territory, look for the Asian red pandas (cousins to the black-and-white ones), which look like beautiful raccoons. Lithe sea lions frolic in the central pool area with beguiling style. Despite their pool and piles of ice, the polar bears still look sad.

The entire zoo is good for short attention spans; you can cover the whole thing in 1½ to 3 hours, depending on the size of the crowds and how long you like to linger. It's also very kid-friendly, with lots of well-written and -illustrated placards. For the littlest ones, there's the **Tisch Children's Zoo.** With sheep, llamas, pot-bellied pigs, and more, a real blast for the 5-and-under set.

830 Fifth Ave. (at 64th St., just inside Central Park). ℭ **212/861-6030.** www.wcs.org/zoos. Admission $3.50 adults, $1.25 seniors, 50¢ children 3–12, free for children under 3. Apr–Oct Mon–Fri 10am–5pm; Sat–Sun 10am–5:30pm. Nov–Mar daily 10am–4:30pm. Subway: N, R to Fifth Ave.

ACTIVITIES

The 6-mile (9.5km) rolling road circling the park, **Central Park Drive,** has a lane for bikers, joggers, and in-line skaters. The best time to use it is when the park is closed to traffic: Monday to Friday from 10am to 3pm (except Thanksgiving to New Year's) and 7 to 10pm. It's also closed from 7pm Friday to 6am Monday, but when the weather is nice, the crowds can be hellish.

BIKING   Off-road mountain biking isn't permitted; stay on Central Park Drive or your bike may be confiscated by park police.

You can rent bikes as well as tandems in Central Park at the **Loeb Boathouse,** midpark near 72nd Street and Park Drive North, just in from Fifth Avenue (ℭ **212/517-2233** or 212/517-3623), for $9 to $20 an hour, with a selection of kids' bikes, cruisers, tandems, and the like ($200 deposit required); at **Metro Bicycles,** 1311 Lexington Ave., at 88th Street (ℭ **212/427-4450**), for about $7 an hour, or $35 a day; and at **Toga Bike Shop,** 110 West End Ave., at 64th Street (ℭ **212/799-9625;** www.togabikes.com), for $30 a day. No matter where you rent, be prepared to leave a credit-card deposit.

BOATING   From March through November, gondola rides and rowboat rentals are available at the **Loeb Boathouse,** midpark near 74th Street and Park Drive North, just in from Fifth Avenue (ℭ **212/517-2233** or 212/517-3623). Rowboats are $10 for the first hour, $2.50 every 15 minutes thereafter, and a $30 deposit is required; reservations are accepted but usually unnecessary.

HORSE-DRAWN CARRIAGE RIDES   At the entrance to the park at 59th Street and Central Park South, you'll see a line of **horse-drawn carriages** waiting to take passengers through the park or along certain streets. You won't need me to tell you how forlorn most of these horses look—skip it.

ICE-SKATING   Wollman Rink 🐦, on the east side of the park between 62nd and 63rd streets (© **212/439-6900;** www.wollman skatingrink.com), is the city's best outdoor skating spot, more spacious than the rink at Rockefeller Center. It's open for skating from mid-October to mid-April, depending on the weather. Rates are $7 for adults, $3.50 for seniors and kids under 12, and skate rental is $3.50; lockers are available (locks are $6.75).

IN-LINE SKATING   Central Park is the city's most popular place for blading. You can rent skates for $20 a day from **Blades Board and Skate,** 120 W. 72nd St., between Broadway and Columbus Avenue (© **212/787-3911;** www.blades.com). Wollman Rink (see above) also rents in-line skates for park use at similar rates.

PLAYGROUNDS   Nineteen playgrounds are scattered through the park, perfect for jumping, sliding, swinging, and digging. At Central Park West and 81st Street is the **Diana Ross Playground** 🐦, voted the city's best by *New York* magazine. Also on the west side is the **Spector Playground,** at 85th Street and Central Park West, and, farther north, the **Wild West Playground** at 93rd Street. On the east side is the **Rustic Playground,** at 67th Street and Fifth Avenue, rife with islands, bridges, and slides; and the **Pat Hoffman Friedman Playground,** behind the Metropolitan Museum of Art at East 79th Street, is geared toward older toddlers.

6 Affordable Sightseeing Tours

Reservations are required on some tours listed below, but even if they're not, call ahead to confirm prices, times, and meeting places.

HARBOR CRUISES

Circle Line Sightseeing Cruises 🐦🐦   Circle Line is the only tour company that circumnavigates the entire 35 miles (56km) around Manhattan, and I love this ride. The **Full Island** cruise takes 3 hours and passes by the Statue of Liberty, Ellis Island, the Brooklyn Bridge, the United Nations, Yankee Stadium, the George Washington Bridge, and more. The panorama is riveting, and the commentary isn't bad. The big boats are basic but fine, with lots of deck room for everybody. Snacks, soft drinks, coffee, and beer are available onboard for purchase.

If 3 hours is more than you can handle, go for either the 1½-hour **Semi-Circle** or **Sunset/Harbor Lights** cruise, both of which show you the highlights of the skyline. There's also a 1-hour **Seaport Liberty** version that sticks close to the south end of the island. The kids might like **The Beast,** a speedboat ride offered in summer only.

In addition, a number of adults-only **Live Music and DJ Cruises** sail from the seaport from May through September ($20–$40 per person). Depending on the night, you can groove to the sounds of jazz, Latin, gospel, dance tunes, or blues as you sail along.

Departing from Pier 83, at W. 42nd St. and Twelfth Ave. Also departing from Pier 16 at South St. Seaport, 207 Front St. © 212/563-3200. www.circleline.com, www. ridethebeast.com, and www.seaportmusiccruises.com. Sightseeing cruises $13–$25 adults, $11–$20 seniors, $7–$12 children 12 and under. Subway to Pier 83: A, C, E to 42nd St. Subway to Pier 16: J, M, Z, 2, 3, 4, 5 to Fulton St.

SPECIALTY TOURS
MUSEUMS & CULTURAL ORGANIZATIONS

The **Municipal Art Society** (© 212/439-1049 or 212/935-3960; www.mas.org) offers excellent historical and architectural walking tours aimed at intelligent, individualistic travelers. A qualified guide gives insights into the buildings, neighborhoods, and history. Topics range from the history of Greenwich Village to "Mies and the Moderns," examining the architectural legacy of Mies van der Rohe. Weekday walking tours cost $12; weekend tours cost $15. Reservations may be required depending on the tour, so call ahead. A full schedule is available online or by calling © 212/439-1049.

The **92nd Street Y** (© 212/415-5500 or 212/415-5628; www.92ndsty.org) offers a variety of walking and bus tours. Subjects can range from "Diplomat for a Day at the U.N." to "Secrets of the Chelsea Hotel," from "Artists of the Meat-Packing District" to "Jewish Harlem." Prices range from $20 to $60 (sometimes more for bus tours), but may include ferry rides, afternoon tea, dinner, or whatever suits the program. Guides are experts on their subjects. Advance registration is required for all walking and bus tours. Check the website for tours that might interest you.

INDEPENDENT OPERATORS

One of the most highly praised sightseeing organizations in New York is **Big Onion Walking Tours** (© 212/439-1090; www.big onion.com). Big Onion guides (all hold degrees in history) peel back the layers of history to reveal the city's secrets. The 2-hour

Value Absolutely Free Walking Tours

A number of organizations and Business Improvement Districts (BIDs) offer guided walks of their neighborhoods. These freebies are worth seeking out:

The **Municipal Art Society** (ⓒ **212/935-3960;** www.mas. org) offers a free walking tour of Grand Central Terminal on Wednesday at 12:30pm, which meets at the information booth on the Grand Concourse. The **Grand Central Partnership** (ⓒ **212/697-1245**) runs its own free tour every Friday at 12:30pm, meeting outside the station in front of the Whitney Museum at Philip Morris gallery, at 42nd Street and Park Avenue. Call to confirm the schedule and meeting spot before you set out to meet either tour.

The Alliance for Downtown New York offers a free 90-minute **Wall Street Walking Tour** 𝕲 every Thursday and Saturday at noon, rain or shine. This guided tour explores the history and architecture of the nation's first capital and the world center of finance. Stops include the New York Stock Exchange, Trinity Church, Federal Hall National Monument, and other sites. Tours meet on the steps of the U.S. Customs House at 1 Bowling Green (subway: 4, 5 to

tours are offered mostly on weekends, and subjects include "The Bowery," "Presidential New York," "Historic Harlem," and the ever-popular "Multiethnic Eating Tour" of the Lower East Side, where you munch on everything from dim sum and dill pickles to fresh mozzarella. Tour prices range from $12 to $18 for adults, $10 to $16 for students and seniors. No reservations are necessary, but Big Onion *recommends that you call to verify schedules.*

All tours from **Joyce Gold History Tours of New York** 𝕲 (ⓒ 212/242-5762; www.nyctours.com) are offered by Joyce Gold herself, an instructor of history at New York University and the New School, who has been conducting walks around New York since 1975. Her tours can cut to the core of this town; Joyce is full of fascinating stories about Manhattan and its people. Tours are arranged around themes like "The Colonial Settlers of Wall Street," "The Genius and Elegance of Gramercy Park," "Downtown Graveyards," and "TriBeCa: The Creative Explosion." Tours are offered most weekends March to December and last from 2 to 4 hours, and the

Bowling Green). Reservations are not required (unless you're a group), but you can call ✆ **212/606-4064** or visit **www.downtownny.com** to confirm the schedule.

The **Orchard Street Bargain District Tour** (✆ **888/825-8374** or 212/226-9010; www.lowereastsideny.com) explores the history and retail culture of the Lower East Side. This is a good bet for bargain-hunters, who will learn about the old-world shops and newer outlet stores in this discount-shopping destination. The free tours are given Sunday at 11am from April to December, rain or shine; no reservation is required. Meet up with the guide in front of Katz's Delicatessen, 205 E. Houston St., at Ludlow Street.

If you're looking to tour a specific neighborhood, call **Big Apple Greeter** (✆ **212/669-8159**; www.bigapplegreeter.org). This organization consists of specially trained New Yorkers who volunteer to take visitors around town for a free 2- to 4-hour tour of a neighborhood. Reservations must be made at least 1 week ahead of your arrival. Big Apple Greeter is also well suited to accommodate travelers with disabilities.

price is $12 per person; no reservations are required. Private tours can be arranged year-round for individuals or groups.

Behind the scenes is the focus of **Adventure on a Shoestring** 🏃🏃 (✆ **212/265-2663**), which offers 90-minute public walking tours on weekends (and some weekdays and holidays) year-round for just $5. Howard Goldberg has provided unique views of New York since 1963, exploring Manhattan's neighborhoods with a breezy, man-of-the-people style. Tours run the gamut from historical and architectural walks of artsy SoHo, elegant Sutton Place, or little-known Roosevelt Island to themed walks. It's one of the best budget bargains in New York. Walks go on regardless of the weather. Call for reservations.

Would you like to cruise by Monica and Chandler's apartment building? How about the courthouse where the prosecutors of *Law & Order* fight the good fight? **On Location Tours** (✆ **212/ 334-0492** or 212/935-0168; www.sceneontv.com) offers narrated minibus tours on their **Manhattan TV Tour;** tickets are $20 for adults, $10 for kids 6 to 9, free for 5 and under. Or, if you want to see Carrie Bradshaw's Big Apple, take the 2½-hour *Sex in the City* **Tour;** tickets cost $25. There's a 3-hour *Sopranos* **Tour** that will take you to New Jersey for $30. Reservations are a must.

Recommended by the Harlem Travel and Tourism Association, **A La Carte New York Tours** (© **212/828-7360;** www.alacartecity. com) offers a slate of walking, bus, architecture, jazz, Apollo Theatre, and gospel tours of the Upper Manhattan neighborhood. Prices run from $15 to $75, depending on the options you choose. All guides are licensed and extremely knowledgeable.

7 Talk of the Town: Free TV Tapings

The trick to getting tickets for TV tapings is to be from out of town. Visitors have a better chance than we New Yorkers; producers are gun-shy about filling their audiences with obnoxious locals and see everybody who's not from New York as being from the heartland—their target TV audience.

If your heart's set on getting tickets to a show, request them as early as possible—6 months ahead isn't too early. You're usually asked to send a postcard. Always include the number of tickets you want, your preferred dates of attendance (be as flexible as you can), and your address *and* phone number. Tickets are always free. And even if you send in your request early, don't be surprised if tickets arrive as late as 1 or 2 weeks before tape date.

If you come to town without tickets, all hope is not lost. Because they know that not every ticket holder will make it, many studios give out standby tickets the day of taping. If you can get up early and don't mind standing in line for a couple (or a few) hours, you may get one. Only one standby ticket per person is allowed, so everybody who wants one has to stand in line. Standby ticket holders are seated only after the regular ticket holders are in. Still, chances are good.

For information on getting tickets for other shows taped in the Big Apple, call the NYCVB at © **212/484-1222.** And remember—you don't need a ticket to be on the *Today* show.

The Daily Show with Jon Stewart Comedy Central's irreverent, often hilarious mock newscast tapes every Monday through Thursday at 5:45pm, at 513 W. 54th St. Make your advance ticket requests by phone at © **212/586-2477,** or check with them for any cancellation tickets for the upcoming week; the line is open Monday through Thursday from 10:30am to 4pm for tickets.

Good Morning America   Fans of ABC's weekday morning show can join Diane Sawyer and Charlie Gibson in their street-facing studio at Broadway and 44th Street as part of the live audience. To witness the 7 to 9am broadcast, fill out the online request at www. abcnews.go.com/sections/GMA (click on "GMA Tickets"), or call ☎ **212/580-5176** during business hours.

Late Night with Conan O'Brien   Conan tix might not quite have the cachet of a Dave ticket, but they're a very hot commodity. Tapings are Tuesday through Friday at 5:30pm (arrive by 4:45pm), and you must be 16 or older to attend. You can reserve up to four tickets by calling ☎ **212/664-3056.** Standby tickets are distributed the day of taping at 9am outside 30 Rockefeller Plaza, on the 49th Street side of the building (under the NBC Studios awning).

The Late Show with David Letterman   Here's the most in-demand TV ticket in town. Tapings are Monday through Thursday at 5:30pm (arrive by 4:15pm), with a second taping Thursday at 8pm (arrive by 6:45pm). You must be 18 or older to attend. Send your postcard 6 to 9 months in advance (two tickets max; one request only, or all will be disregarded), to *Late Show* Tickets, Ed Sullivan Theater, 1697 Broadway, New York, NY 10019. You can also register at www.cbs.com/latenight/lateshow (click on "Get Tickets") to be notified of tickets that may become available for specific dates you select over the next 3 months. On tape days, there are no standby lines; call ☎ **212/247-6497** at 11am for up to two standby tickets; start dialing early, because the machine will kick in as soon as all standbys are gone. If you do get through, you may have to answer a trivia question about the show to score tickets.

Live! with Regis and Kelly   Tapings with Regis Philbin and Kelly Ripa are Monday through Friday at 9am at the ABC Studios at 7 Lincoln Sq. (Columbus Ave. and W. 67th St.) on the Upper West Side. You must be 10 or older to attend (under 18s must be accompanied by a parent). Send your postcard (four tickets max) at least a *full year* in advance to *Live!* Tickets, Ansonia Station, P.O. Box 230777, New York, NY 10023-0777 (☎ **212/456-3054**). Standby tickets are sometimes available. Arrive at the studio no later than 7am and request a standby number.

Montel Williams Show   Order tickets by calling ☎ **212/989-8101.** Shows typically tape on Wednesday and Thursday at 11:30am, 1:30pm, and 3:30pm. You must be 18 or older to attend.

The Ricki Lake Show   Tickets can be requested by calling ℂ **800/ GO-RICKI,** or filling out the online form at www.ricki.com. You can also use this line, or register on the website, to volunteer yourself as a guest for shows such as "Stop Being Naked Around My Man!" You must be 18 or older to attend.

Saturday Night Live   SNL tapings are Saturday at 11:30pm from fall to late spring (arrival time 10pm); there's also a dress rehearsal at 8pm (arrival time 7pm). You must be 16 or older to attend. Tickets are so in demand that the lottery system for advance tickets is usually suspended. However, you can try for standby tickets on the day of the taping, which are distributed at 7am outside 30 Rockefeller Plaza, on the 49th Street side of the building, on a first-come, first-served basis. If you want to try your luck with advanced tickets, call ℂ **212/664-3056** *as far in advance of your arrival in New York as possible* to determine the current ticket-request procedure.

The *Today* Show   Anybody can be on TV with Katie, Matt, and weatherman Al Roker. All you have to do is show up outside *Today's* glass-walled studio at Rockefeller Center, on the southwest corner of 49th Street and Rockefeller Plaza. Tapings are Monday through Friday from 7am to 10am, but come at the crack of dawn if your heart's set on being in front. Who knows? If it's a nice day, you may even get to chat with Katie, Matt, or Al in a segment. Come extra early to attend a Friday Summer Concert Series show.

The View   ABC's popular girl-power gabfest tapes live Monday through Friday at 11am (ticket holders must arrive by 9:30am). Requests, which should be made 12 to 16 weeks in advance, can be submitted online (www.abc.go.com/theview) or via postcard to Tickets, *The View,* 320 W. 66th St., New York, NY 10023. Because exact date requests are not usually accommodated, try standby: Arrive at the studio before 10am and put your name on the standby list; earlier is better, because tickets are handed out on a first-come, first-served basis. You must be 18 or older to attend.

8 Shopping Highlights for Bargain Hunters

THE TOP SHOPPING STREETS & NEIGHBORHOODS
CHINATOWN
Don't expect to find the purchase of a lifetime, but there's some quality browsing. The fish markets along Canal, Mott, Mulberry, and Elizabeth streets are fun for their bustle and exotica. Dispersed

---

(Finds) New York's Most Dramatic Bookstore

At 80 years old, the **Drama Book Shop** (© 212/944- 0595; www.dramabookshop.com) at 250 W. 40th St. (btw. Eighth & Ninth aves.) is hardly a newcomer. But since its move from cramped, second-floor digs in Times Square at the end of 2001, the theatrical bookstore has reinvented itself in a large new space, complete with the **Arthur Seelen Theatre,** an in-house performance venue, complete with a resident theatre company, Back House Productions. The theatre also hosts discussions and book signings with members of the theatre community, ranging from playwright Tina Howe to critic Mel Gussow.

Offering thousands of plays, from translations of Greek classics to this season's hits hot off the presses, the shop also offers books, magazines and newspapers on the craft and business of the theatre, ranging from biographies, criticism, directing, makeup, and lighting to how to get an agent. The shop is open from 10am to 8pm Monday through Saturday, and from noon to 6 on Sundays.

---

among them (especially along **Canal St.**), you'll find a mind-boggling collection of knock-off sunglasses and watches, backpacks, leather goods, and souvenirs. It's a fun browse, but don't expect quality, and be sure to bargain before you buy. **Mott Street,** between Pell Street and Chatham Square, boasts the most interesting off-Canal shopping, with an antiques shop or two among the storefronts selling blue-and-white Chinese dinnerware. The highlight is the **Pearl River** Chinese emporium on Broadway just north of Canal St. (© 212/431-4770; www.pearlriver.com), and with a second location on Grand Street between Mott and Mulberry streets.

THE LOWER EAST SIDE

The bargains aren't what they used to be in the **Historic Orchard Street Shopping District**—which runs from Houston to Canal along Allen, Orchard, and Ludlow streets, spreading outward along both sides of Delancey Street—but prices on leather bags, shoes, luggage, and fabrics on the bolt are good. Be aware that the hard sell on Orchard Street can be hard to take. Still, the district is a nice place to discover a part of New York that's disappearing. Come during the week, because most stores are Jewish-owned and close Friday afternoon and all day Saturday. Sunday tends to be a madhouse.

The artists and other trendsetters who have been turning this neighborhood into a bastion of hip have added a cutting edge to its shopping scene. You'll find a growing crop of alterna-shops south of Houston and north of Grand Street, between Allen and Clinton streets to the east and west, specializing in up-to-the-minute fashions and club clothes for 20-somethings, plus funky retro furnishings, Japanese toys, and offbeat items. Before you browse, stop into the **Lower East Side Visitor Center,** 261 Broome St., between Orchard and Allen streets (**© 888/825-8374** or 212/226-9010; subway: F to Delancey St.), for a guide that includes vendors both old-world and new. Or you can see the list online at www.lowereastsideny.com. *Money-saving tip:* Check the website or call the center for details about the **Go East card,** which will score cardholders discounts at more than 70 neighborhood merchants.

SOHO

People love to complain about super-fashionable SoHo—it's become too trendy, too tony, too Mall of America. True, **J. Crew** is one of the big names that has supplanted the artists and galleries that used to inhabit the cast-iron buildings. But SoHo is still one of the best shopping neighborhoods in the city, and fun to browse. You'll find few bargains, as merchants have to cover those high rents. This is the epicenter of cutting-edge couture, with designers like Anna Sui and British legend Vivienne Westwood in residence. Most of these shops are likely to be *way* out of your price range, but the streets are full of unique boutiques, some hawking more affordable wares, and the eye candy is tops. End-of-season sales, when racks are cleared for incoming merchandise, are the best bet if you want to buy.

SoHo's prime shopping grid is from Broadway east to Sullivan Street and from Houston down to Grand Street.

THE EAST VILLAGE

The East Village remains the standard of bohemian hip, and is one of the city's best neighborhoods for wallet-friendly shopping. The easiest subway access is the 6 train to Astor Place, which lets you out by **Kmart,** and is just across from **Astor Wines & Spirits,** which is an excellent discount stop for bargain-hunting oenophiles; from here, it's just a couple blocks east to the prime hunting grounds.

East 9th Street ✿ between Second Avenue and Avenue A has become one of my favorite shopping strips in the city. Lined with an increasingly smart collection of boutiques, it proves that the East Village isn't just for kids anymore. Up-and-coming designers sell affordably priced fashions for women here, and a branch of **Eileen Fisher,** 314 E. 9th St. (© **212/529-5715;** www.eileenfisher.com), caters to bargain hunters by serving as the chain's outlet store. This is also an excellent stretch for gifts and little luxuries. Most of these shops don't open until around 1pm, and most are closed Mondays.

If it's strange, illegal, or funky, it's probably available on **St. Marks Place,** 8th Street, running east from Third Avenue to Avenue A. It's like a permanent street market, with countless T-shirt and jewelry stands.

GREENWICH VILLAGE

The West Village is great for browsing and gift shopping. Specialty book- and record stores, antiques and crafts shops, and gourmet food markets dominate. Head for **8th Street** between Broadway and Sixth Avenue for trendy footwear and affordable fashions, and the stretch of Broadway from 8th Street south to Houston, which is anchored by **Urban Outfitters** and dotted with skate and sneaker shops.

The prime drag for strolling is **Bleecker Street,** where you'll find lots of leather shops and record stores interspersed with interesting, artsy boutiques. **Christopher Street,** just east of Seventh Avenue, is fun and loaded with Village character. Serious browsers should also wander west of **Seventh Avenue,** where boutiques are tucked among the brownstones, and along **Hudson Street.**

THE FLATIRON DISTRICT & UNION SQUARE

The epitome of uptown fashion a hundred years ago, **Sixth Avenue** from 14th to 23rd streets has grown into the city's discount shopping center. Superstores and off-pricers fill the cast-iron buildings: **Filene's Basement, TJ Maxx,** and **Bed Bath & Beyond,** are all at 620 Sixth Ave., and **Old Navy** is next door; **Barnes & Noble** is just a couple of blocks away at Sixth Avenue near 22nd Street.

HERALD SQUARE & THE GARMENT DISTRICT

Herald Square—where 34th Street, Sixth Avenue, and Broadway converge—is dominated by **Macy's,** the self-proclaimed world's biggest department store, and other famous-name shopping. At Sixth Avenue and 33rd Street is the **Manhattan Mall** (© **212/ 465-0500;** www.manhattanmallny.com), home to mall standards such as Foot Locker, LensCrafters, and Radio Shack.

A long block over on Seventh Avenue, not much goes on in the Garment District. This is, however, where you'll find that unique New York experience, the sample sale. You won't know where to find them if you just walk the streets, so check **www.nysale.com**; **www. nymetro.com** also regularly announces sample sales.

TIMES SQUARE & THE THEATER DISTRICT

This neighborhood has become increasingly family-oriented: with the **Virgin Megastore; Gap** at 42nd and Broadway; the **Toys "R" Us** flagship on Broadway and 44th Street (✆ **800/869-7787**), with its own Ferris wheel; and the **E-Walk** retail and entertainment complex on 42nd Street between Seventh and Eighth avenues, overflowing with mall-familiar shops like the **Museum Company.**

West 47th Street between Fifth and Sixth avenues is the city's **Diamond District.** More than 90% of the diamonds sold in the United States come through this neighborhood, so there are some great deals if you're in the market for a nice rock or a piece of fine jewelry. The street is lined with showrooms; be ready to wheel and deal with the largely Hasidic dealers, who offer quite a juxtaposition to the crowds. For an introduction to the district, visit **www.47th-street.com**. If you're in the market for wedding rings, head for Herman Rotenberg's **1,873 Unusual Wedding Rings,** 4 W. 47th St., booth 86 (✆ **800/877-3874** or 212/944-1713; www.unusual weddingrings.com).

Shopper's alert: You'll notice a wealth of electronics stores throughout the neighborhood, many with GOING OUT OF BUSINESS sales. These guys have been going out of business since the Stone Age. That's the bait and switch; pretty soon you've spent too much money for not enough MP3 player. If you want to check out what they have, go in knowing what the going price is on what you want. You can make a good deal if you know exactly what the market is, but these guys will be happy to suck you dry given half a chance.

FIFTH AVENUE & 57TH STREET

The heart of Manhattan retail is the corner of Fifth and 57th. Home to high-ticket names like Gucci, Chanel, and Cartier, this tony neighborhood has long been the province of the über-rich. In recent years, however, both Fifth Avenue and 57th Street have become more accessible as wallet-friendlier retailers such as the **NBA Store,** 666 Fifth Ave., at 52nd Street (✆ **212/515-NBA1;** www.nbastore. com), have arrived. You'll also find kid wonderland **FAO Schwarz,** 767 Fifth Ave., at 58th Street (✆ **212/644-9400;** www.fao.com), as well as a number of national names such as **Banana Republic** and **Liz Claiborne,** which have further democratized Fifth by setting up their flagships along the avenue.

High traffic flow and real estate costs keep prices up, and the flagships tend to send their sale merchandise to lower-profile shops. Still, the window-shopping is classic. And if you, like Holly Golightly, always dreamed of shopping at **Tiffany & Co.,** 727 Fifth Ave., at 57th Street (✆ **212/755-8000;** www.tiffany.com), the world's most famous jewelry store is worth a stop. The multilevel showroom is so full of tourists that it's easy to browse. If you want to indulge, head upstairs to the gift level, where you'll find a number of items to suit a $75 budget. Everything comes packaged in the classic little blue box with an impeccable white ribbon.

THE BEST DEPARTMENT STORES FOR BARGAIN HUNTERS

Bloomingdale's   Bloomie's is more accessible than Barneys or Bergdorf's and more affordable than Saks, but still has the pizzazz that Macy's and Lord & Taylor now largely lack. Taking up a city block, it has just about anything you could want, from clothing (both designer and everyday basics) and fragrances to a full range of housewares. The frequent sales can yield unbeatable bargains. 1000 Third Ave. (Lexington Ave. at 59th St.). ✆ 212/705-2000. www.bloomingdales. com. Subway: 4, 5, 6 to 59th St.

Century 21 *(Value*   Despite suffering severe damage in the terrorist attacks on the World Trade Center, Century 21 reopened its doors last March. The designer discount store is back, and better than ever. Prices on designer goods are 40% to 70% off what you would pay at a department store or designer boutique. Don't think that $250 Armani blazer is a bargain? Look again at the tag—the retail price on it is upward of $800. This is the place to find those $5 Liz Claiborne tees, or the $50 Bally loafers—not to mention underwear, hosiery, and ties so cheap that they're almost free. Kids' clothes, linens, and housewares are also on sale. The price you used to pay to get these deals was wrestling with the aggressive, ever-present throngs, but it's hard to say what the ambience will be now. Avoid the weekday lunch hour and Saturdays. 22 Cortlandt St. (btwn Broadway and Church St.). ✆ 212/227-9092. www.c21stores.com. Subway: 1, 2, 3, 4, 5, M to Fulton St.; A, C to Broadway/Nassau St.; E to Chambers St.

Kmart   Kmart is so out of place in the East Village that it has turned the mundane into marvelous camp: Japanese kids stare at gargantuan boxes of detergent as if they were Warhol designed, and pierced locals navigate the name-brand maze alongside stroller-pushing housewives. Kitsch value aside, this multilevel store is a great bet for discount prices on practical items, from socks to shampoo. You'll also find a pharmacy, a food department where you can stock up on Cocoa Puffs and other kitchen supplies (sale prices on snack foods are rock-bottom), and a photo studio. 770 Broadway (btwn 8th and 9th sts.). ✆ 212/673-1540. Subway: 6 to Astor Place.

Lord & Taylor   Okay, so maybe Lord & Taylor isn't the first place you'd go for a vinyl miniskirt, but I like its understated, elegant mien. Long known as an excellent source of women's dresses and coats, L&T stocks all the major labels for men and women, with a special emphasis on American designers. Their house-brand clothes (khakis, blazers, turtlenecks, and summer sportswear) are well made and a great bargain. Sales, especially around holidays, can be stellar. The store is big enough to have a good selection but doesn't overwhelm. The Christmas window displays are an annual delight. 424 Fifth Ave. (at 39th St.). ✆ 212/391-3344. www.lordandtaylor.com. Subway: F, V to 42nd St.

Macy's   A four-story sign on the side of the building trumpets "MACY'S, THE WORLD'S LARGEST STORE"—hard to dispute, since the 10-story behemoth covers an entire block. Macy's is a hard place to shop: The size is unmanageable, the service is dreadful, the din from the crowds on the ground floor alone will kick your migraine into action. But they do sell *everything*. What's more, sales run constantly, so bargains are guaranteed. And the store provides personal guides/shoppers at no charge. At Christmastime, come as late as you can manage (the store is usually open until midnight in the final shopping days).

Tips for sale seekers: One-day sales usually occur on Wednesdays and sometimes on Saturdays. Call the store when you arrive to find out whether your visit overlaps with one. Or check the *New York Times* for full-page advertisements, which sometimes include coupons for additional 10% to 15% discounts. At Herald Sq., W. 34th St. and Broadway. ✆ 212/695-4400. www.macys.com. Subway: B, D, F, N, Q, R, 1, 2, 3, 9 to 34th St.

6

New York City After Dark

For the latest, most comprehensive arts and entertainment listings, *Time Out New York* (www.timeoutny.com) is my favorite source; a new issue hits newsstands every Thursday. The free *Village Voice* (www.villagevoice.com) is available late Tuesday downtown and early Wednesday in the rest of the city. The *New York Times* (www.nytoday.com) features terrific entertainment coverage, particularly in the Friday "Weekend" section. Other sources are "Goings on About Town" in the *New Yorker* (www.newyorker.com); and *New York* magazine (www.newyorkmag.com). *New York*'s www.nymetro.com site is an excellent Web source.

1 The Theater Scene

Nobody does theater better than New York. No other city—not even London—has a scene with so much breadth and depth, with so many alternatives. Broadway gets the most ink and airplay: This is where you'll find the big stage productions, from crowd-pleasers like *Phantom of the Opera* and *42nd Street* to newer phenomena like *The Lion King* and *The Producers*. But today's scene thrives beyond the bounds of Broadway.

Despite this vitality, plays and musicals close all the time, often with little warning. Before you arrive, or even once you get here, check the **publications** and **websites** at the beginning of this chapter to get an idea of what you might like to see. One source is the **Broadway Line** (℃ **888/BROADWAY** or 212/302-4111; www.broadway.org), where you can obtain details and descriptions on current shows, hear about special offers and discounts, and can be transferred to TeleCharge or Ticketmaster to buy tickets. There's also **NYC/Onstage** (℃ **212/768-1818;** www.tdf.org), providing the same kind of service for Broadway and Off-Broadway productions.

Value   How to Save on Theater Tickets

For Advance Planners You might be able to purchase **reduced-price theater tickets** over the phone (or at the box office) by joining an online theater club. Membership is free and can garner you discounts of up to 50% on select Broadway and Off-Broadway shows. The deals are available to club members at **Broadway.com** (www.broadway.com), **Playbill Online** ⚘ (www.playbill.com or www.playbillclub. com), and **TheaterMania** (www.theatermania.com).

You can sign up with the **Hit Show Club** (✆ 212/581-4211; www.hitshowclub.com), a free subscription club that offers its members discounts to Broadway and Off-Broadway shows. Once you sign up, you can find offers online or stop by their offices at 630 Ninth Ave. (between 44th and 45th sts., 8th floor; open Mon–Fri 9am–4pm), and pick up discount coupons for theater, dining, and attractions.

For In-Towners The best deal on same-day tickets for Broadway and Off-Broadway shows is the **Times Square Theatre Centre** ⚘⚘⚘, better known as the **TKTS** booth run by the nonprofit Theatre Development Fund at Duffy Square, 47th Street and Broadway (open 3–8pm for evening performances, 10am–2pm for Wed and Sat matinees, from 11am on Sun for all performances). Tickets for that day's performances are usually offered at half-price, with a few reduced 25%, plus a $2.50 per ticket service charge. Boards outside the ticket windows list available shows; you're unlikely to find the biggest hits, but most other shows turn up. Only cash and traveler's checks are accepted (no credit cards). There's often a line, so show up early and be prepared to wait—but the crowd is part of the fun. If you don't have a specific show in mind, you can go later in the day and something is always available.

Offering the same discounts is the **TKTS Downtown Theatre Centre,** at the corner of Front and John streets at

TOP TICKET-BUYING TIPS

BEFORE YOU LEAVE HOME   If you want to guarantee yourself a seat at a particular show, it's almost impossible to get around paying full price. (The only exception is to register for one or more of the online theater clubs, which offer advance-purchase discounts the South Street Seaport (open Mon–Sat 11am–6pm, Sun 11am–3:30pm; subway: 2, 3, 4, 5, E, J, Z, M to Fulton St.; A, C to Broadway-Nassau). All the same policies apply. The advantages to coming down here are that the lines are generally shorter, and matinee tickets are sold one day in advance, so you can plan ahead.

Visit **www.tdf.org** or call **NYC/Onstage** at © **212/768-1818** and press "8" for the latest TKTS information.

Many shows, particularly long-running ones, offer **twofers,** which allow you to purchase two tickets for the price of one for certain performances. You can find these coupons all over the city: in hotel lobbies, in shops, even at restaurant cash registers. They are always available at the **Times Square Visitors Center,** 1560 Broadway, between 46th and 47th streets (© **212/768-1560**); at the **NYCVB Visitor Information Center** at 810 Seventh Ave., between 52nd and 53rd streets (© **212/484-1222**); and at the information window on the main concourse of **Grand Central Terminal,** near the ticket-purchase windows directly across from the information kiosk.

For Theater Fans Willing to Go the Extra Mile Broadway shows sometimes have a limited number of tickets set aside for **students and seniors,** and they might be available at the last minute; many Off-Broadway houses make "rush" seats available to students 30 minutes to an hour before curtain. Call the box office to inquire about their discount policies.

If you don't mind staying on your feet, you can save big bucks—and often gain access to sold-out shows—with **standing-room** tickets, offered by many Broadway shows. A limited number are usually sold on the day of show, and cost between $10 and $20. Call the box office and they can fill you in on their standing-room policy.

to members; see "How to Save on Theater Tickets," below.) Phone ahead or go online for tickets to the most successful or popular shows as far in advance as you can; with shows such as *The Lion King* or *The Producers,* it's never too early.

Buying tickets can be simple, if the show you want isn't sold out. Call such general numbers as **TeleCharge** (© 212/239-6200; www. telecharge.com), which handles most Broadway and Off-Broadway shows and some concerts; or **Ticketmaster** (© 212/307-4100; www.ticketmaster.com), which also handles Broadway and Off-Broadway shows and concerts. If you're an American Express cardholder, check to see if tickets are being sold through **American Express Gold Card Events** (© 800/448-TIKS; www.american express.com/gce). You'll pay full price, but Amex has access to blocks of preferred seating for cardholders, so you may be able to get tickets to a show that's otherwise sold out, or better seats than you would otherwise be able to buy.

Theatre Direct International (TDI) is a ticket broker that sells tickets to select Broadway and Off-Broadway shows, including some of the most popular, to individuals and travel agents. Check to see if they have seats to the shows in which you're interested by calling © 800/BROADWAY or 212/541-8457; you can also order tickets through TDI via their website, **www.broadway.com**. Because there's a service charge of $15 per ticket, try Ticketmaster or TeleCharge first; but because they act as a consolidator, TDI may have tickets for a specific show if the major outlets don't.

If you don't want to pay a service charge, call the **box office.** Broadway theaters don't sell tickets over the phone—the major exception is the **Roundabout Theatre** (© 212/719-1300; www. roundabouttheatre.org), which charges a $5-per-ticket "convenience" fee—but a number of Off-Broadway theaters do.

WHEN YOU ARRIVE   Getting your hands on good tickets can take some smarts—and failing those, cash. Even if it seems unlikely that seats are available, always **call the box office** first. Single seats are often easiest to obtain, so people willing to sit apart may find themselves in luck.

Also try the **Broadway Ticket Center,** run by the League of American Theaters and Producers at the Times Square Visitors Center, 1560 Broadway, between 46th and 47th streets (open Mon–Sat 9am–7pm, Sun 10am–6pm). They often have tickets available for otherwise sold-out shows, both for advance and same-day purchase, and charge about $5 extra per ticket.

If you want to deal with a broker, **Keith Prowse & Co.** has an office that accommodates drop-ins at 234 W. 44th St., between Seventh and Eighth avenues, Suite 1000 (© 800/223-6108; open Mon–Sat 9am–6pm).

One **insiders' trick** is to make the rounds of Broadway theaters at about 5 or 6pm, when unclaimed house seats are made available to the public. These tickets—reserved for VIPs, friends of the cast, the press, and so on—offer great seats and are sold at face value.

2 The Performing Arts: Major Concert Halls & Companies

Bargemusic *Value*   Many thought Olga Bloom peculiar when she transformed a 40-year-old barge into a chamber-music concert hall. More than 20 years later, Bargemusic is an internationally renowned recital room boasting more than 100 chamber-music performances a year. There are three shows per week, on Thursday and Friday evenings at 7:30pm and Sunday afternoon at 4pm. The musicians perform on a small stage in a cherry-paneled, fireplace-lit room accommodating 130. The barge may creak a bit and an occasional boat may speed by, but the music is wonderful—and the panoramic view through the glass wall behind the stage can't be beat. Neither can the price: Tickets cost $35 ($20 students), or $40 for performances by larger ensembles. Reserve well in advance. At Fulton Ferry Landing (just south of the Brooklyn Bridge), Brooklyn. (*C*) **718/624-2083** or 718/624-4061. www.bargemusic.org. Subway: 2, 3 to Clark St; A, C to High St.

Brooklyn Academy of Music *Finds*   BAM is the city's most renowned contemporary arts institution, presenting cutting-edge theater, opera, dance, and music. Offerings have included presentations of baroque opera by William Christie and Les Arts Florissants; Marianne Faithfull singing Kurt Weill; dance by Mark Morris and Mikhail Baryshnikov; the Philip Glass ensemble accompanying screenings of *Koyannisqatsi* and Lugosi's original *Dracula;* the Royal Dramatic Theater of Sweden directed by Ingmar Bergman; and much more. Tickets run anywhere from $5 to $95, depending on the performance and the seats; most performances offer a $25-to-$75 range. Of particular note is the **Next Wave Festival,** from September through December, this country's foremost showcase for new experimental works. 30 Lafayette Ave. (off Flatbush Ave.), Brooklyn. (*C*) **718/636-4100**. www.bam.org. Subway: 2, 3, 4, 5, M, N, Q, R, W to Pacific St./Atlantic Ave.

Carnegie Hall   One of the most famous venues in the world, Carnegie Hall offers everything from classics to the music of Ravi Shankar. The **Isaac Stern Auditorium,** the 2,804-seat main hall, welcomes visiting orchestras. The legendary hall is both visually and acoustically brilliant. There's also the intimate 284-seat **Weill**

⟨*Value*⟩ The Classical Learning Curve

The **Juilliard School,** 60 Lincoln Center Plaza (Broadway at 65th St.; ⓒ **212/769-7406** or 212/721-6500; www.juilliard.edu), the nation's premier music education institution, sponsors about 550 performances of high quality—at low prices—throughout the school year. With most concerts free and $20 as a maximum, Juilliard is one of New York's great cultural bargains. Though most would assume that the school presents only classical music, Juilliard offers other music as well as drama, dance, opera, and interdisciplinary works. Call, visit the website (click on "Calendar of Events"), or consult the bulletin board in the building's lobby. Watch for master classes and discussions featuring celebrity guest artists.

Recital Hall, used to showcase chamber music and vocal and instrumental recitals. Carnegie Hall has also reclaimed the underground Zankel Concert Hall, occupied by a movie theater for 38 years; it should reopen as a 650-seat third stage in 2003. *Money-saving tip:* In addition to same-day senior and student rush tickets, Carnegie Hall offers some limited-view tickets for $10 (on sale Sat at 11am for the week's upcoming performances), and presents some free events through its neighborhood concert series. Check for details. 881 Seventh Ave. (at 57th St.). ⓒ 212/247-7800. www.carnegiehall.org. Subway: B, N, Q, R to 57th St.

City Center Modern dance usually takes center stage in this Moorish dome-topped performing-arts palace. The companies of Merce Cunningham, Martha Graham, Alvin Ailey, Twyla Tharp, the Dance Theatre of Harlem (in residence in Sept), and the American Ballet Theatre are often on the calendar. Don't expect cutting edge—but do expect excellence. 131 W. 55th St. (btwn Sixth and Seventh aves.). ⓒ 877/581-1212 or 212/581-1212. www.citycenter.org. Subway: F, N, R, Q, W to 57th St.; B, D, E to Seventh Ave.

Joyce Theater Housed in an old Art Deco movie house, the Joyce has grown into a modern dance institution. You can see everything from Native American dance to the works of Pilobolus to the Martha Graham Dance Company. In residence annually is Eliot Feld's company, Ballet Tech, which WQXR radio's Francis Mason called "better than a whole month of namby-pamby classical ballets." 175 Eighth Ave. (at 19th St.). ⓒ 212/242-0800. www.joyce.org. Subway:

C, E to 23rd St.; 1, 9 to 18th St. Joyce SoHo at 155 Mercer St. (btwn Houston and Prince sts.; ℭ **212/431-9233;** subway: N, R to Prince St.).

Lincoln Center for the Performing Arts   New York is the world's premier performing-arts city, and Lincoln Center is its premier institution. Lincoln Center's many buildings serve as permanent homes to their own companies as well as major stops for world-class performance troupes from around the globe.

Resident companies include the **Metropolitan Opera** (ℭ **212/ 362-6000;** www.metopera.org), whose full productions of the classics, starring world-class grand sopranos and tenors, make this the world's premier opera house. The **American Ballet Theatre** (www. abt.org) is in residence each spring; the Met also hosts such visiting companies as the Kirov, Royal, and Paris Opéra ballets.

At the New York State Theater, the superb **New York City Opera** (ℭ **212/870-5630;** www.nycopera.com), attempts to reach a wider audience than the Metropolitan with its more "human" scale and lower prices. It's committed to adventurous premieres, newly composed operas, the occasional avant-garde work, American musicals presented as operettas (such as *Sweeney Todd, Porgy and Bess*), and even obscure works by mainstream or lesser-known composers. The same venue serves as home base for the **New York City Ballet** (ℭ **212/870-5570;** www.nycballet.com). The cornerstone of the annual season is the Christmastime production of *The Nutcracker;* tickets usually become available in early October.

Symphony-wise, you'd be hard-pressed to do better than the **New York Philharmonic** (ℭ **212/875-5656** or 212/875-5030; www. newyorkphilharmonic.org), performing at Avery Fisher Hall. The country's oldest orchestra is under the guidance of Lorin Maazel. **Jazz at Lincoln Center** (ℭ **212/258-9800;** www.jazzatlincolncenter. org) is led by Wynton Marsalis, with the orchestra usually performing at the more intimate Alice Tully Hall.

The **Chamber Music Society of Lincoln Center** (ℭ **212/875- 5788;** www.chamberlinc.org) performs at Alice Tully Hall or the Daniel and Joanna S. Rose Rehearsal Studio, often with such high-caliber guests as Anne Sofie Von Otter and Midori. The **Film Society of Lincoln Center** (ℭ **212/875-5600;** www.filmlinc.com) screens a daily schedule of movies at the Walter Reade Theater, and hosts film and video festivals as well as the Reel to Real program for kids, pairing silent-screen classics with live performance. **Lincoln Center Theater** (ℭ **212/362-7600;** www.lct.org) consists of the Vivian Beaumont Theater, a modern, comfortable venue with great

**Park It! Shakespeare, Music &
Other Free Fun**

As the weather warms, New York comes outdoors to play.

Shakespeare in the Park, held at Central Park's Delacorte
Theater, is the city's most famous alfresco arts event.
Organized by the late Joseph Papp's Public Theater, the
schedule consists of one or two summer productions, usually
of the Bard's plays. Productions often feature big names and
range from traditional (Andre Braugher as an armor-clad
Henry V) to avant-garde (Morgan Freeman and Tracy
Ullman in *Taming of the Shrew* as a Wild West showdown).
The theater, next to Belvedere Castle near 79th Street and
West Drive, is a dream—on a starry night, there's no better
stage in town. Tickets are given out free on a first-come,
first-served basis (two per person), at 1pm on the day of the
performance at the theater. The Delacorte might have 1,881
seats, but each is a hot commodity, so people line up next to
the theater 2 to 3 hours or more in advance. You can also
pick up same-day tickets between 1 and 3pm at the Public
Theater, at 425 Lafayette St. Call the Public Theater at
ⓒ 212/539-8750 or the Delacorte at ⓒ 212/861-7277, or go
online at www.publictheater.org.

The most active music stage in Central Park is
SummerStage, at Rumsey Playfield, midpark around 72nd
Street. Recent offerings have included concerts by Hugh

sightlines that has been home to much Broadway drama, and the
Mitzi E. Newhouse Theater, an Off-Broadway house.

Tickets for all performances at Avery Fisher and Alice Tully halls
can be purchased through **CenterCharge** (ⓒ 212/721-6500) or at
www.lincolncenter.org (click on "Box Office & Schedule"). Tickets
for all Lincoln Center Theater performances can be purchased
through **TeleCharge** (ⓒ 212/239-6200; www.telecharge.com).
Tickets for New York State Theater productions (New York City
Opera and Ballet companies) are available through **Ticketmaster**
(ⓒ 212/307-4100; www.ticketmaster.com), while tickets for films
showing at the Walter Reade Theater can be bought up to 7 days
in advance by calling ⓒ 212/496-3809. 70 Lincoln Center Plaza (at
Broadway and 64th St.). ⓒ 212/546-2656 or 212/875-5456. www.lincolncenter.
org. Subway: 1, 9 to 66th St.

Masekela, the Jon Spencer Blues Explosion; "Viva, Verdi!" festival performances by the New York Grand Opera; cabaret nights; and more. The season usually lasts from mid-June to August. While some big-name shows charge admission, tickets aren't usually required. Call the hot line at © **212/360-2777** or visit www.summerstage.org.

The calendar of free events heats up throughout the city's parks in summertime. You can find out what's happening by calling the **Parks and Recreation Special Events Hot Line** at © **888/NY-PARKS** or 212/360-3456, or pointing your browser to **nycparks.completeinet.net.**

HBO sponsors the **Bryant Park Summer Film Festival,** in which a classic film—like *Dr. Zhivago* or *Viva Las Vegas*—is shown on a screen under the stars every Monday evening at sunset. Admission is free; bring a blanket and a picnic. Rain dates are Tuesdays. For the schedule, call © **212/512-5700** or visit www.hbobryantparkfilm.com.

In Lower Manhattan, Trinity Church, at Broadway and Wall Street, hosts a chamber-music and orchestral **Noonday Concert** series year-round each Monday and Thursday at 1pm. This program isn't quite free, but almost: A $2 contribution is requested. Call the concert hot line at © **212/602-0747** or visit www.trinitywallstreet.org.

92nd Street Y Tisch Center for the Arts (Value) This community center offers a phenomenal slate of cultural happenings, from classical to folk to jazz to world music to cabaret to literary readings. Great performers—Janos Starker, Nadja Salerno-Sonnenberg—give recitals here. The concert calendar often includes luminaries such as Max Roach, John Williams, and Judy Collins; Jazz at the Y from Dick Hyman and guests; the longstanding Chamber Music at the Y series; the classical Music from the Jewish Spirit series; and regular cabaret programs. The lectures and literary-readings calendar is unparalleled, with featured speakers ranging from Lorne Michaels to David Halberstam to Jeff Bezos (CEO of Amazon) to Katie Couric to Elie Wiesel. There's a regular schedule of modern dance, too. Readings and lectures are usually priced between $20 and $30

(Value) Lincoln Center Alert: Last-Minute & Discount Ticket-Buying Tips

The **New York Philharmonic** offers bargain hunters a range of options. When subscribers can't attend, they may return their tickets to the theater, which resell them at the last moment. Ticket holders can return tickets until curtain time, so those not available in the morning may be available (at full price) later in the day. The hopefuls form "cancellation lines" 2 hours or more before curtain.

Periodically, some **same-day orchestra tickets** are set aside at the box office, and sold in the morning for $25 (maximum two). They usually go on sale at 10am weekdays, 1pm Saturday (noon if there's a matinee). **Senior/student/ disabled rush tickets** may be available for $10 (maximum two) on concert day, but never at Friday matinees or Saturday evening performances. To check availability for any of these programs, call **Audience Services** at © 212/875-5656.

You're also invited to watch the Philharmonic at work by attending an **Open Rehearsal** for just $14.

Families with teenagers can participate in **Phil Teens,** which allows you and your teen (from ages 12 to 17) to attend a New York Philharmonic Rush Hour Concert for $10 each. Rush Hour concerts start at 6:45pm and last an hour.

Lincoln Center's **Alice Tully Hall** (where the Chamber Music Society performs and other concerts are held), **Jazz at Lincoln Center,** the **Metropolitan Opera,** and the **New York City Opera,** offer last-minute-purchase and discount

for nonmembers, dance is usually $20, and concert tickets generally go for $15 to $50—half or a third of what you'd pay at comparable venues. 1395 Lexington Ave. (at 92nd St.). © 212/996-1100. www.92ndsty.org. Subway: 4, 5, 6 to 86th St.; 6 to 96th St.

3 Live Rock, Jazz, Blues & More

I've highlighted a few choice venues below, but the city has many more. For a complete list of what's happening and where to find it, check the publications and websites listed at the start of this chapter.

programs. Policies differ; for instance, the **New York City Ballet** offers Student Rush tickets only, at $10 a pop, while the New York City Opera allows students to buy tickets a week in advance at half-price ($13–$53), and offers same-day rush tickets (Rush Hot Line: ℂ **212/870-5630**).

The **Met Opera** offers **standing-room** tickets for $12 to $16, which can be a bargain for budget-minded fans. It's not a bad situation, because you get to lean against plush red bars. (If subscribers fail to show, I've seen standees with eagle eyes fill the empty seats at intermission.) Wheelchair-access standing-room places are also available. Tickets go on sale Saturday at 10am for the following week's perform-ances (Sat–Fri). The line sometimes forms much earlier, so plan ahead. Keep in mind that special performances may not be available to potential standees. Call ℂ **212/362-6000** for details. It never hurts to inquire about standing-room availability at other venues as well.

Summer visitors should also keep in mind that both the **Philharmonic** and the **Met Opera** offer **free concerts in the parks** throughout the five boroughs, including Central Park, in July and August. For the current schedule, call ℂ **212/ 875-5656** or 212/362-6000. The Philharmonic maintains a list of their upcoming park gigs throughout the five boroughs at **www.newyorkphilharmonic.org**.

Arlene Grocery This casual Lower East Side club boasts a friendly bar and a good sound system; the quality of the artists is usually pretty high, and the cover is around $5. Arlene Grocery serves as a showcase for hot bands looking for a deal or promoting their self-pressed record. The crowd is a mix of club-hoppers, rock fans looking for a new fix, and industry scouts looking for new blood. 95 Stanton St. (btwn Ludlow and Orchard sts.). ℂ **212/358-1633.** www.arlene-grocery.com. Subway: F to Second Ave.

Blue Note Celebrating its 20th birthday in 2001, the Blue Note attracts the biggest names in jazz to its intimate setting. Just about everyone has played here. The sound system is excellent, and every seat has a sightline to the stage. A night here can get expensive—the cover is usually $30 to $35 per person—but how often do you get to enjoy jazz of this caliber? There are two shows per night, and dinner is served. 131 W. 3rd St. (at Sixth Ave.). ✆ 212/475-8592. www.bluenote.net. Subway: A, C, E, F, V to W. 4th St.

The Bottom Line The Bottom Line built its reputation by serving as a showcase for the likes of Bruce Springsteen, and it remains one of the city's most well-respected venues. With table seating, waiter service, decent burgers, and a no-smoking policy, it's also one of the city's most comfortable. It's renowned for its sound and bookings of the best singer/songwriters in the business. Usually two shows nightly. Tickets run $15 to $30, with most $20 or less. 15 W. 4th St. (at Mercer St.). ✆ **212/502-3471** or 212/228-6300. www.bottomline cabaret.com. Subway: N, R to Astor Place; A, C, E, F, V to W. 4th St.

Bowery Ballroom This marvelous space is run by the same people behind the Mercury Lounge (see below). The Bowery is bigger, accommodating 500 or so. The stage is big and raised to allow good sightlines. The sound couldn't be better, and Art Deco details give the place a sophistication not often found in general-admission halls. It's a favorite with alt-rockers as well as established acts who thrive in an intimate setting. Tickets run $10 to $30, with most under $20. *Money-saving tip:* Save on the service charge and day-of-show higher pricing by buying advance tickets at Mercury's box office. 6 Delancey St. (at Bowery). ✆ **212/533-2111.** www.boweryballroom. com. Subway: F, J, M, Z to Delancey St.

CBGB The original downtown club has seen better days, but no other spot is so rich with rock history. This was the launching pad for New York punk and New Wave: the Ramones, Blondie, the Talking Heads, Television, Patti Smith—everybody got started here. These days, you've probably never heard of most acts here. Never mind—CB's still rocks. Come early if you have hopes of actually seeing the stage. Cover usually runs $6 to $10. 315 Bowery (at Bleecker St.). ✆ 212/982-4052, or 212/677-0455 for CB's 313 Gallery. www.cbgb.com. Subway: F to Second Ave.; 6 to Bleecker St.

Jazz at the Cajun *(Finds* This casual New Orleans–themed supper club is the best venue in town for prewar big-band and Dixieland jazz—think Jelly Roll Morton, Scott Joplin, early Duke. The crowd comes from all walks of life, united in their love of the old school. There's no cover charge, and food is affordable and just fine, with entrees in the low and mid-teens; reserve in advance. 129 Eighth Ave.

(btwn 16th and 17th sts.). © 212/691-6174. www.jazzatthecajun.com. Subway: A, C, E to 14th St. L to 8th Ave.

The Knitting Factory   New York's premier avant-garde music venue has four spaces, each showcasing performances ranging from experimental jazz and folk to spoken-word and poetry to multimedia. There are often two shows a night in the main performance space, so it's easy to work a show around other activities. Prices usually run $7 to $20, with most between $10 and $15. The Old Office Lounge offers an extensive list of microbrews and free live entertainment. 74 Leonard St. (btwn Broadway and Church St.). © 212/219-3006. www.knittingfactory.com. Subway: 1, 9 to Franklin St.

Lenox Lounge *(Finds)*   Harlem's best jazz club is this beautifully renovated classic. Said to be a favorite of Billie Holliday's, the intimate, Art Deco–cool back room—complete with zebra stripes on the walls and banquettes—hosts top-flight jazz vocalists, trios, and quartets for a crowd that comes to listen and be wowed. The cover never goes higher than $15 (one-drink minimum). Well worth the trip uptown for those who want a genuine Harlem jazz experience. 288 Malcolm X Blvd. (Lenox Ave.; btwn 124th and 125th sts.). © 212/427-0253. Subway: 2, 3 to 125th St.

Mercury Lounge   The Merc is everything a top-notch live-music venue should be: unpretentious, civilized, and with a killer sound system. The rooms are nothing special: a front bar and an intimate back-room performance space with a low stage and a few tables lining the brick walls. The calendar is filled with a mix of accomplished local rockers and national acts like Frank Black, Dave Pirner (of Soul Asylum), and the Mekons. The crowd is grown-up and easygoing. The only downside is that it's ususally packed thanks to the high quality of the entertainment and pleasing nature of the experience. The cover is usually $8 and $10, maybe more for national acts. 217 E. Houston St. (at Essex St./Ave. A). © 212/260-4700. www.mercuryloungenyc.com. Subway: F to Second Ave.

Rodeo Bar *(Value)*   Here's New York's oldest—and finest—honky-tonk. Hike up your Wranglers and head inside, where you'll find longhorns on the walls, peanut shells underfoot, and Tex-Mex on the menu. But this place is really about the music: urban-tinged country, bluegrass, swinging rockabilly, and Southern-flavored rock. A 10-gallon hat full o' fun—and best of all, the music is always free! It's happy hour until 7pm; the music starts around 9:30pm nightly, and goes until at least 3am. 375 Third Ave. (at 27th St.). © 212/683-6500. www.rodeobar.com. Subway: 6 to 28th St.

Terra Blues This artsy blues club hosts an active calendar of local and national acts, with a $5 to $10 cover, even on weekends; plan on a two-drink minimum. 149 Bleecker St. (btwn Thompson St. and LaGuardia Place). ② 212/777-7776. www.terrablues.com. Subway: A, C, E, F, V to W. 4th St.

Village Underground *Finds* The folks behind dear departed Tramps have opened this intimate, even romantic subterranean venue (which has a "no smoking" policy in the performance space). Some big-name talent turns up—but even if you don't recognize the names, you can count on quality music. Tickets run from $7 to $25; advance tickets can be purchased at www.ticketweb.com or ② **866/ 468-7619**. 130 W. 3rd St. (btwn Sixth Avenue and MacDougal St.). ② 212/777-7745. www.thevillageunderground.com. Subway: A, C, E, F, V to W. 4th St. (use W. 3rd St. exit).

The Village Vanguard What CBGB is to rock, the Village Vanguard is to jazz. Expect a mix of established names and high-quality local talent, including the Vanguard's own jazz orchestra on Monday nights. The sound is great, but sightlines are terrible, so come early for a front table. Covers range from $15 to $30; Sunday through Thursday nights are cheapest. 178 Seventh Ave. S. (just below 11th St.). ② 212/255-4037. www.villagevanguard.net. Subway: 1, 2, 3, 9 to 14th St.

4 Stand-Up Comedy

Comedy Cellar *Finds* This subterranean spot is the club of choice for stand-up fans in the know, thanks to the most consistently impressive lineups in the business. I'll always love the Comedy Cellar for introducing an unknown comic named Ray Romano to me a few years ago. $10 weekdays, $12 weekends, two-drink minimum. *Money-saving tip:* Check the website to order free tickets and free drinks for select nights. 117 MacDougal St. (btwn Bleecker and W. 3rd sts.). ② 212/254-3480. www.comedycellar.com. Subway: A, C, E, F, V to W. 4th St. (use 3rd St. exit).

New York Comedy Club *Value* With a $7 cover charge on weekdays ($10 Fri–Sat) plus two-beverage minimum, this small club offers the best value for your money. Despite what the owners call their "Wal-Mart approach" to comedy, the club has presented Damon Wayans, Chris Rock, and Brett Butler, among others, in its two showrooms. Monday's Open Mike Night (5pm) is $3 with unlimited soft drinks, and you're welcome to get on stage for your 5 minutes of fame. Weekends set aside time for African-American and Latino comics. Come early for a good seat. 241 E. 24th St. (btwn Second and Third aves.). ✆ 212/696-5233. www.newyorkcomedyclub.com. Subway: 6 to 23rd St.

5 Bars & Cocktail Lounges

DOWNTOWN

Barramundi   This nice lounge is notable for its fairy-tale outdoor garden, friendly staff, and settled-in feel in a neighborhood overrun by hipster copycats. Come on a weeknight to snare a table in the little corner of heaven out back. A fireplace makes Barramundi almost as appealing on cool nights. 147 Ludlow St. (btwn Stanton and Rivington sts.). ✆ 212/569-6900. Subway: F to Second Ave.

Bowlmor   Super-cool Bowlmor isn't your daddy's bowling alley: deejays spin, martinis flow, candy-colored balls knock down day-glo pins, and strikes and spares are automatically tallied into the wee hours. Frankly, Bowlmor is a blast. 110 University Pl. (btwn 12th and 13th sts.). ✆ 212/255-8188. www.bowlmor.com. Subway: 4, 5, 6, L, N, R to 14th St./ Union Sq.

dba *(Finds*   dba has bucked the loungey trend that has taken over the city, instead remaining an unpretentious neighborhood bar. Everyone is welcome in this beer- and scotch-lover's paradise, which posts a massive drink menu on chalkboards. Owner Ray Deter specializes in British-style cask-conditioned ales (the kind that you pump by hand) and stocks a phenomenal collection of single-malt scotches. Excellent jukebox, too. 41 First Ave. (btwn 2nd and 3rd sts.). ✆ 212/475-5097. www.drinkgoodstuff.com. Subway: F to Second Ave.

Merc Bar   Notable for its long tenure in the fickle world of beautiful-people bars, upscale Merc Bar has mellowed nicely. The decor bespeaks civilized rusticity with warm woods, a canoe over the bar, copper-top tables, and butter-leather banquettes. A great place to nestle into a comfortable couch with your honey, splurge on a classy cocktail, and enjoy the scene. Look carefully, because there's no sign. 151 Mercer St. (btwn Prince and Houston sts.). ✆ 212/966-2727. www.merc bar.com. Subway: N, R to Prince St.

MIDTOWN

Bull & Bear   The name speaks to its business-minded clientele; there's even a stock ticker in constant service for those three-martini lunches. The Bull & Bear is like a gentlemen's pub, with leather chairs, a waistcoated staff, and a troika-shaped mahogany bar polished to a high sheen at the center of the room. Ask Oscar, who's been here for more than 30 years, or one of the other bartenders to blend you a classic cocktail. Or just order a beer—either way, you'll be right at home here. An ideal place to kick back after a hard day of sightseeing. At the Waldorf-Astoria. 301 Park Ave. (btwn 49th and 50th sts.). ✆ 212/872-4900. Subway: 6 to 51st St.

Mickey Mantle's   Of course, it's terribly sad that the Mick, who gave his life to the bottle, should have his name on a bar. But if you're a fan, it's worth a visit to his mahogany-and-brass sports bar and restaurant, which chronicles his life and career in photos. The crowd is a laid-back mix of white-collar workers and tourists. Moderately priced burger fare is available, plus the requisite souvenirs. 42 Central Park S. (btwn Fifth and Sixth aves.). ✆ 212/688-7777. www. mickeymantles.com. Subway: F to 57th St.

Pete's Tavern   The oldest continually operating establishment in the city, Pete's opened while Lincoln was president. It reeks of history—and more importantly, there's Guinness on tap and a terrific happy hour. The crowd is a mix of locals from Gramercy Park and more down-to-earth types. 129 E. 18th St. (at Irving Place). ✆ 212/473-7676. www.petestavern.com. Subway: 4, 5, 6, L, N, R, Q, W to 14th St./Union Sq.

Serena (Finds)   This plush and popular basement boîte has managed to stay fresh by reinventing itself. Done in deep, sexy reds, Serena is again as hip as can be—I've even spotted Moby here. Dress the part if you want to make it past the doorman. The crowd is young and pretty, and the music mix is a blast—think Fatboy Slim meets ABBA meets Foghat and you'll get the picture. In the basement level of the Hotel Chelsea, 222 W. 23rd St. (btwn Seventh and Eighth aves.). ✆ 212/255-4646. Subway: C, E, 1, 9 to 23rd St.

Tír Na Nóg   This place is a standout among the Irish pubs that line Eighth Avenue near Penn Station. The decor lends the place a real Celtic vibe, as does the Murphy's on tap. The bar has established itself among both locals and bridge-and-tunnel types for its unpretentious, lively air. There's upscale pub grub, a dance floor, and live foot-stompin' Irish music Friday and Saturday nights. 5 Penn Plaza (Eighth Ave. between 33rd and 34th sts.). ✆ 212/630-0249. www.tirnanognyc. com. Subway: A, C, E to 34th St./Penn Station.

UPTOWN

Amsterdam Billiard Club   A straight-ahead, top-flight billiard bar with a completely unpretentious ambience, good beers on tap, and a lively local crowd make this one of the best pool bars in NYC.

344 Amsterdam Ave. (btwn 76th and 77th sts.). ✆ 212/496-8180. Subway: 1, 9 to 79th St. Also at 210 E. 86th St. (btwn Second and Third aves.; ✆ 212/570-4545; subway: 6 to 86th St.).

Brandy's Piano Bar   A mixed crowd—Upper East Side locals, waiters off work, gays, straights, all ages—comes to this intimate, old-school piano bar for the atmosphere and nightly entertainment. The talented wait staff does most of the singing while waiting for their big break, but patrons regularly join in. The sounds tend to adult-contemporary radio hits and cabaret tunes. This place is so unhip that it's cool; it makes for a fun, affordable night on the town. No cover charge; two-drink minimum. 235 E. 84th St. (btwn Second and Third aves.). ✆ 212/650-1944. Subway: 4, 5, 6 to 86th St.

Great Hall Balcony Bar *Moments*   One of Manhattan's best cocktail bars is only open on Friday and Saturday—and only from 4 to 8:30pm, to boot. The Metropolitan Museum of Art transforms the lobby's mezzanine level into a cocktail-and-classical music lounge twice weekly, offering an only-in-New-York experience. The music is usually provided by a grand piano and string quartet. The setting couldn't be grander. You'll have to pay the $10 admission, but the galleries are open until 9pm. At the Metropolitan Museum of Art, Fifth Ave. at 82nd St. ✆ 212/535-7710. www.metmuseum.org. Subway: 4, 5, 6 to 86th St.

6 Dance Clubs & Party Scenes

Finding and going to the latest hot spot is not worth agonizing over. My rule of thumb is that if I know about a place, it must not be hip anymore. Just find someplace that amuses you, and enjoy the crowd.

"Clubs" as actual, physical spaces don't mean much anymore. The hungry-for-nightlife crowd follows events of certain party "producers" who switch venues and times each week. *Time Out New York* is a great source to check, as it lists cover charges for the week's big events and clearly indicates which are free.

No matter what, **always call ahead,** because schedules change constantly and can do so at the last minute. Even better: You also may be able to put your name on a guest list that will save you a few bucks at the door. Also check **newyork.sheckys.com** for VIP guest list access. And always check the clubs' websites for special deals.

Baktun   This club has been hot since the word go. Baktun was conceived in 2000 as a multimedia lounge, and incorporates video projections (shown on a double-sided video screen) into its dance parties as well as live cybercasts. The music tends toward electronica, with some live acts. At press time, Saturday's Direct Drive was still the key drum 'n' bass party in town. The cover runs $3 to $10. 418 W. 14th St. (btwn Ninth Ave. and Washington St.). ✆ **212/206-1590**. www. baktun.com. Subway: A, C, E, L to 14th St.

Cafe Wha?   You'll find a carefree crowd dancing in this casual basement club any night of the week. From Wednesday through Sunday, the stage features the house's own Wha Band, which does an excellent job of cranking out crowd-pleasing covers of familiar rock-and-roll hits from the '70s, '80s, and '90s. Monday night is the hugely popular Brazilian Dance Party, while Tuesday night is Classic Funk Night. Expect to be surrounded by lots of Jersey kids and out-of-towners on the weekends, but so what? Reservations are a good idea. The cover runs from free to $10, making Wha a good value to boot. 115 MacDougal St. (btwn Bleecker and 3rd sts.). ✆ **212/254-3706**. www. cafewha.com. Subway: A, B, C, D, E, F, V to W. 4th St.

Nell's *Finds*   Nell's calls itself "The Classic New York Nightclub," and it has earned the moniker. It was the first to establish a lounge-like atmosphere. It has been endlessly copied. Nell's attracts a grown-up crowd that ranges from homeboys to Wall Streeters, and it's as marvelous as ever. Although the entertainment can run the gamut from comedy to Cuban sounds, most of the parties have a soulful edge. The gem of the New York nightlife scene! The cover is a well-worth-it $7 to $15. Dress nicely—Nell's deserves respect. 246 W. 14th St. (btwn Seventh and Eighth aves.). ✆ **212/675-1567**. www.nells. com. Subway: A, C, E, 1, 2, 3, 9 to 14th St.

S.O.B.'s *Finds*   The city's top world-music venue, specializing in Brazilian, Caribbean, and Latin sounds. The packed house dances and sings along nightly to calypso, samba, mambo, African drums, reggae, or other global grooves, united in the high-energy, feel-good vibe. Bookings include top-flight performers from around the globe, from Astrud Gilberto to Beausoleil. The room's Tropicana Club style has island pizzazz that carries through to the Caribbean-influenced cooking and extensive tropical drinks menu. This place is so popular that it's an excellent idea to book in advance. The cover runs $10 to $25, but often stays at or below the $15 mark. *Money-saving tip:* Check the website for a $5 off coupon. 204 Varick St. (at Houston St.). ✆ **212/243-4940**. www.sobs.com. Subway: 1, 9 to Houston St.

13 *Value*   This little lounge is a great place to dance the night away. It's stylish but unpretentious, with a steady roster of fun weekly parties. Sunday night's no-cover Britpop fest Shout! lives on, and with no cover, to boot. The rest of the week runs the gamut from '70s and '80s New Wave and glam night to progressive house and trance to poetry slams and performance art. If there's a cover, it's usually $5, occasionally $7 or $10. Happy hour offers two-for-one drinks (no cover) from 4 to 8pm. 35 E. 13th St. (btwn Broadway and University Place), 2nd floor. (© 212/979-6677. www.bar13.com. Subway: 4, 5, 6, N, R, L, Q, W to 14th St./Union Sq.

Vinyl *(Finds)* No alcohol is served at Vinyl—but that doesn't keep the masses at bay. This TriBeCa club welcomes a mixed black/white, gay/straight crowd to the best roster of weekly parties on the planet—mainly hip-hop- and house-flavored party nights ruled by a first-rate crop of deejays. The legendary Body and Soul (www.bodyandsoul-nyc.com) is a Sunday-afternoon party extraordinaire. Even better is Friday's Be Yourself, deejay Danny Tenaglia's weekly rave, which doesn't relent until the Saturday-morning cartoon hours. 6 Hubert St. (btwn Hudson and Greenwich sts.). (© 212/343-1379. Subway: A, C, E to Canal St.; 1, 9 to Franklin St.

7 The Gay & Lesbian Scene

To get a thorough, up-to-date take on what's happening in gay and lesbian nightlife, pick up copies of *HX* (www.hx.com), *New York Blade* (www.nyblade.com), *Next* (www.nextnyc.com), and *Gay City News* (www.gaycitynews.com), available for free in bars and clubs all around town, at news boxes throughout the city, or at the **Lesbian, Gay, Bisexual & Transgender Community Center,** at 208 W. 13th St., between Seventh and Eighth avenues ((© 212/620-7310; www.gaycenter.org).

Barracuda Chelsea is central to gay life—and gay bars. This trendy, loungey place is a continuing favorite, voted "Best Bar" by *HX* and *New York Press* for 2 years running, while *Paper* magazine singles out the hunky bartenders. There's a sexy bar for cruising out front and a comfy lounge in back. Look for the regular drag shows. 275 W. 22nd St. (btwn Seventh and Eighth aves.). (© 212/645-8613. Subway: C, E, 1, 9 to 23rd St.

Big Cup Big Cup isn't a bar but a coffeehouse. Still, you'd be hard-pressed to find a cooler, comfier pickup joint. This is where all the Chelsea boys hang; just think of it as a living room–style lounge without the alcohol. By the way, it also happens to be a fab coffee-house. 228 Eighth Ave. (btwn 21st and 22nd sts.). (© 212/206-0059. Subway: C, E to 23rd St.

Crazy Nanny's   This lesbian bar and club is huge, friendly, and perpetually trendy. There are two floors, two bars, a groovy jukebox, dancing, a pool table, video games, and a variety of theme nights, including Dance Party on Thursday, and karaoke on Sunday and Wednesday (free cover). Out-of-towners are welcome. There's usually an $8 cover; drinks are half-price Monday through Friday from 4 to 7pm. 21 Seventh Ave. S. (at Leroy St.). ℭ **212/366-6312.** www.crazynannys. com. Subway: 1, 9 to Houston St.

Meow Mix   Owner Brooke Webster has made this funky, divey East Village bar a great hangout since 1994. It draws in a young, attractive riot *grrrrl* crowd with nightly diversions like deejays and live bands, a pool table and authentic Ms. PacMan machine in the basement lounge, and is the place to watch New York Liberty away games on the big-screen TV. Two-for-one happy hour daily from 5 to 8pm. 269 E. Houston St. (at Suffolk St.) ℭ **212/254-0688.** www.meowmix chix.com. Subway: F to Second Ave.

Splash/SBNY   After 10 years, this campy and fun dance club is still one of the hottest scenes on the men's circuit. An end-of-2001 rebirth has breathed new life into the scene; *New York* magazine chose it best gay dance club for 2002. Beautiful bartenders, video screens, New York's best drag queens—Splash has it all. Theme nights are a big deal. Best of the bunch is Musical Mondays, dedicated to Broadway video clips and music. Musical Mondays' famous singalongs are such a blast that they draw a crossover gay/straight mixed crowd. 50 W. 17th St. (btwn Fifth and Sixth aves.). ℭ **212/691-0073.** www.splashbar.com. Subway: F, V to 14th St.; 4, 5, 6, N, R, L, Q, W to 14th St./ Union Sq.

Stonewall Bar   The spot where it all started. A mixed gay and lesbian crowd—old and young—makes this an easy place to begin. At least pop in to relive a defining moment in queer history. 53 Christopher St. (east of Seventh Ave.). ℭ **212/463-0950.** Subway: 1, 9 to Christopher St.

View Bar *(Finds*   View Bar is more Will Truman than Jack McFarland, if you know what I mean. Up front is a very attractive and comfortable lounge, in back is a pool room with the name-worthy view; throughout you'll find friendly bartenders, affordable drinks, and Kenneth Cole–dressed boys who could pass on either side of bi. A welcome addition to the scene. 232 Eighth Ave. (btwn 21st and 22nd sts.). ℭ **212/929-2243.** Subway: C, E to 23rd St.

Index

See also Accommodations and Restaurant indexes, below.

ACCOMMODATIONS

RESTAURANTS

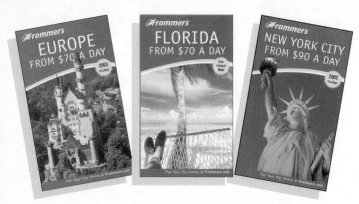

FROMMER'S® COMPLETE TRAVEL GUIDES

Alaska
Alaska Cruises & Ports of Call
Amsterdam
Argentina & Chile
Arizona
Atlanta
Australia
Austria
Bahamas
Barcelona, Madrid & Seville
Beijing
Belgium, Holland & Luxembourg
Bermuda
Boston
Brazil
British Columbia & the Canadian Rockies
Budapest & the Best of Hungary
California
Canada
Cancún, Cozumel & the Yucatán
Cape Cod, Nantucket & Martha's Vineyard
Caribbean
Caribbean Cruises & Ports of Call
Caribbean Ports of Call
Carolinas & Georgia
Chicago
China
Colorado
Costa Rica
Denmark
Denver, Boulder & Colorado Springs
England
Europe
European Cruises & Ports of Call
Florida

France
Germany
Great Britain
Greece
Greek Islands
Hawaii
Hong Kong
Honolulu, Waikiki & Oahu
Ireland
Israel
Italy
Jamaica
Japan
Las Vegas
London
Los Angeles
Maryland & Delaware
Maui
Mexico
Montana & Wyoming
Montréal & Québec City
Munich & the Bavarian Alps
Nashville & Memphis
Nepal
New England
New Mexico
New Orleans
New York City
New Zealand
Northern Italy
Nova Scotia, New Brunswick & Prince Edward Island
Oregon
Paris
Philadelphia & the Amish Country
Portugal
Prague & the Best of the Czech Republic

Provence & the Riviera
Puerto Rico
Rome
San Antonio & Austin
San Diego
San Francisco
Santa Fe, Taos & Albuquerque
Scandinavia
Scotland
Seattle & Portland
Shanghai
Singapore & Malaysia
South Africa
South America
South Florida
South Pacific
Southeast Asia
Spain
Sweden
Switzerland
Texas
Thailand
Tokyo
Toronto
Tuscany & Umbria
USA
Utah
Vancouver & Victoria
Vermont, New Hampshire & Maine
Vienna & the Danube Valley
Virgin Islands
Virginia
Walt Disney World® & Orlando
Washington, D.C.
Washington State

FROMMER'S® DOLLAR-A-DAY GUIDES

Australia from $50 a Day
California from $70 a Day
Caribbean from $70 a Day
England from $75 a Day
Europe from $70 a Day

Florida from $70 a Day
Hawaii from $80 a Day
Ireland from $60 a Day
Italy from $70 a Day
London from $85 a Day

New York from $90 a Day
Paris from $80 a Day
San Francisco from $70 a Day
Washington, D.C. from $80 a Day

FROMMER'S® PORTABLE GUIDES

Acapulco, Ixtapa & Zihuatanejo
Amsterdam
Aruba
Australia's Great Barrier Reef
Bahamas
Berlin
Big Island of Hawaii
Boston
California Wine Country
Cancún
Charleston & Savannah
Chicago
Disneyland®
Dublin
Florence

Frankfurt
Hong Kong
Houston
Las Vegas
London
Los Angeles
Los Cabos & Baja
Maine Coast
Maui
Miami
New Orleans
New York City
Paris
Phoenix & Scottsdale

Portland
Puerto Rico
Puerto Vallarta, Manzanillo & Guadalajara
Rio de Janeiro
San Diego
San Francisco
Seattle
Sydney
Tampa & St. Petersburg
Vancouver
Venice
Virgin Islands
Washington, D.C.

FROMMER'S® NATIONAL PARK GUIDES

Banff & Jasper
Family Vacations in the National Parks
Grand Canyon

National Parks of the American West
Rocky Mountain

Yellowstone & Grand Teton
Yosemite & Sequoia/ Kings Canyon
Zion & Bryce Canyon

FROMMER'S® MEMORABLE WALKS

Chicago
London

New York
Paris

San Francisco
Washington, D.C.

FROMMER'S® GREAT OUTDOOR GUIDES

Arizona & New Mexico
New England

Northern California
Southern New England

Vermont & New Hampshire

SUZY GERSHMAN'S BORN TO SHOP GUIDES

Born to Shop: France
Born to Shop: Hong Kong,
   Shanghai & Beijing

Born to Shop: Italy
Born to Shop: London

Born to Shop: New York
Born to Shop: Paris

FROMMER'S® IRREVERENT GUIDES

Amsterdam
Boston
Chicago
Las Vegas
London

Los Angeles
Manhattan
New Orleans
Paris
Rome

San Francisco
Seattle & Portland
Vancouver
Walt Disney World®
Washington, D.C.

FROMMER'S® BEST-LOVED DRIVING TOURS

Britain
California
Florida
France

Germany
Ireland
Italy
New England

Northern Italy
Scotland
Spain
Tuscany & Umbria

HANGING OUT™ GUIDES

Hanging Out in England
Hanging Out in Europe

Hanging Out in France
Hanging Out in Ireland

Hanging Out in Italy
Hanging Out in Spain

THE UNOFFICIAL GUIDES®

Bed & Breakfasts and Country
   Inns in:
   California
   Great Lakes States
   Mid-Atlantic
   New England
   Northwest
   Rockies
   Southeast
   Southwest
Best RV & Tent Campgrounds in:
   California & the West
   Florida & the Southeast
   Great Lakes States
   Mid-Atlantic
   Northeast
   Northwest & Central Plains

   Southwest & South Central
      Plains
   U.S.A.
Beyond Disney
Branson, Missouri
California with Kids
Chicago
Cruises
Disneyland®
Florida with Kids
Golf Vacations in the Eastern U.S.
Great Smoky & Blue Ridge Region
Inside Disney
Hawaii
Las Vegas
London

Mid-Atlantic with Kids
Mini Las Vegas
Mini-Mickey
New England and New York with
   Kids
New Orleans
New York City
Paris
San Francisco
Skiing in the West
Southeast with Kids
Walt Disney World®
Walt Disney World® for Grown-ups
Walt Disney World® with Kids
Washington, D.C.
World's Best Diving Vacations

SPECIAL-INTEREST TITLES

Frommer's Adventure Guide to Australia &
   New Zealand
Frommer's Adventure Guide to Central America
Frommer's Adventure Guide to India & Pakistan
Frommer's Adventure Guide to South America
Frommer's Adventure Guide to Southeast Asia
Frommer's Adventure Guide to Southern Africa
Frommer's Britain's Best Bed & Breakfasts and
   Country Inns
Frommer's Caribbean Hideaways
Frommer's Exploring America by RV
Frommer's Fly Safe, Fly Smart
Frommer's France's Best Bed & Breakfasts and
   Country Inns
Frommer's Gay & Lesbian Europe

Frommer's Italy's Best Bed & Breakfasts and
   Country Inns
Frommer's New York City with Kids
Frommer's Ottawa with Kids
Frommer's Road Atlas Britain
Frommer's Road Atlas Europe
Frommer's Road Atlas France
Frommer's Toronto with Kids
Frommer's Vancouver with Kids
Frommer's Washington, D.C., with Kids
Israel Past & Present
The New York Times' Guide to Unforgettable
   Weekends
Places Rated Almanac
Retirement Places Rated